TURBO PASCAL TOOLBOX

A PROGRAMMER'S GUIDE

PAUL GARRISON

TAB

TAB BOOKS Inc.

Blue Ridge Summit, PA 17214

FIRST EDITION
FIRST PRINTING

Library of Congress Cataloging in Publication Data

Garrison, Paul.
Turbo Pascal toolbox—a programmer's guide.

Includes index.
1. PASCAL (Computer program language) 2. Turbo Toolbox (Computer programs) I. Title.
QA76.73.P2G375 1987 005.13'3 86-29990
ISBN 0-8306-0152-X
ISBN 0-8306-2852-5 (pbk.)

Contents

Introduction

Welcome to the Turbo Pascal Toolbox, a collection of programs that greatly enhances the usefulness of your Turbo Pascal program, whether you use your Turbo Pascal to write programs for your business or profession, write programs to market commercially, or do so simply for the fun and enjoyment of it. This book covers four different programs that are designed specifically to be used in conjunction with Turbo Pascal, and two others that simply make life a little easier.

If you do not already own any of the programs that are described in this book, reading the different introductory paragraphs and the related text will help you decide which of the programs you might wish to use; not all are necessarily of practical value for each and every Turbo Pascal user.

The four programs are the **Turbo Editor Toolbox**, the **Turbo Database Toolbox**, the **Turbo Graphix Toolbox** and the **Turbo Gameworks**, and the two convenience programs are **Turbo Lightning** and **Sidekick**.

The **Turbo Editor Toolbox** is a utility program consisting of individual procedures and functions that can be used to design your own text editor. It also includes a simple text editor that is ready to use, and a fairly sophisticated one that might be described as a word-processor (though not a true word-processor like WordStar, despite its resemblance to it), designed to be used in program writing or to generate text. Though intended to be used to write programs in Pascal, both can just as easily be used to write programs in BASIC or any other language.

The **Turbo Database Toolbox** is a utility program that simplifies the task of creating different types of database programs, rivaling in sophistication those that are marketed commercially at rather steep prices.

The **Turbo Graphix Toolbox** is supposed to make writing graphics programs a breeze. The programs can be still or animated, monochrome or in color, designed to be used in business or scientific applications, or simply for the fun of it.

The **Turbo Gameworks** lets you play chess, go-moku or bridge. It can be used as a utility program in the design of other game programs, and some of the decision-making procedures can also be incorporated into other types of programs that call for a decision based on a given set of circumstances.

Those are the four programs that are designed to be used specifically with Turbo Pascal. Each one includes the source code for each of the programs that make up the software package, making it possible for the user to modify or change programs in order to satisfy any type of individual requirement.

The other two programs are **Turbo Lightning**, a fairly ingenious spelling checker, dictionary, and thesaurus, and **Sidekick**, a RAM-resident notepad, calculator, and a general electronic "Man Friday."

None of the programs are copy protected. Be sure to make at least one copy of each before you start fooling around with the contents of the disks. And, because Borland International's Philippe Kahn is revolutionizing the software industry by selling software at reasonable prices, return the favor by making copies only for yourselves, not for friends and relatives.

Although it is illegal to sell, give away, or otherwise distribute the procedures, functons and programs that make up each software package, according to the Borland International end-user agreement, it is perfectly legal to incorporate those procedures and functions into programs of your own design, and to then sell or otherwise distribute those programs of yours.

Now that you've taken a quick look at what you're in for, let's briefly take a closer look at the makeup of "modular program designs," because nearly all of the programs use modular construction. After that, you will be ready to get started with real hands-on practice.

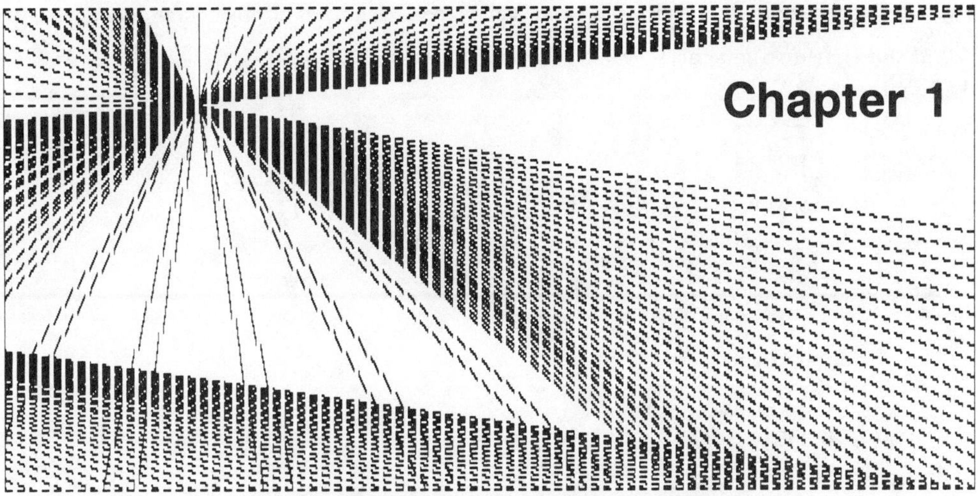

Chapter 1

A Word About Modular Programs

The term **modular program** implies that a program consists of a bunch of individual modules that interact with a main program. Most well-designed programs, especially those written in Pascal or C, are indeed collections of subprograms, called procedures and functions. Usually, however, all of these procedures and functions are included as part of one long source code, under a single program heading.

This is not the case with the majority of the programs that are included in the various Turbo Toolboxes. The source code for most of these programs, appearing on the distribution disk as PROGRAM.PAS, is often quite short, because it will contain a number of *include directives* that look like {$I FILENAME.EXT}. This tells the Turbo Pascal compiler that the procedures and functions that make up FILENAME.EXT are to be included during the compilation process. These modules, which will subsequently be included with the main program, may consist of as few or as many procedures and/or functions as necessary. Some advantages are likely to be lost, however, if these files are too long.

To illustrate, let's look at two versions of a fairly simple Pascal program. It's a word game program that's quite a bit of fun to play. The program displays three letters at random. You're asked to type as many words as you can think of, from three to six letters in length, that include those three letters. The program keeps score, and checks to make sure that each word uses all three letters and is not longer than six letters.

Figure 1-1 is the source code for the program written in the conventional manner, with all of its components included under one program heading. Figure 1-2, on the other hand, is just the source code for the main program, with a number of {$I . . . } directives to tell the compiler to include the modules that are named in those directives:

```
{ $I PICKLET.MOD }
{ $I WORDLEN.MOD }
{ $I MISSLET.MOD }
{ $I NUMWORD.MOD }
```

Fig. 1-1. The conventional version of the Word Game program contains all procedures under one file name in a single file.

```
{A word-game program}
{WRDGME.P   }

label       FIRST, QUIT;
const       num = 90;
var         W, Y, T, LEN, Z, A, L1, L2, L3 : integer;
            WORD   :  array[1..50] of string[10];
            C      :  array[1..6] of char;
            X      :  char;

procedure PickLetter;
begin
     randomize;
     repeat
     L1 := random(num);
     until L1 > 64;

     repeat
     L2 := random(num);
     until L2 > 64;

     repeat
     L3 := random(num);
     until L3 > 64;
end;

procedure WordLength;
begin
     writeln;
     LEN := 0;
     LEN := length(WORD[Z]);
            begin
               if LEN > 6 then
               writeln('       Word is too long.  Try again.');
            end;
            begin
               if LEN > 6 then A := A - 1;
     end;
end;

procedure MissedLetter;
begin
     LEN := length(WORD[Z]);
     for W := 1 to LEN do
         begin
            C[W] := copy(WORD[Z],W,1);
         end;
     T := 0;
     for Y := 1 to LEN do
          begin
             if (C[Y] = chr(L1)) or
                (C[Y] = chr(L2)) or
                (C[Y] = chr(L3)) then
             T := T + 1;
          end;
     begin
          if (T < 3) and (WORD[Z] <> '0') then A := A - 1;
```

```
     begin
          writeln;
          if (T < 3) and (WORD[Z] <> '0') then
          writeln('You''ve used only ',T,' of the letters.  Try again.');
          writeln;
     end;
  end;
end;

procedure NumberOfWords;
begin
     A := A - 1; writeln;
     writeln('You''ve found a total of ',A,' words so far.');
     writeln;
     write('Press ENTER to continue          ');
     readln(X);
end;

begin
     A := 0;
     clrscr;  gotoxy(1,10);
     writeln('I''ll display groups of three letters.  Type as many words');
     writeln('as you can think of that include all three letters.  Your');
     writeln('words may be up to six letters long.');
     writeln('............................................................');
     writeln('Press ENTER after each word and 0 after the last one.');
     writeln;
     write('Press ENTER to start.          ');
     readln(X);
repeat
      if A = 0 then goto FIRST;
      NumberOfWords;
FIRST:
      clrscr;
      PickLetter;
      gotoxy(23,10);
      writeln(chr(L1),'   ',chr(L2),'   ',chr(L3));
      gotoxy(23,11);
      writeln('=========');
      writeln('How many words of six letters or less can you find that');
      writeln('include the letters ',chr(L1),', ',chr(L2),' and ',
      chr(L3),'?');
      writeln;
      writeln('                    Use only CAPITAL LETTERS!');
      writeln('                    ========================');
      writeln('ENTER after each word, 0 after the last word, Q to quit.');
      writeln;
      repeat
           Z := Z + 1;
           write(chr(L1),' ',chr(L2),' ',chr(L3),':     ');
           readln(WORD[Z]);
           A := A + 1;
           if WORD[Z] = 'Q' then goto QUIT;
           WordLength;
           MissedLetter;
      until WORD[Z] = '0';
      until WORD[Z] = 'Q';
QUIT:
end.
```

Fig. 1-2. The modular version of the Word Game has a main program with explanations, and four include directives that call the procedures in the include files.

```
{A word-game program}
{WRDGME.P   }

label       FIRST, QUIT;
const       num = 90;
var         W, Y, T, LEN, Z, A, L1, L2, L3 : integer;
            WORD  :  array[1..50] of string[10];
            C     :  array[1..6] of char;
            X     :  char;

{$I PICKLET.MOD}
{$I WORDLEN.MOD}
{$I MISSLET.MOD}
{$I NUMWORD.MOD}

begin
     A := 0;
     clrscr;  gotoxy(1,10);
     writeln('I''ll display groups of three letters.  Type as many words');
     writeln('as you can think of that include all three letters.  Your');
     writeln('words may be up to six letters long.');
     writeln('.........................................................');
     writeln('Press ENTER after each word and 0 after the last one.');
     writeln;
     write('Press ENTER to start.          ');
     readln(X);
repeat
      if A = 0 then goto FIRST;
      NumberOfWords;
FIRST:
      clrscr;
      PickLetter;
      gotoxy(23,10);
      writeln(chr(L1),'   ',chr(L2),'   ',chr(L3));
      gotoxy(23,11);
      writeln('=========');
      writeln('How many words of six letters or less can you find that');
      writeln('include the letters ',chr(L1),', ',chr(L2),' and ',chr(L3),'?');
      writeln;
      writeln('                    Use only CAPITAL LETTERS!');
      writeln('                    ========================');
      writeln('ENTER after each word, 0 after the last word, Q to quit.');
      writeln;
      repeat
            Z := Z + 1;
            write(chr(L1),' ',chr(L2),' ',chr(L3),':     ');
            readln(WORD[Z]);
            A := A + 1;
            if WORD[Z] = 'Q' then goto QUIT;
            WordLength;
            MissedLetter;
      until WORD[Z] = '0';
      until WORD[Z] = 'Q';
QUIT:
end.
```

Fig. 1-3. The first include file, PICKLET.MOD, picks three letters at random.

```
{First include file for the word-game program}


procedure PickLetter;
begin
     randomize;
     repeat
     L1 := random(num);
     until L1 > 64;

     repeat
     L2 := random(num);
     until L2 > 64;

     repeat
     L3 := random(num);
     until L3 > 64;
end;
```

They are shown in Figs. 1-3 through 1-6. The first include file was given the name PICKLET.MOD. It is used to pick three letters at random. Notice that the last "end" in include files is followed by a semicolon rather than a period. The second include file was saved under the file name WORDLEN.MOD, and it is used to determine whether or not the word entered by the player is within the six-letter limit. The third of these include files, named MISSLET.MOD, is used by the program to make sure that the word that was typed does, in fact, include the three displayed random letters. The last include file, called NUMWORD.MOD, keeps track of the total number of words typed by the player.

When both programs are compiled, they produce .COM files of exactly the same length. These compiled versions function identically when they are run.

There are a number of advantages to placing procedures and/or functions into separate files that are included in the main program only during the compilation procedure. One advantage deals with multi-purpose procedures that can be used in many different programs. Instead of retyping such procedures or functions whenever you're writing a program that can use one, you simply copy it onto the disk that is currently being used. In this manner, you will eventually have

Fig. 1-4. The second include file, WORDLEN.MOD, checks whether the word typed by the player is within the six-letter limit.

```
{Second include file for the word-game program}

procedure WordLength;
begin
     writeln;
     LEN := 0;
     LEN := length(WORD[Z]);
            begin
               if LEN > 6 then
               writeln('       Word is too long.  Try again.');
            end;
            begin
               if LEN > 6 then A := A - 1;
     end;
end;
```

Fig. 1-5. The third include file, MISSLET.MOD, makes sure that all three random letters are used in the word that was typed by the player.

```
{Third include file for the word-game program}


procedure MissedLetter;
begin
     LEN := length(WORD[Z]);
     for W := 1 to LEN do
         begin
             C[W] := copy(WORD[Z],W,1);
         end;

     T := 0;
     for Y := 1 to LEN do
          begin
              if (C[Y] = chr(L1)) or
                 (C[Y] = chr(L2)) or
                 (C[Y] = chr(L3)) then
              T := T + 1;
          end;
     begin
          if (T < 3) and (WORD[Z] <> '0') then A := A - 1;
     begin
          writeln;
          if (T < 3) and (WORD[Z] <> '0') then
          writeln('You''ve used only ',T,' of the letters.  Try again.');
          writeln;
     end;
  end;
end;
```

Fig. 1-6. The fourth include file, NUMWORD.MOD, keeps track of the number of words found by the player, displaying the running totals.

```
{Fourth include file for the word-game program}

procedure NumberOfWords;
begin
     A := A - 1; writeln;
     writeln('You''ve found a total of ',A,' words so far.');
     writeln;
     write('Press ENTER to continue        ');
     readln(X);
end;
```

many useful procedures recorded as include files that can be copied to the active work disk whenever they're needed. Another advantage is that the chances for typographical errors are reduced to a minimum, because short chunks of source code are easy to edit and correct. And, finally, programs are much easier to read and understand when you're not confronted with thousands of lines of source code, no matter how much explanatory text is included.

These include files don't have to be used verbatim in different programs. It's easy to make minor adjustments, such as changing variable names to conform to the program in which they'll be used. Also, it is generally good practice to give all the files that are to be used in a given program the same extension. They can, after they've been copied, be renamed to any file name that appeals to you. If you use file name extensions of less than three letters, be sure to leave spaces(s) between the last letter and the closing brace. Otherwise, the compiler might think that the closing brace is part of the file name: .AZ } or .Z } are acceptable, but .AZ} or .Z } or .Z} are not.

Chapter 2

The Turbo Editor Toolbox

The Turbo Editor Toolbox contains the material, procedures, and functions necessary to design a text editor or word processor.

The terms "text editor" and "word processor" are often considered to be synonymous, but, in fact, there are considerable differences between the various types of programs that can be used to generate text. A true word processor, such as WordStar or WordStar 2000, is often referred to as a WYSIWYG (What You See Is What You Get) system, meaning that you can look at your screen display and see how the final printed copy will look. Simpler systems might lack a word-wrap function, or won't show you where the page breaks are going to occur. I prefer to describe these as text editors or line editors. They are fine for program writing, and they can be used to write short texts, such as letters or memos, but for the purpose of writing entire articles or books, they are ill-suited.

The Turbo Editor Toolbox consists of two 5.25-inch disks and a documentation book of about 244 pages. The disks contain a simple line editor, and a fairly sophisticated word processor that in many aspects is similar (though not identical) to WordStar, with a plethora of functions and procedures that represent the actions the computer takes in response to various editing commands. There's also a program called README.COM which you should call up (type README and ENTER) before you do anything else, because it contains valuable information, including any changes that might have been made since the documentation book was printed.

The hardware and software requirements are an IBM PC, XT, AT, 3270, PCjr, or any true compatible, with a minimum of 192K RAM, PC DOS, MS-DOS 2.0 (or a later version), and Turbo Pascal 3.0. A color monitor, while not a requirement, is of considerable advantage when the windowing capability of some of the programs is used.

The documentation requires a fair amount of study because much of it isn't easy to understand. One of the problems, of course, is that users expect to take the program disks that come with software packages and, after making a work copy, simply shove them into the drive, expecting them to either run or prompt us for some type of input. But those disks contain actual programs, rather than utilities that are to be used when you write your own programs.

This "toolbox," like the others, is primarily designed to help you write programs that are tailored to your specific requirements. Actually using the tools—the individual procedures and functions—is a rather complicated process, requiring a fair degree of programming expertise. On the other hand, all of the programs, with the possible exception of the Turbo Graphix Toolbox, contain fully functional programs that you can use without modification. For instance, there are two ready-to-run text editors included in this program, and the database and game programs respectively contain a ready-to-use database program and three game programs.

GETTING STARTED IN A HURRY

Unless one of the two disks that make up this package contains a file named FIRST-ED.COM, you'll have to compile the file FIRST-ED.PAS, using your Turbo Pascal compiler. (If you are uncertain about how to do this, see Appendix B.) Once the compiled version, the one with the .COM extension, is available, and the computer is showing the A > prompt (assuming FIRST-ED.COM is in the A: drive), type FIRST-ED and ENTER (or RETURN). What you'll see is a status line reading:

```
Window: 1 File:NONAME          Line:1          Col:1          INS
```

meaning that you're now ready to type text into a file called NONAME, the cursor is located in the first column in the top line, and the INSERT function is on. The idea of having a file called NONAME might not be appealing; you might want to start out by renaming that file. But how? Nowhere in the documentation book did I find any instruction on how to name a file.

By trial and error, I found that the following method produces the desired result (^ means that Ctrl key is being pressed): press ^K^S followed by ^K^X to save the empty file, and return to the A> prompt. Now you have an empty file called NONAME on your disk. Rename that file, using the DOS command REN NONAME FIRST.TST, which changes the name to FIRST.TST. Next, type FIRST-ED again, and there's that silly status line, saying that the file is still called NONAME. To fix that, type ^K^R. When the display asks which file to read, type FIRST.TST (or whatever name you gave that file), and your status line will change to FILE:FIRST.TST.

The commands that are available with FIRST-ED are printed on Page 33 of the documentation book. If you're familiar with WordStar (the older version, not WordStar 2000), you'll have little trouble using these commands. Most are identical to those used by WordStar, but there are some differences. One important command is ^O^W, which switches the word-wrap feature on or off. When typing ordinary text, you'll want that feature on. But if you want to type a program, which is a non-document file, you'll want word-wrap off.

Once you've familiarized yourself with the commands, or at least with the ones you're likely to use, experiment by typing any arbitrary material, using the various commands to see the results that can be achieved. You'll find that this Turbo Editor is really a fairly sophisticated word processor.

Its main shortcoming is the fact that you can type hundreds of lines, and there will never be an indication of a page break. It's therefore up to you to watch the line numbers and to skip the appropriate number of lines wherever a pagebreak will occur, if you want your material printed. By the way, there is no command that causes the printer to print what you have written. To get your document sent to the printer, exit FIRST-ED and use the appropriate PRINT command from your DOS prompt. Some of the attributes associated with PRINT vary among different DOS versions, so be sure to check your DOS manual for the correct command to print the contents of a file.

Another drawback is the lack of a line-spacing command (^O^S in WordStar). The best way I have been able to figure out to produce a double-spaced document is to type it single-spaced and, when you're finished, insert blank lines using the ^N (insert line) command.

If you want to use this program for serious work, I suggest that, with FIRST-ED in drive A:, you place a formatted blank work disk into drive B: and then type B: and ENTER, to switch the logged drive from A: to B:. Now type A:FIRST-ED, to call up the program that is in the A: drive. Now, everything you type will be saved (using ^K^S) on the disk in the B: drive.

CUSTOMIZING FIRST-ED

The next step in exploring the potential capabilities of the Turbo Edit Toolbox is to make some minor change in the program, to find out how that sort of thing works. The modification doesn't have to serve any particular practical purpose; this is simply meant to be an exercise.

I decided to add a title page, and to have the program ask for a file name immediately upon activation. The first step is to make a copy of FIRST-ED.PAS, and all files with the .ED extension, onto a formatted blank disk. Those files with the .ED extension are the ones that contain all of the procedures and functions that constantly call one another during the execution of the program. Once that is done, put the newly created disk into drive B: and WordStar into drive A: (instead of WordStar, you could use the Turbo Pascal program disk in the Edit function, or any other text editor or word processor). Then, call up FIRST-ED.PAS to get a look at the source code (it is reproduced in the documentation book on pages 30 and 31). Next, delete most of the comments (all that stuff between braces), because I think it simply tends to clutter up the program.

Once that is done, a nice clean program of some 60 lines remains, ready to accept whatever modification you might want to make. I searched through the part of the documentation book entitled "Turbo Editor Toolbox Procedures and Functions" (pages 117 through 240), which lists the procedures and functions alphabetically, gives a brief description of each, and the name of the file in which it is contained. I was looking for one that would require that a file name be typed in, and found EditCprfw (page 151), which is part of the file called K.ED. Insert **EditCprfw;** between **EditInitialize;** and **EditSystem;** in the main program, which should have the desired effect.

Next, insert a new procedure called TitlePage (Fig. 2-1) above the main program. This procedure consists of two loops that produce horizontal lines of 80 hyphens. Between the loops insert a writeln command with the title of the program; in my case, MY FIRST EDITOR. A **Delay(2000);** line is also added to hold the title on the screen for a given period of time before continuing with program execution. Insert **TitlePage;** between **EditInitialize;** and **EditCprfw;** and save the edited version on disk. Then exit WordStar (or whatever editor you're using), and replace the WordStar disk with the Turbo Pascal disk. With the Turbo Pascal menu in display, type OCQC, followed by FIRST-ED.PAS, and Turbo Pascal will start the compiling procedure.

The source code is very short and, logically, the compile should be very quick. Not so. The compile goes on and on and on because it incorporates all those procedures and functions that call one another during the execution of the program. When the compilation is finally complete, you'll find that the .COM version of the program consists of 56,088 bytes, while the source code is only 1,800 bytes long.

Once the compilation is complete, exit Turbo Pascal by typing Q and, with the B> prompt up (assuming that your FIRST-ED.COM disk is still in drive B:), type FIRST-ED and ENTER. The title of the program will be displayed for approximately a second and a half, after which the status line appears preceded by <**Read file**>:. There is no work file on that disk, so you can simply press ENTER, which produces an error message, and then type ^K^X to exit.

Remove the FIRST-ED disk from drive B: and replace it with a formatted disk onto which you want to write your document. Type A:TURBO and, from the Turbo Pascal main menu, select the Edit function to create one (or several) empty files(s), by typing file name(s) and then saving those empty file(s). Once that's done, remove the Turbo Pascal disk and replace it with your newly created FIRST-ED disk. With the B> prompt still up, type A:FIRST-ED and

Fig. 2-1. The slightly modified version of the simple text editor demonstration program, adds a title page and an input prompt for the file name to be used.

```
{$C-,I-,K-}
program FirstEditor;

{$I VARS.ED }

procedure UserCommand(var ch : byte);
begin
end;

procedure UserError(var Msgno : byte);
begin
end;

procedure userStatusline(Var TWindow:Byte;
                         Column,line:Integer;
                         Insertflag:Insflag;
                         WW,AI: boolean);
begin
end;

procedure UserReplace(var ch : byte);
begin
end;

procedure UserTask;
begin
end;

{$I USER.ED       }
{$I SCREEN.ED     }

{$I INIT.ED       }
{$I KCMD.ED       }
{$I OCMD.ED       }
{$I QCMD.ED       }
{$I CMD.ED        }

{$I K.ED          }
{$I O.ED          }
{$I Q.ED          }
{$I DISP.ED       }
{$I TASK.ED       }
{$I INPUT.ED      }

procedure TitlePage;
var X : integer;
begin
clrscr; gotoxy(1,10);
for X := 1 to 80 do begin
write('-');
end;
writeln;
writeln('                         MY FIRST EDITOR');
for X :=1 to 80 do begin
write('-');
end;
```

```
writeln;
delay(2000);
 clrscr;
end;
begin
  EditInitialize;
  TitlePage;
  EditCprfw;
  EditSystem;
  ClrScr;
end.
```

ENTER, and you'll see a repeat of what was described above. Now, however, you can enter one of the file names you've stored on the disk in drive B:, and the NONAME in the status line will be repeated with your FILENAME.EXT—or whatever you called your file.

Because the source code includes all lines that start with "{$I," all of the 123 procedures and functions are available for inclusion, exclusion or modification. Using the Edit function of Turbo Pascal, WordStar or any other text editor, you can examine the source code of any of these procedures and functions by calling up the file in which it is contained. Whenever you decide to fool around with any of this material, be sure you do it on a copy disk, leaving at least one, preferably several, untouched copies, because at first you're likely to make all kinds of mistakes. You can also create a file consisting of procedures and/or functions of your own design. You'd then have to add a {$I YOURFILE.ED} in order to permit the program to include the procedures or functions that you want your version of the program to use.

THE MICROSTAR PROGRAM

The second ready-to-run program in the Turbo Editor Toolbox is called MicroStar. It is on the disk as MS.PAS (MS.COM is the compiled version). MicroStar is a rather impressive looking program that imitates WordStar in a great many ways, even adding a number of features that are unavailable in WordStar. But, again, it does not allow for automatic page breaks, so if you use the program to generate text that is to be printed, you will have to keep track of line numbers. Also, as in FIRST-ED, there appears to be no way to produce double-spaced text without going through the routine that I described earlier in the "Getting Started . . ." section of this chapter.

There is, in fact, very little practical difference between the two programs. The real difference is primarily cosmetic, in that MicroStar looks extremely dramatic, especially if you're using a color monitor, because it makes extensive use of colors to accentuate prompts and such.

When you're ready to experiment with the program, place the disk that contains MS.COM, all files with the .ED extension, and the MS.000 overlay into drive A:, and a formatted blank disk into drive B:. Change the logged drive to B: and type A:MS and ENTER. You'll see a title page with a copyright notice and a line beneath it reading **Open File:**. After you've typed a file name of your choice (I used SAMPLE.TXT), the display adds a second line reading **File is new. Continue (Y/N):**. Type Y in answer to that question, and the display will change to two lines at the top, providing the following information:

```
File B:SAMPLE.TXT                                   IN  Line:  1 Col:  1
Block Search Go to Text format Window File WW       F10 for pulldown menu
```

The IN on the top line indicates that insert is on, and the WW below it indicates that word-wrap is also on. Block, Search, etc., to the left of the WW, represent the names of various pulldown menus that can be called at any time during editing by pressing the function key F10.

These pulldown menus display a number of choices, with the top one highlighted. Each choice consists of one capital letter, with the rest in lowercase. The choices can be selected by typing the capital letter followed by ENTER, or by moving the highlighting to the desired choice, using the arrow keys, and then pressing ENTER. Here are the choices offered by these menus:

Block:	Begin	
	End	
	Copy	
	Move	
	Read	
	Write	
	Delete	
	Hide/show	
	Spell check	[This can be used only if Turbo Lightning is resident in RAM]
Search:	Find	
	find/Replace	
	Next	
Go to:	Top of file	
	End of file	
	Begin block	
	end block	
	Line	
	Column	
	Go marker	
	Set marker	
Text format:	Insert	ON (OFF)
	Word wrap	ON (OFF)
	Auto indent	ON (OFF)
	Left margin:	1
	Right margin:	65
	Tab size:	8
	Undo limit:	20
	Save settings	
Window:	Select	
	open	
	Close	
File:	Open	
	Close	
	Save	
	save As	
	Directory	
	Logged drive	
	Print	

copy
Rename
Erase
Quit

When you press the F10 function key, the message to the right of WW on the second line changes to **ESC to exit menu**, and the first menu name (Block) is highlighted. If you press ENTER, that block menu will appear above your typed text. If you want one of the other menus, simply move the highlighting, using the right-arrow key to the desired menu name, and press ENTER.

You don't have to use menus to produce the results that are offered by their choices. If you can remember the command structure, you can simply use the commands that are listed on page 45 of the documentation book. Note: there are some errors at the very bottom—^K^S means save the file, ^K^Y is delete block and ^K^X is exit program.

I suggest that you experiment with the program by writing some text (a dozen or so lines should suffice) and using the various choices offered by the pulldown menus. Also, try the different commands that are listed in the book. You don't necessarily have to try them all; just pick the ones that you're likely to want to use frequently.

Whether you want to use the Turbo Editor Toolbox to write a text editor to your personal liking, or whether you'll simply use the programs as they are, the attractive price ($69.95 is the suggested retail price at this writing) makes it by far the best buy in text editors.

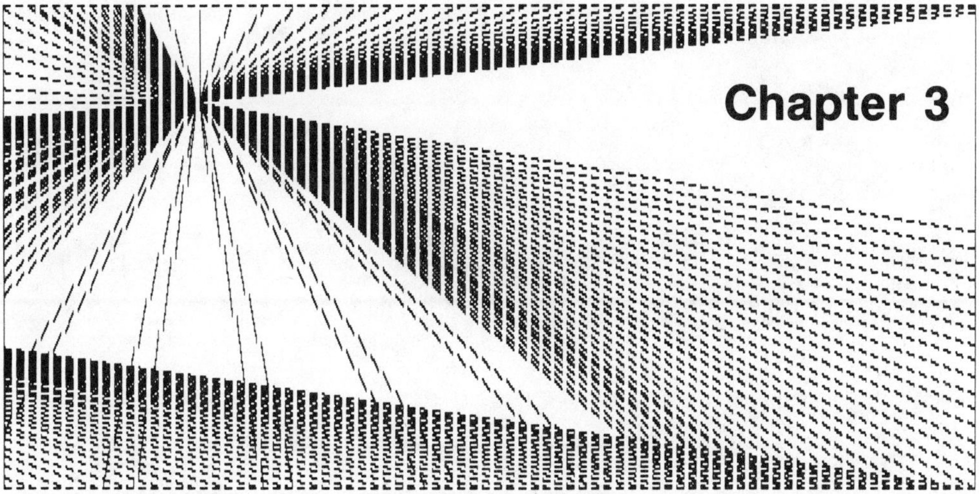

Chapter 3

The Turbo Database Toolbox

Databases are among the most useful types of computer programs for every-day use in your business, profession or home. The term "database" is simply a fancy way of referring to lists, any kind of lists, such as inventories, addresses, birthdays, recipes—you name it. In other words, all of the information that was kept on index cards, filed alphabetically or numerically, can now be dumped into an appropriately designed database program in any order. Additionally, any single record or group of related records can be accessed and retrieved, based on whatever criteria you might want to use.

Simple database programs are not particularly difficult to write, but they can get a bit complicated when you want to include sorting capabilities, either alphabetical or numerical, or a large variety of access criteria.

I have included a program listing in Pascal of a catch-all database program that I had, some time ago, designed for my own use. It illustrates the relative simplicity of such a program, if you're willing to do without gimmicks that may improve the program cosmetically, but add little to its usefulness.

Take a few moments to study the program (Fig. 3-1), because a clear understanding of what takes place here will also help you understand how the Turbo Database Toolbox functions. The program was originally designed to keep track of magazine articles, which explains some of the variable and procedure names. Any of these names can, of course, be changed to any other name that might appeal to you.

As with most Pascal programs, examine it starting at the bottom. The main program consists of just three lines, calling the procedure Menu until the user decides to exit the program by selecting Choice 0 from the menu. Choice 1 is used to enter new data. It calls the procedure Enter. Choices 2 through 5 offer the user an opportunity to retrieve data by any one of four parameters, sending the computer to one of four different procedures. Choice 6 is activated when the program is being used for the first time, or when all previously stored data are to be erased. It sends the computer to the procedure Start, which first displays a warning and then creates an empty data file that will accept entries.

Fig. 3-1. This sample all-purpose database program, with no index files, works fine if not too many records are stored. Otherwise, it proves rather slow.

```
{A sample database program}

program Sample;

var ARTICLE : file of string[50];

    KEY1, KEY2, KEY3, KEY4, KEY5, KEY6, KEY7, KEY8 : string[50];
    COMP, PERS, SUBJ, OTKY                         : string[50];
    WHICH                                          : integer;
    Y                                              : char;

procedure Print;
begin
     writeln(Lst,' ');
     writeln(Lst,'Key1 data.....................',KEY1);
     writeln(Lst,'Key2 data.....................',KEY2);
     writeln(Lst,'Key3 data.....................',KEY3);
     writeln(Lst,'Key4 data.....................',KEY4);
     writeln(Lst,'Key5 data.....................',KEY5);
     writeln(Lst,'Key6 data.....................',KEY6);
     writeln(Lst,'Key7 data.....................',KEY7);
     writeln(Lst,'Key8 data.....................',KEY8);
end;

procedure Display;
begin
     writeln('Key1 data.....................',KEY1);
     writeln('Key2 data.....................',KEY2);
     writeln('Key3 data.....................',KEY3);
     writeln('Key4 data.....................',KEY4);
     writeln('Key5 data.....................',KEY5);
     writeln('Key6 data.....................',KEY6);
     writeln('Key7 data.....................',KEY7);
     writeln('Key8 data.....................',KEY8);
     writeln;
     write('Printout?      (Y/N)            ');
     readln(Y);
               if UpCase(Y) = 'Y' then
     Print;
     writeln;
     write('Press ENTER to go on            ');
     readln(Y);
end;

procedure Enter;
begin
            clrscr;  gotoxy(1,10);
            repeat
     assign(Article,'ARTCL.FIL');
     reset(Article);
     seek(Article,FileSize(Article));
     write('Enter key1 data                     ');
     readln(KEY1);
     write('Enter key2 data                     ');
     readln(KEY1);
     write('Enter key3 data                     ');
```

```
        readln(KEY1);
        write('Enter key4 data                          ');
        readln(KEY1);
        write('Enter key5 data                          ');
        readln(KEY1);
        write('Enter key6 data                          ');
        readln(KEY1);
        write('Enter key7 data                          ');
        readln(KEY1);
        write('Enter key8 data                          ');
        readln(KEY1);
        write(Article,KEY1);
        write(Article,KEY2);
        write(Article,KEY3);
        write(Article,KEY4);
        write(Article,KEY5);
        write(Article,KEY6);
        write(Article,KEY7);
        write(Article,KEY8);
        writeln;
        write('Another entry?    (Y/N)                  ');
        readln(Y);
            until UpCase(Y) = 'N';
end;

Procedure Company;
begin
       clrscr;  gotoxy(1,10);
    write('Enter key4 data                          ');
    readln(COMP);
    assign(Article,'ARTCL.FIL');
    reset(Article);
       repeat
    read(Article,KEY1);
    read(Article,KEY2);
    read(Article,KEY3);
    read(Article,KEY4);
    read(Article,KEY5);
    read(Article,KEY6);
    read(Article,KEY7);
    read(Article,KEY8);
       if COMP = KEY4 then
    Display;
       until eof(Article);
    close(Article);
end;

procedure Personality;
begin
       clrscr;  gotoxy(1,10);
    write('Enter key5 data                          ');
    readln(PERS);
    assign(Article,'ARTCL.FIL');
    reset(Article);
       repeat
    read(Article,KEY1);
    read(Article,KEY2);
    read(Article,KEY3);
    read(Article,KEY4);
```

```
    read(Article,KEY5);
    read(Article,KEY6);
    read(Article,KEY7);
    read(Article,KEY8);
        if PERS = KEY5 then
    Display;
        until eof(Article);
    close(Article);
end;

procedure Subject;
begin
        clrscr;  gotoxy(1,10);
    write('Enter key6 data                         ');
    readln(SUBJ);
    assign(Article,'ARTCL.FIL');
    reset(Article);
        repeat
    read(Article,KEY1);
    read(Article,KEY2);
    read(Article,KEY3);
    read(Article,KEY4);
    read(Article,KEY5);
    read(Article,KEY6);
    read(Article,KEY7);
    read(Article,KEY8);
        if SUBJ = KEY6 then
    Display;
        until eof(Article);
    close(Article);
end;
procedure Other;
begin
        clrscr;  gotoxy(1,10);
    write('Enter key7 data                         ');
    readln(OTKY);
    assign(Article,'ARTCL.FIL');
    reset(Article);
        repeat
    read(Article,KEY1);
    read(Article,KEY2);
    read(Article,KEY3);
    read(Article,KEY4);
    read(Article,KEY5);
    read(Article,KEY6);
    read(Article,KEY7);
    read(Article,KEY8);
        if OTKY = KEY7 then
    Display;
        until eof(Article);
    close(Article);
end;

procedure Start;
begin
         clrscr;  gotoxy(1,10);
    writeln('          WARNING!  All previous entries will be erased!');
    writeln('          ==========================================');
    write('          Go ahead?  (Y/N)     ');
```

```
     readln(Y);
          if UpCase(Y) = 'Y' then begin
     assign(Article,'ARTCL.FIL');
     rewrite(Article);
     close(Article);
          end
          else
end;

procedure Menu;
begin
          clrscr;  gotoxy(1,6);
     writeln('                                   SAMPLE DATABASE');
     writeln('                                   ***************');
     writeln;
     writeln('                              1   Enter new data');
     writeln;
     writeln('                              2   Retrieve data by key4');
     writeln('                              3   Retrieve data by key5');
     writeln('                              4   Retrieve data by key6');
     writeln('                              5   Retrieve data by key7');
     writeln;
     writeln('                              6   Erase;  start from scratch');
     writeln;
     writeln('                              0   Exit program');
     writeln('                              -------------------------------');
     write('                           Which?        ');
     readln(WHICH);
          case WHICH of
     1 : Enter;
     2 : Company;
     3 : Personality;
     4 : Subject;
     5 : Other;
     6 : Start;
     0 : end;
end;

begin
         repeat
     menu;
         until WHICH = 0;
end.
```

Each of the four retrieve-data procedures (here called Company, Personality, Subject, and Other) are identical in structure. Each asks that the user enter some type of key data. The computer then searches through the entire data file for data that match the key data. Once it finds a match, it calls the procedure Display, which causes the record containing the desired data to be displayed, and asks whether or not you want a hard copy. If you do, the procedure Print is called. This process is repeated until all records have been examined.

If, for example you wanted to use this program as a name-and-address database, you might change the variables KEY1 through KEY8 and the displayed text key1 through key8 as follows:

key1: First Name	KEY1: NAMEF
key2: Last Name	KEY2: NAMEL
key3: Address or P.O. Box	KEY3: ADDR

key4: City	KEY4: CTY
key5: State ID	KEY5: STATE
key6: Zip code	KEY6: ZIP
key7: Area code	KEY7: AREA
key8: Phone number	KEY8: PHON

Two lines in the four retrieve-data procedures will also have to be changed to permit the use of last names, city or state, the first two digits of the zip code, and the area code as keys to retrieve data. The two lines are **write('Enter . . .** and **if VARIABLE NAME = VARIABLE NAME then . . . .** If you want to use the first two digits of the zip code, you'll have to use the copy(ZIP,1,2) function in order to separate those two digits from the rest of the zip code.

I used no index files in this version, which makes the program simpler to write and understand. Depending on the number of records in the data file, however, it can be somewhat slower than programs that do use index files to access records.

The Turbo Database Toolbox consists of one 5.25-inch disk and a 151-page documentation book. The disk contains a huge number of functions and procedures, all supposedly designed to simplify the task of creating database programs that can rival such well-known software as VisiCalc or DataStar in sophistication and versatility. The documentation, while extremely thorough, is occasionally a bit obscure, requiring a greater amount of expertise than many users actually possess. By providing step-by-step explanations in conjuction with some actual examples, I hope to simplify the task of using this rather remarkable program.

The hardware and software requirements are a minimum of 64K RAM, operating under one of the following:

- MS DOS or PC DOS 2.0 (or a later version) and Turbo Pascal 2.0 (or later).
- CP/M-86 1.1 (or later) with Turbo Pascal 2.1 (or later).
- CP/M-80 2.2 (or later) with Turbo Pascal 2.0 (or later).

THE COMPONENTS OF DATABASE PROGRAMS

Sophisticated database programs—those electronic card files full of data such as names and addresses, inventories, or whatever—are usually made up of a number of components that must be understood before it is possible to create and write such programs for your own use and to your own specifications.

Data Files are the files into which you dump the data that you want stored for future retrieval. Unlike card files, where you have to store the cards manually in alphabetical order, data can be entered into data files in any order. The task of arranging data in alphabetical or numerical order is handled by a sorting program that is part of the database program system.

Record is the term used for each group of data that consists of closely related information. For instance, a record might consist of first name, last name, address, city, state, zip code, area code, phone number, extension, birth date and remarks. Or it might contain a product description, inventory amount, reorder number, wholesale and retail price, and so on. The databases created with the Turbo Database Toolbox can store up to 65,535 records, which is more than ample for most purposes.

Keys might be described as record identifiers. In other words, when you want to retrieve a given record, you'll have to tell the computer what record you're interested in by typing a given key. Keys can be strings of letters, numbers, or a combination of the two.

Index Files are structured much like data files, but instead of storing records, they store keys—up to 65,535 of them. The access portion of a database program uses the keys that are stored in the index files to manage the records contained in the data files.

Data files and index files are normally stored on the same disk, but they are entirely separate entities. When you try to access a record, the program goes back and forth between the two types of files, using the key that is associated with the desired record. In addition, in the sample database programs that are part of the Turbo Database Toolbox, every record in the data file is also assigned a number so that the program can locate the correct record when there are duplicate keys, such as several persons named Smith when last names are used as keys.

INTRODUCING THE SAMPLE PROGRAMS

Two demonstration programs are included on the distribution disk under the file names TBDEMO.PAS and BTREE.PAS. TBDEMO.PAS is the source code for what might be described as a "bare bones" database program. Although it can be used, it lacks most of the refinements that you're likely to be looking for. You can, however, modify this program, adding some of those refinements. BTREE.PAS, on the other hand, is a rather sophisticated program. It can be used as is, or it, too, can be modified, but here major changes require a considerable amount of programming expertise.

Before either one of the programs can be used, you'll have to compile them (See Appendix B).

PLAYING AROUND WITH TBDEMO

The first database program (TBDEMO.PAS) that's described in the documentation book is a fairly simple one, and much less sophisticated than the one that takes up most of the book (BTREE.PAS). Exactly because of its relative simplicity, it is much better suited to show what's going on and, in turn, to make some modifications.

In order to run the program as is, you must compile it (see Appendix B for details), creating a program called TBDEMO.COM that can be run by typing TBDEMO and ENTER. Once you've done that, you will probably see areas in which you'll want to make changes, even if those changes are only to produce a more attractive display.

Use the Turbo Pascal text editor (or any other text editor) to take a look at the source code. You'll find that, not counting the four include directives ({$I ACCESS.BOX }, {$I ADDKEY .BOX }, {$I DELKEY.BOX }, and {$I GETKEY.BOX }), the program consists of more than 450 lines of code. Despite the plentiful explanations, it's pretty difficult to figure out what's going on in the various program segments. Even if you make a hard copy (eight pages), it's still difficult to determine the exact workings of the program.

Before you begin to decipher it, copy TBDEMO.PAS on a formatted blank disk. Then, using your text editor or word processor, break the program down into its components, turning each of these components into a newly created separate {$I . . . } file with its own file name. In this manner, I created 16 files with names starting with PG for simpler identification. I ended up with 16 short program segments on separate sheets of paper, making it much easier to examine and understand each of the segments individually.

If you compare these 16 program segment files with the original code, you'll notice that I already made a few changes, purely cosmetic in nature, consisting mostly of some added **writeln;**s and some **clrscr; gotoxy(,);**s in order to reduce unnecessary clutter in the display. I also changed the file name of the main program from TBDEMO.PAS to MYDB.PAS. In its new form (Fig. 3-2) it takes up just one page.

The first line is a new include file called PG.BOX (Fig. 3-3) which contains the constants that are required by the program. These constants change if you decide to use different values for your records and keys, so changes can now be made with ease in the eight lines that make up the constant declaration.

That line is followed by four lines that consist of the standard include directives that were part of the original source code. Then come two new include directives, followed by the unchanged procedure Stop—I can't imagine why anyone would want to make any changes there. Next, 13

Fig. 3-2. Here is the main module of the demonstration program. All of the remaining portions have been moved into new include files with names starting with PG.

```
Program MyDatabase;

{$I PG.BOX      }
{$I ACCESS.BOX }
{$I ADDKEY.BOX }
{$I DELKEY.BOX }
{$I GETKEY.BOX }

{$I PGREC.BOX  }
{$I PGGLOB.BOX }

  procedure Stop;
  begin
    GotoXY(1,24);
    Writeln;
    Writeln;
    Writeln;
    Writeln('Customer database program aborted.');
    Halt;
  end

{$I PGFILE.BOX }
{$I PGINFO.BOX }
{$I PGINDX.BOX }
{$I PGSCRN.BOX }
{$I PGACCS.BOX }
{$I PGCODE.BOX }
{$I PGSRCH.BOX }
{$I PGNEXT.BOX }
{$I PGPREV.BOX }
{$I PGADDC.BOX }
{$I PGDELC.BOX }
{$I PGUPDT.BOX }
{$I PGMENU.BOX }

var
  Finished: Boolean;
begin
  Finished := false;
  OpenDataFile(CustFile,'CustFile.dat',SizeOf(CustRec));
  OpenIndexFile(CodeIndx,'CodeFile.Ndx',
                SizeOf(Customer.CustCode) - 1,NoDuplicates);
  repeat
    case Menu of
      '1','L': ListCustomers(CustFile);
      '2','F': FindCustomer(CustFile,CodeIndx);
      '3','S': SearchCustomer(CustFile,CodeIndx);
      '4','N': NextCustomer(CustFile,CodeIndx);
      '5','P': PreviousCustomer(CustFile,CodeIndx);
      '6','A': AddCustomer(CustFile,CodeIndx);
      '7','U': UpdateCustomer(CustFile,CodeIndx);
      '8','D': DeleteCustomer(CustFile,CodeIndx);
      '9','R': RebuildIndex(CustFile,CodeIndx);
      '0','E': Finished := true;
      else     Write('Choose 0 - 9: ');
    end;
```

```
  until Finished;
  CloseIndex(CodeIndx);
  CloseFile(CustFile);
end.
```

include directives go to the different newly created program modules. Finally, the main program opens the data and index files, and sends the computer to the appropriate procedures, based on the selection from the menu made by the user.

PG.BOX has already been discussed, but note that changing the value assigned to NoDuplicates from zero to any other will cause the program to accept, rather than reject, duplicate keys.

PGREC.BOX (Fig. 3-4) is the module containing type definitions. The number of permissible characters is determined for each category here, and can be changed if necessary. But remember, if you change the overall record length or the number of permissible characters under CustCode, you'll have to make the appropriate changes in PG.BOX.

PGGLOB.BOX (Fig. 3-5) simply defines three global variables.

PGFILE.BOX (Fig. 3-6) opens an existing data file. If none exists, it creates a new and empty data file with a description represented by the *fname* variable.

PGINFO.BOX (Fig. 3-7) is used to enter the data for a new record. This is one place where changes are usually made first, because it is here that the program prompts the user to enter specific types of data. In addition, it would probably be desirable to indicate the number of acceptable characters by adding something like "(to 15 characters)." Remember that changes made in this module, other than those for purely cosmetic reasons, will require comparable changes elsewhere.

PGINDX.BOX (Fig. 3-8) opens, creates, or rebuilds index files. Except during the first run of the program, when no index file exists, this module requires no action on the part of the user. Everything takes place automatically.

PGSCRN.BOX (Fig. 3-9) causes entire records to be displayed on the screen after processing in another module has determined which record is to be displayed.

PGACCS.BOX (Fig. 3-10) is used to access records in sequence, rather than through the interaction of the index file. It is used only if, during the first run, you typed N in reply to the question of whether or not you want an index file created.

PGCODE.BOX (Fig. 3-11) is used when the record associated with a given code is to be found and displayed. The user is asked to enter the code, and the program then displays all data associated with it.

PGSRCH.BOX (Fig. 3-12) comes into play when you can't remember the complete code used for the key. Part of that code is typed in, and the program looks for a likely match, displaying the appropriate record when such a match has been found.

PGNEXT.BOX (Fig. 3-13) displays the next record in line, based on an examination of the codes. Whether the codes are numerical or alphabetical, they are represented as strings within the program and, thus, are examined alphabetically.

```
{PG.BOX}
{Required constants}

const
MaxDataRecSize  =  342;
MaxKeyLen       =   15;
PageSize        =   16;
PageStackSize   =   10;
Order           =    8;
MaxHeight       =    5;
NoDuplicates    =    0;
```

Fig. 3-3. The include file PG.BOX contains the constants required during program execution.

Fig. 3-4. PGREC.BOX is the include file that performs the type-definitions.

```
{PGREC.BOX}
{Type definitions}

TYPE
  CustRec = record
    CustStatus : integer;
    CustCode   : string[15];
    EntryDate  : string[8];
    FirstName  : string[15];
    LastName   : string[30];
    Company    : string[40];
    Addr1      : string[40];
    Addr2      : string[40];
    Phone      : string[15];
    PhoneExt   : string[5];
    Remarks1   : string[40];
    Remarks2   : string[40];
    Remarks3   : string[40];
  end;

  FilenameType = string[64];
```

Fig. 3-5. PGGLOB.BOX contains the global variables used throughout the program.

```
{PGGLOB.BOX       }
{Global variables}

var
  CustFile : DataFile;
  CodeIndx : IndexFile;
  Customer : CustRec;
```

Fig. 3-6. PGFILE.BOX opens a data file, or creates one if none exists.

```
{PGFILE.BOX}
{Open or create a file}

  procedure OpenDataFile(var CustFile : DataFile;
                             Fname: FilenameType;
                             Size : integer     );
  var
    create : char;
  begin
    OpenFile(CustFile, fname, Size);
    if not OK then
    begin
      clrscr; gotoxy(1,10);
      Writeln(' The data file: ',fname,' was not found.'); writeln;
      Write('Do you wish to create it? ');
      Read(KBD, Create);
      Writeln(Create);
      if UpCase(create) = 'Y' then
        MakeFile(CustFile,fname,Size)
      else stop;
    end;
    If not OK Then stop;
  end;
```

Fig. 3-7. PGINFO.BOX is the include file that contains the input prompts used to enter new customer data.

```
{PGINFO>BOX}
{Data input}

  procedure InputInformation(var Customer : CustRec);
  begin
    Writeln;
    Writeln(' Enter Customer Information ');
    Writeln;
    with Customer do
    begin
      CustStatus := 0;
      Write('Customer code: '); Readln(CustCode);
      Write('Entry date    : '); Readln(EntryDate);
      Write('First name    : '); Readln(FirstName);
      Write('Last name     : '); Readln(LastName);
      Write('Company       : '); Readln(Company);
      Writeln('Address ');
      Write('    Number & Street    : '); Readln(Addr1);
      Write('    City, State & Zip : '); Readln(Addr2);
      Write('Phone     : '); Readln(Phone);
      Write('Extention : '); Readln(PhoneExt);
      Write('Remarks   : '); Readln(Remarks1);
      Write('Remarks   : '); Readln(Remarks2);
      Write('Remarks   : '); Readln(Remarks3);
    end;
    Writeln;
  end;
```

Fig. 3-8. PGINDX.BOX rebuilds an index file after it has been compromised in some way.

```
{PGINDX.BOX}
{Open or create or rebuild index file}

  procedure RebuildIndex(VAR CustFile: DataFile;
                         VAR CodeIndex: IndexFile);
  var
    RecordNumber : integer;
  begin
    InitIndex;
    MakeIndex(CodeIndex,'CodeFile.ndx',
              SizeOf(Customer.CustCode)-1,NoDuplicates);
    for RecordNumber := 1 to FileLen(CustFile) - 1 do
    begin
      GetRec(CustFile,RecordNumber,Customer);
      if Customer.CustStatus = 0 then
        AddKey(CodeIndex,RecordNumber,Customer.CustCode);
    end
  end;

  procedure OpenIndexFile(var CodeIndx  : IndexFile;
                              Fname     : FilenameType;
                              KeySize   : integer;
                              Dups      : integer);
  var
    create: char;
  begin
    InitIndex;
```

```
  OpenIndex(CodeIndx, Fname,KeySize,Dups);
  if not OK then
  begin
    clrscr; gotoxy(1,10);
    Writeln(' The index file: ',fname,' was not found.'); writeln;
    Write('Do you wish to create it? ');
    Read(KBD, Create);
    if UpCase(Create) = 'Y' then
      RebuildIndex(CustFile,CodeIndx)
    else
      Stop;
  end;
  If not OK then Stop;
end;
```

Fig. 3-9. PGSCRN.BOX is used to display the data that make up a given record, on the screen.

```
{PGSCRN.BOX}
{Display information on the screen}

  procedure DisplayCustomer(Customer: CustRec);

  begin
    with Customer do
    begin
      Writeln;
      WriteLn('    Code: ',CustCode,'     Date: ',EntryDate);
      Writeln('    Name: ',FirstName,' ',LastName);
      WriteLn('Company: ',Company);
      Writeln('Address: ',Addr1);
      Writeln('         ',Addr2);
      Writeln('   Phone:',Phone,' ext. ',PhoneExt);
      WriteLn('Remarks: ',Remarks1);
      Writeln('         ',Remarks2);
      WriteLn('         ',Remarks3);
    end;
    Writeln;

  end;
```

Fig. 3-10. PGACCS.BOX accesses and displays records sequentially. The "Press any key to continue . . ." line is needed to hold data on the screen long enough to read.

```
{PGACCS.BOX}
{Access records sequentially}

    procedure ListCustomers(var CustFile: DataFile);
    var
      NumberOfRecords,
      RecordNumber     : integer;
      Pause            : char;
    begin
      NumberOfRecords := FileLen(CustFile);
      Writeln('                   Customers  ');
      Writeln;
      for RecordNumber := 1 to NumberOfRecords - 1 do
      begin
        GetRec(CustFile,RecordNumber,Customer);
```

```
      if Customer.CustStatus = 0 then DisplayCustomer(Customer);
    end;
    Writeln;
    Write(' Press any key to continue . . .');
    Read(KBD,Pause); Writeln;
  end;
```

Fig. 3-11. PGCODE.BOX searches for a record, using the customer's identification code.

```
{PGCODE.BOX}
{Find data by code}

  procedure FindCustomer(var CustFile: DataFile;
                         var CodeIndx: IndexFile );
  var
    RecordNumber : integer;
    SearchCode   : string[15];
    Pause        : char;

  begin
    Write('Enter the Customer code: '); ReadLn(SearchCode);
    FindKey(CodeIndx,RecordNumber,SearchCode);
    if OK then
    begin
      GetRec(CustFile,RecordNumber,Customer);
      DisplayCustomer(Customer);
    end
    else
      Writeln('A record was not found for the key ',SearchCode);
    Writeln('Press any key to continue . . .');
    Read(KBD,Pause);
  end;
```

Fig. 3-12. PGSRCH.BOX uses the SearchKey function to search for records based on partial customer identification codes.

```
{PGSRCH.BOX}
{Search data by code}

  procedure SearchCustomer(var CustFile: DataFile;
                           var CodeIndx: IndexFile );
  var
    RecordNumber : integer;
    SearchCode   : string[15];
    Pause        : char;
  begin
    Write('Enter the Partial Customer code: '); ReadLn(SearchCode);
    SearchKey(CodeIndx,RecordNumber,SearchCode);
    if OK then
    begin
      GetRec(CustFile,RecordNumber,Customer);
      DisplayCustomer(Customer);
    end
    else
      Writeln('A record was not found greater than the key ',SearchCode);
    Writeln('Press any key to continue  . . .');
    Read(KBD,Pause);
  end;
```

Fig. 3-13. PGNEXT.BOX displays the next record, after the current one has been displayed.

```
{PGNEXT.BOX}
{Next data by code}

  procedure NextCustomer(var CustFile: DataFile;
                         var CodeIndx: IndexFile );
  var
    RecordNumber : integer;
    SearchCode   : string[15];
    Pause        : char;
  begin
    NextKey(CodeIndx,RecordNumber,SearchCode);
    if OK then
    begin
      clrscr; gotoxy(1,5);
      GetRec(CustFile,RecordNumber,Customer);
      Writeln('The next customer is : ');  writeln;
      DisplayCustomer(Customer);
    end
    else
      Writeln('The end of the database has been reached.');
      writeln;
    Writeln('Press any key to continue  . . .');
    Read(KBD,Pause);
  end;
```

PGPREV.BOX (Fig. 3-14) is similar to PGNEXT.BOX, but it displays the record preceding the last one accessed.

PGADDC.BOX (Fig. 3-15) is used when new records are to be added. It calls the procedure InputInformation in the module PGINFO.BOX.

Fig. 3-14. PGPREV.BOX displays the record that precedes the current one.

```
{PGPREV.BOX}
{Previous data by code}

  procedure PreviousCustomer(var CustFile: DataFile;
                             var CodeIndx: IndexFile);
  var
    RecordNumber : integer;
    SearchCode   : string[15];
    Pause        : char;
  begin
    PrevKey(CodeIndx,RecordNumber,SearchCode);
    if OK then
    begin
      clrscr; gotoxy(1,5);
      GetRec(CustFile,RecordNumber,Customer);
      Writeln('The previous customer is : ');  writeln;
      DisplayCustomer(Customer);
    end
    else
      Writeln('The start of the database has been reached.');
      writeln;
    Writeln('Press any key to continue  . . .');
    Read(KBD,Pause);
  end;
```

Fig. 3-15. PGADDC.BOX is used to add new records to the file.

```
{PGADDC.BOX}
{Adds records to files}

  procedure AddCustomer(var CustFile: DataFile;
                        var CodeIndx: IndexFile);
  var
    RecordNumber     : integer;
    Response         : char;
  begin
    repeat
      clrscr;  gotoxy(1,5);
      InputInformation(Customer);
      FindKey(CodeIndx,RecordNumber,Customer.CustCode);
      If not OK then
      begin
        AddRec(CustFile,RecordNumber,Customer);
        AddKey(CodeIndx,RecordNumber,Customer.CustCode);
        Write('Add another record? ');
      end
      else
        Write('Duplicate code exists. Try another code? ');
      Read(KBD,Response); Writeln(UpCase(Response));
    until UpCase(Response) <> 'Y';
  end;
```

PGDELC.BOX (Fig. 3-16) asks the user to type in the code for a record that is to be deleted. This works fine if duplicate codes are not allowed (NoDuplicate = 0 in PG.BOX). If last names, company names, or such are to be used as codes, then duplicates must be allowed. In that case, this module would have to be changed to display each record that matches the code, and ask whether or not that specific record is to be deleted.

PGUPDT.BOX (Fig. 3-17) is used when the data previously entered are to be changed. This one, too, is going to need some work, because, as it stands, all data for each category must be reentered. Otherwise, you will end up with empty fields.

PGMENU.BOX (Fig. 3-18) simply displays the available choices. Here, again, certain modifications might be desired, depending on how the database is to be used. Again, remember that changes made here will require changes elsewhere.

Now that all of these bits and pieces are on the work disk, you're going to have to compile the program in order to make sure that it works. After the first few lines have been compiled, you'll be confronted by **ERROR: 90 File not found** because the compiler has reached the include directive that asks for ACCESS.BOX, which is not on the disk. In order to successfully compile the program, you must copy ACCESS.BOX, ADDKEY.BOX, DELKEY.BOX, and GETKEY.BOX onto the work disk. Once that's been done, the compilation will be successful and the program will run the way it's supposed to.

Run the program, after having created data and index files with at least five or six records, and select the first choice, List Customer Records, from the menu. You'll find that the individual records scroll by on the screen much too fast to be read. Here is the first reason to make a change.

MODIFYING THE LIST SELECTION

To change the program to display only one record at a time when List Customer Records is selected from the menu, you must first find out which modules are called upon to execute the command.

Fig. 3-16. PGDELC.BOX is used to delete records from the file.

```
{PGDELC.BOX}
{Delete records}

  procedure DeleteCustomer(var CustFile: DataFile;
                           var CodeIndx: IndexFile);
  var
    RecordNumber    : integer;
    Response        : char;
    CustomerCode    : string[15];
  begin
    repeat
      clrscr; gotoxy(1,5);
      Write(' Enter code of customer to be deleted: '); Readln(CustomerCode);
      FindKey(CodeIndx,RecordNumber,Customer.CustCode);
      if OK then
      begin
        DeleteKey(CodeIndx,RecordNumber,Customer.CustCode);
        DeleteRec(CustFile,RecordNumber);
        Write('Delete another record? ');
      end
      else
        Write('Customer code was not found. Try another code? ');
      Read(KBD,Response);
    until UpCase(Response) <> 'Y';
  end;
```

Fig. 3-17. PGUPDT.BOX is used to update or otherwise edit the data contained in a data file.

```
{PGUPDT.BOX}
{Updates recorded data}

  procedure UpdateCustomer(var  CustFile: DataFile;
                           var  CodeIndx: IndexFile);
    var
      RecordNumber    : integer;
      Response        : char;
      CustomerCode    : string[15]; { Same as CustRec.CustCode field }
    begin
      repeat
        Write('Enter code of customer to be updated: ');
        Readln(CustomerCode);
        FindKey(CodeIndx,RecordNumber,CustomerCode);
        if OK then
        begin
          GetRec(CustFile,RecordNumber,Customer);
          DisplayCustomer(Customer);
          InputInformation(Customer);
          PutRec(CustFile,RecordNumber,Customer);
          If CustomerCode <> Customer.CustCode Then
          begin
            DeleteKey(CodeIndx,RecordNumber,CustomerCode);
            AddKey(CodeIndx,RecordNumber,Customer.CustCode);
          end;
          Write('Update another record? ');
        end
        else
          Write('Customer code was not found. Try another code? ');
```

```
      Read(KBD,Response); Writeln(UpCase(Response));
    until UpCase(Response) <> 'Y';
end;
```

Fig. 3-18. PGMENU.BOX offers the choice of ten selections from the menu.

```
{PGMENU.BOX}
{Main menu}

  function Menu: char;
  var
    action: char;
  begin
    ClrScr;
    GotoXY(1,3);
    Writeln('    Enter Number or First Letter');
    Writeln;
    Writeln(' 1)  List Customer Records ');
    Writeln(' 2)  Find a Record by Customer Code ');
    Writeln(' 3)  Search on Partial Customer Code ');
    Writeln(' 4)  Next Customer');
    Writeln(' 5)  Previous Customer');
    Writeln(' 6)  Add to Customer Database ');
    Writeln(' 7)  Edit a Customer Record ');
    Writeln(' 8)  Delete a Customer Record ');
    Writeln(' 9)  Rebuild Index files ');
    Writeln(' 0)  Exit ');
    Writeln(' ');
    Read(KBD,Action);
    Writeln;
    Menu := UpCase(action);
  end;
```

Take a look at the main program in MYDB.PAS. In the **case Menu of** section you will find the name of the procedure that is being called when either 1 or L has been typed from the main menu. That name is ListCustomers, and it can be found in the module PGACCS.BOX.

The loop that causes the records to be displayed is initiated by the line:

```
for RecordNumber := 1 to NumberOfRecords - 1 do
```

It starts with **begin** and ends with the **end:** in the fifth line from the bottom. The changes will have to be made here.

First, we want to see only one record on the screen at a time, meaning that the screen must be cleared before each new record is displayed. This is accomplished by adding **clrscr;** between **begin** and the line that starts with **GetRec**. This would cause the record to be displayed at the very top of the screen, which is all right, but doesn't look very good. Let's, therefore, add **gotoxy(1,8);** to more or less center the display.

There must be a means of holding each individual record on the screen for as long as necessary. The simplest way of doing that is to ask for some type of input to trigger the display of the next record. To achieve this, we insert two lines ahead of the **end;** which represents the end of the loop:

```
write(' Press ENTER   ');
readln(X);
```

This requires that X be declared at the top of the procedure by changing the fifth line from the top to read:

```
Pause, X      : char;
```

That's all that's needed to accomplish the change (Fig. 3-19).

Now compile the program once more, and then run it. Selecting the first choice from the menu, you'll find that each individual record is neatly displayed near the center of the screen, and that it stays there until you press ENTER to go on to the next record.

You might want selected records to be printed. There are, of course, a number of ways to accomplish this. The simplest and cleanest involves creating one more module, that performs the print function. I've called it PGPRNT.BOX (Fig. 3-20). The include directive for it must be added to the main program (MYDB.PAS) before the include directive for PGACCS.BOX, because the procedure PrintCustomers is contained in PGPRNT.BOX and is called by PGACCS.BOX. Figure 3-21 is a listing of the revised version of MYDB.PAS.

Now PGACCS.BOX must be modified, because it should include the option to have the displayed record printed. To do that we add five lines:

```
write(' Do you want this record printed? (Y/N) ');
readln(X);
     case X of
     'Y' : PrintCustomers(Customer);
     'N' : end;
```

Everything else stays the way it was before (Fig. 3-22). When you recompile and run the program, the display of each record is accompanied by the above question. If you answer by typing Y and ENTER, the line printer will print the record exactly as it is displayed (Fig. 3-23).

Fig. 3-19. This is the edited version of the PGACCS.BOX include file.

```
{PGACCS.BOX}
{Access records sequentially}

    procedure ListCustomers(var CustFile: DataFile);
    var
      NumberOfRecords,
      RecordNumber     : integer;
      Pause, X         : char;
    begin
      NumberOfRecords := FileLen(CustFile);
      Writeln('                    Customers   ');
      Writeln;
      for RecordNumber := 1 to NumberOfRecords - 1 do
      begin
        clrscr;  gotoxy(1,8);
        GetRec(CustFile,RecordNumber,Customer);
        if Customer.CustStatus = 0 then DisplayCustomer(Customer);
      write(' Press ENTER   ');
      readln(X);
      end;
      Writeln;
      Write(' Press any key to continue . . .');
      Read(KBD,Pause); Writeln;
    end;
```

Fig. 3-20. PGPRNT.BOX is used when the print option is exercised.

```
{PGPRNT.BOX}
{Prints the selected record}

procedure PrintCustomers(Customer: CustRec);
  begin
    with Customer do
    begin
      Writeln(Lst,' ');
      WriteLn(Lst,'   Code: ',CustCode,'     Date: ',EntryDate);
      Writeln(Lst,'   Name: ',FirstName,' ',LastName);
      WriteLn(Lst,'Company: ',Company);
      Writeln(Lst,'Address: ',Addr1);
      Writeln(Lst,'         ',Addr2);
      Writeln(Lst,'  Phone:',Phone,' ext. ',PhoneExt);
      WriteLn(Lst,'Remarks: ',Remarks1);
      Writeln(Lst,'         ',Remarks2);
      WriteLn(Lst,'         ',Remarks3);
    end;
    Writeln(Lst,' ');
  end;
```

Fig. 3-21. The main program now contains include directives to the modules of the new or edited files.

```
Program MyDatabase;

{$I PG.BOX     }
{$I ACCESS.BOX }
{$I ADDKEY.BOX }
{$I DELKEY.BOX }
{$I GETKEY.BOX }

{$I PGREC.BOX  }
{$I PGGLOB.BOX }

  procedure Stop;
  begin
    GotoXY(1,24);
    Writeln;
    Writeln;
    Writeln;
    Writeln('Customer database program aborted.');
    Halt;
  end;

{$I PGFILE.BOX }
{$I PGINFO.BOX }
{$I PGINDX.BOX }
{$I PGSCRN.BOX }
{$I PGPRNT.BOX }
{$I PGACCS.BOX }
{$I PGCODE.BOX }
{$I PGSRCH.BOX }
{$I PGNEXT.BOX }
{$I PGPREV.BOX }
{$I PGADDC.BOX }
{$I PGDELC.BOX }
{$I PGUPDT.BOX }
```

```
{$I PGMENU.BOX }

var
  Finished: Boolean;
begin
  Finished := false;
  OpenDataFile(CustFile,'CustFile.dat',SizeOf(CustRec));
  OpenIndexFile(CodeIndx,'CodeFile.Ndx',
                SizeOf(Customer.CustCode) - 1,NoDuplicates);
  repeat
    case Menu of
      '1','L': ListCustomers(CustFile);
      '2','F': FindCustomer(CustFile,CodeIndx);
      '3','S': SearchCustomer(CustFile,CodeIndx);
      '4','N': NextCustomer(CustFile,CodeIndx);
      '5','P': PreviousCustomer(CustFile,CodeIndx);
      '6','A': AddCustomer(CustFile,CodeIndx);
      '7','U': UpdateCustomer(CustFile,CodeIndx);
      '8','D': DeleteCustomer(CustFile,CodeIndx);
      '9','R': RebuildIndex(CustFile,CodeIndx);
      '0','E': Finished := true;
      else     Write('Choose 0 - 9: ');
    end;
  until Finished;
  CloseIndex(CodeIndx);
  CloseFile(CustFile);
end.
```

Fig. 3-22. Here, PGACCS.BOX has been modified again.

```
{PGACCS.BOX}
{Access records sequentially}

    procedure ListCustomers(var CustFile: DataFile);
    var
      NumberOfRecords,
      RecordNumber     : integer;
      Pause, X         : char;
    begin
      NumberOfRecords := FileLen(CustFile);
      Writeln('                        Customers  ');
      Writeln;
      for RecordNumber := 1 to NumberOfRecords - 1 do
      begin
        clrscr;  gotoxy(1,8);
        GetRec(CustFile,RecordNumber,Customer);
        if Customer.CustStatus = 0 then DisplayCustomer(Customer);
      write(' Do you want this record printed?  (Y/N)    ');
      readln(KBD,X);
           case X of
           'Y','y' : PrintCustomers(Customer);
           'N','n' : end;
      write(' Press ENTER   ');
      readln(X);
      end;
      Writeln;
      Write(' Press any key to continue . . .');
      Read(KBD,Pause); Writeln;
    end;
```

Fig. 3-23. This is a sample printout produced by the print option of the modified version of the program.

```
    Code: 101     Date: 6/10/86
    Name: FRANK JONES
 Company: ABC CONSTRUCTION CO.
 Address: 186 MICHIGAN AVENUE
          CHICAGO, IL 60606
   Phone:312 555 3456 ext. 12
 Remarks: CREDIT LIMIT $150,000



    Code: 102     Date: 6/12/86
    Name: SHIRLEY BROWN
 Company:
 Address: P.O. BOX 2217
          SANTA FE, NM 87504
   Phone:505 555 8741 ext.
 Remarks: DANCER, ACTRESS



    Code: 103     Date: 6/12/86
    Name: CLARK ROBINSON
 Company: PPG PROGRAMS
 Address: 555 FIFTH AVENUE
          NEW YORK, NY 10016
   Phone:212 555 9876 ext. 2
 Remarks: PROGRAMS IN TURBO PASCAL
          FOR IBM PC AND COMPATIBLES
```

ANOTHER MODIFICATION

In the previous section we tackled the first selection from the menu. In this one we'll look at the seventh, which is used to edit records that were entered at some previous date. Editing a record, as the program now stands, necessitates reentering every item. After displaying the original version of the record, it simply deleted the record in its entirety, replacing it with the new one in exactly the same manner as when new records are added.

Reentering the entire record is a big nuisance when only one item needs to be edited. If, for example there is a change of address, the purpose of the attempted modification is to retain the data in fields that require no editing. For this purpose, one of the program modules was changed and renamed, another was created from scratch, and some minor changes were made in the source code of the main program which, for this version, I've renamed DB.P.

Originally, when the seventh choice was selected from the menu, the program called the UpdateCustomer procedure contained the module PGUPDT.BOX. The new version of this module, now renamed UPDTPG.BOX, consists of a slightly changed procedure, now called Customer Update. In it, the call for DisplayCustomer has been changed to a call for a procedure called CustomerDisplay, and the call for the procedure InputInformation has been eliminated altogether (Fig. 3-24).

CustomerDisplay is contained in a newly created program module called PGDSPL.BOX, in which the individual data for each field of a record is displayed sequentially, along with the question **Edit? (Y/N)**. An **if . . . then** statement examines the reply, going directly to the data in the next field if the answer was negative, or offering an opportunity to edit the data if the answer was affirmative (Fig. 3-25).

Fig. 3-24. This is the edited version of PGUPDT.BOX, used to update the customer information in existing records.

```
{UPDTPG.BOX}
{Updates recorded data}

  procedure CustomerUpdate(var  CustFile: DataFile;
                           var  CodeIndx: IndexFile);

    var
      RecordNumber      : integer;
      Response          : char;
      CustomerCode      : string[15]; { Same as CustRec.CustCode field }
    begin
      repeat
        clrscr;  gotoxy(1,8);
        Write('Enter code of customer to be updated: ');
        Readln(CustomerCode);
        FindKey(CodeIndx,RecordNumber,CustomerCode);
        if OK then
        begin
          GetRec(CustFile,RecordNumber,Customer);
          CustomerDisplay(Customer);
          PutRec(CustFile,RecordNumber,Customer);
          If CustomerCode <> Customer.CustCode Then
          begin
            DeleteKey(CodeIndx,RecordNumber,CustomerCode);
            AddKey(CodeIndx,RecordNumber,Customer.CustCode);
          end;
          Write('Update another record? ');
        end
        else
          Write('Customer code was not found. Try another code? ');
        Read(KBD,Response); Writeln(UpCase(Response));
      until UpCase(Response) <> 'Y';
  end;
```

Fig. 3-25. This include file displays the individual fields that make up the selected record, asking in each case whether correction is to be made.

```
{PGDSPL.BOX}
{Edit information on the screen}

  procedure CustomerDisplay(Customer: CustRec);
var X : char;
  begin
    with Customer do
    begin
      writeln;
      write('   Code: ',CustCode,'                  Edit?  (Y/N)    ');
      readln(X);
      if (X = 'Y') or (X = 'y') then begin
                     writeln;
                     write('Enter new code    ');
                     readln(CustCode);
                     end
                     else
      write('    Date: ',EntryDate,'              Edit?  (Y/N)    ');
      readln(X);
      if (X = 'Y') or (X = 'y') then begin
                     writeln;
```

```
                write('Enter new date    ');
                readln(EntryDate);
                end
                else
write('   First name: ',FirstName,'        Edit?  (Y/N)    ');
readln(X);
if (X = 'Y') or (X = 'y') then begin
                writeln;
                write('Enter new first name    ');
                readln(FirstName);
                end
                else
write('   Last name: ',LastName,'          Edit?  (Y/N)    ');
readln(X);
if (X = 'Y') or (X = 'y') then begin
                writeln;
                write('Enter new last name    ');
                readln(LastName);
                end
                else
write('Company: ',Company,'                Edit?  (Y/N)    ');
readln(X);
if (X = 'Y') or (X = 'y') then begin
                writeln;
                write('Enter new company name    ');
                readln(Company);
                end
                else
write('Street address: ',Addr1,'          Edit?  (Y/N)    ');
readln(X);
if (X = 'Y') or (X = 'y') then begin
                writeln;
                write('Enter new street address    ');
                readln(Addr1);
                end
                else
write('City, State, Zip: ',Addr2,'         Edit?  (Y/N)    ');
readln(X);
if (X = 'Y') or (X = 'y') then begin
                writeln;
                write('Enter new address data   ');
                readln(Addr2);
                end
                else
write('  Phone:',Phone,'                   Edit?  (Y/N)    ');
readln(X);
if (X = 'Y') or (X = 'y') then begin
                writeln;
                write('Enter new phone data   ');
                readln(Phone);
                end
                else
write('  Extension:',PhoneExt,'            Edit?  (Y/N)    ');
readln(X);
if (X = 'Y') or (X = 'y') then begin
                writeln;
                write('Enter new phone extension   ');
                readln(PhoneExt);
```

```
                    end
                    else
    write('Remarks: ',Remarks1,'                    Edit?  (Y/N)     ');
    readln(X);
    if (X = 'Y') or (X = 'y') then begin
                    writeln;
                    write('Enter new remarks    ');
                    readln(Remarks1);
                    end
                    else
    write('Remarks: ',Remarks2,'                    Edit?  (Y/N)     ');
    readln(X);
    if (X = 'Y') or (X = 'y') then begin
                    writeln;
                    write('Enter new remarks    ');
                    readln(Remarks2);
                    end
                    else
    write('Remarks: ',Remarks3,'                    Edit?  (Y/N)     ');
    readln(X);
    if (X = 'Y') or (X = 'y') then begin
                    writeln;
                    write('Enter new remarks    ');
                    readln(Remarks3);
                    end
                    else
    end;
  Writeln;
end;
```

In the source code for the main program only three changes had to be made. In line seven of the **case Menu of** section, UpdateCustomer had to be changed to CustomerUpdate. The include directive {$I PGUPDT.BOX } has been changed to {$I UPDTPG.BOX }, and a new include directive, {$I PGDSPL.BOX }, has been added (Fig. 3-26).

ADDING A PRINT OPTION

To add a print option to the second, third, forth, and fifth choices from the main menu, the required modifications are quite minor. In the procedure called DisplayCustomer you simply add five lines at the bottom, asking whether or not the displayed record is to be printed. If the answer is affirmative, the program calls the procedure PrintCustomer, which is in the PGPRNT.BOX module that was created when you modified the first choice from the menu. Also, do not forget to declare the added variable X to avoid an annoying error message during compilation (Fig. 3-27).

To retain the various stages of the different modules used during these progressive modifications, I renamed the module PGSCRN.BOX, containing the DisplayCustomer procedure, to SCRNPG.BOX. I also changed the name of the source code for the main program to BASE.P, thus retaining the .COM versions of each stage in the modification process.

The only changes necessary in the source code of the main program is to change {$I PGSCRN.BOX } to {$I SCRNPG.BOX }, and to move the include directive {$I PGPRNT.BOX } to a position ahead of that. The procedure DisplayCustomer calls the procedure PrintCustomers, so an **unknown identifier** error would occur during compilation if the module containing that identifier were positioned further down in the source code (Fig. 3-28).

When you compile the program and run it, regardless of whether you select the second, third, fourth, or fifth choice from the menu, the program will now offer you the option of having the displayed record printed (Fig. 3-29).

Fig. 3-26. This is the new version of the main program, calling the various modified include files.

```
Program MyDatabase;

{$I PG.BOX      }
{$I ACCESS.BOX }
{$I ADDKEY.BOX }
{$I DELKEY.BOX }
{$I GETKEY.BOX }

{$I PGREC.BOX  }
{$I PGGLOB.BOX }

  procedure Stop;
  begin
    GotoXY(1,24);
    Writeln;
    Writeln;
    Writeln;
    Writeln('Customer database program aborted.');
    Halt;
  end;

{$I PGFILE.BOX }
{$I PGINFO.BOX }
{$I PGINDX.BOX }
{$I PGSCRN.BOX }
{$I PGDSPL.BOX }
{$I PGPRNT.BOX }
{$I PGACCS.BOX }
{$I PGCODE.BOX }
{$I PGSRCH.BOX }
{$I PGNEXT.BOX }
{$I PGPREV.BOX }
{$I PGADDC.BOX }
{$I PGDELC.BOX }
{$I UPDTPG.BOX }
{$I PGMENU.BOX }

var
  Finished: Boolean;
begin
  Finished := false;
  OpenDataFile(CustFile,'CustFile.dat',SizeOf(CustRec));
  OpenIndexFile(CodeIndx,'CodeFile.Ndx',
                SizeOf(Customer.CustCode) - 1,NoDuplicates);
  repeat
    case Menu of
      '1','L': ListCustomers(CustFile);
      '2','F': FindCustomer(CustFile,CodeIndx);
      '3','S': SearchCustomer(CustFile,CodeIndx);
      '4','N': NextCustomer(CustFile,CodeIndx);
      '5','P': PreviousCustomer(CustFile,CodeIndx);
      '6','A': AddCustomer(CustFile,CodeIndx);
      '7','U': CustomerUpdate(CustFile,CodeIndx);
      '8','D': DeleteCustomer(CustFile,CodeIndx);
      '9','R': RebuildIndex(CustFile,CodeIndx);
      '0','E': Finished := true;
```

```
      else      Write('Choose 0 - 9: ');
    end;
  until Finished;
  CloseIndex(CodeIndx);
  CloseFile(CustFile);
end.
```

Fig. 3-27. This file displays the selected record on the screen and asks whether a hard copy is desired.

```
{SCRNPG.BOX}
{Display information on the screen, with printer option}

  procedure DisplayCustomer(Customer: CustRec);

  var X : char;

  begin
    with Customer do
    begin
      clrscr; gotoxy(1,8);
      Writeln;
      WriteLn('    Code: ',CustCode,'     Date: ',EntryDate);
      Writeln('    Name: ',FirstName,' ',LastName);
      WriteLn('Company: ',Company);
      Writeln('Address: ',Addr1);
      Writeln('          ',Addr2);
      Writeln('   Phone:',Phone,' ext. ',PhoneExt);
      WriteLn('Remarks: ',Remarks1);
      Writeln('          ',Remarks2);
      WriteLn('          ',Remarks3);
    end;
    Writeln;
    Write(' Do you wish this record printed?  (Y/N)       ');
    Readln(X);
              case X of
              'Y','y' : PrintCustomers(Customer);
              'N','n' : end;
  end;
```

Fig. 3-28. The main program is changed once more, to accommodate the various modifications.

```
Program MyDatabase;

{$I PG.BOX      }
{$I ACCESS.BOX }
{$I ADDKEY.BOX }
{$I DELKEY.BOX }
{$I GETKEY.BOX }

{$I PGREC.BOX  }
{$I PGGLOB.BOX }

  procedure Stop;
  begin
    GotoXY(1,24);
    Writeln;
    Writeln;
```

```
    Writeln;
    Writeln('Customer database program aborted.');
    Halt;
  end;

{$I PGFILE.BOX }
{$I PGINFO.BOX }
{$I PGINDX.BOX }
{$I PGPRNT.BOX }
{$I SCRNPG.BOX }
{$I PGDSPL.BOX }
{$I PGACCS.BOX }
{$I PGCODE.BOX }
{$I PGSRCH.BOX }
{$I PGNEXT.BOX }
{$I PGPREV.BOX }
{$I PGADDC.BOX }
{$I PGDELC.BOX }
{$I UPDTPG.BOX }
{$I PGMENU.BOX }

var
  Finished: Boolean;
begin
  Finished := false;
  OpenDataFile(CustFile,'CustFile.dat',SizeOf(CustRec));
  OpenIndexFile(CodeIndx,'CodeFile.Ndx',
              SizeOf(Customer.CustCode) - 1,NoDuplicates);
  repeat
    case Menu of
      '1','L': ListCustomers(CustFile);
      '2','F': FindCustomer(CustFile,CodeIndx);
      '3','S': SearchCustomer(CustFile,CodeIndx);
      '4','N': NextCustomer(CustFile,CodeIndx);
      '5','P': PreviousCustomer(CustFile,CodeIndx);
      '6','A': AddCustomer(CustFile,CodeIndx);
      '7','U': CustomerUpdate(CustFile,CodeIndx);
      '8','D': DeleteCustomer(CustFile,CodeIndx);
      '9','R': RebuildIndex(CustFile,CodeIndx);
      '0','E': Finished := true;
      else     Write('Choose 0 - 9: ');
    end;
  until Finished;
  CloseIndex(CodeIndx);
  CloseFile(CustFile);
end.
```

Fig. 3-29. This printout was produced by the revised print option.

```
   Code: 103    Date: 6/12/86
   Name: CLARK ROBINSON
Company: PPG PROGRAMS
Address: 555 FIFTH AVENUE
         NEW YORK, NY 10016
  Phone:212 555 9876 ext. 2
Remarks: PROGRAMS IN TURBO PASCAL
         FOR IBM PC AND COMPATIBLES
```

LOOKING AT BTREE.PAS

Before doing anything with BTREE.PAS you must, of course, compile the program. Even though the actual source code of BTREE.PAS is quite short, the compiling process takes quite a while because of the various include files {$I FILENAME.EXT} that contain the procedures and functions that are responsible for program execution.

You now have a compiled version called BTREE.COM (you might want to rename that file, calling it, say, DATA.COM, because BTREE, which refers to a highly technical concept that is used in this program, is really a rather ridiculous file name). Now type BTREE (or the file name you've selected) and the display greets you with the program title:

```
Turbo-Access Customer Database
```

and a line reading:

```
Data files missing. Create new files? (Y/N)
```

After you've replied with Y, you'll see:

```
TURBO-Access Customer Database 0 Records in use
```

and across the bottom of the screen:

```
Select: U)pdate L)ist Q)uit
```

At this point the data file is still empty, so you'll have to use **U)pdate** in order to enter some data into the file. The display now changes to:

```
Code:                   Date:

First Name:             Last Name:
Company:
Address 1:
Address 2:

Phone:                  Extension:

Remarks 1:
Remarks 2:
Remarks 3:

--------------------------------------------------------------------------------
Update: A)dd   F)ind   Q)uit
--------------------------------------------------------------------------------
```

Type A and an underline appears after **Code:**, asking that you type in an identification of some kind. Because the variable representing the code is declared as STRING[15], you can use digits, letters, or both, with up to 15 characters (I used 101, 102, and so on during my trial runs). You don't have to count the characters because the underline to the right of the word **Code:** is 15 characters long. When a code has been entered and ENTER has been pressed, an underline, eight characters long, appears to the right of **Date:**, allowing for date entry of up to eight characters, something like 5/14/86 or 11/8/86. It doesn't really matter. Now go to **First Name:**, where you might also want to include a middle initial, then **Last Name:, Company:**, etc. **Address 1:** and **Address 2:** are somewhat confusing, but simply mean that you can use two lines for the address. I would have preferred prompts reading ADDRESS for the first line and CITY, STATE, ZIP for the second, but that can always be changed. The rest is self-explanatory. When there's nothing to be entered, for example, no telephone extension, simply press ENTER and the cursor will move to the next item.

After the last item has been taken care of, it takes a second or so for this program to store the new data in the data file, and to internally create or update the index files. If you're planning to use this program to store large numbers of data, copy the .COM version of the program onto a formatted blank disk in order to have plenty of disk space. There isn't a lot of space left on the copy of the distribution disk.

After you type Q to exit, the display returns to the first line of prompts:

```
Select: U)update L)ist Q)uit
```

If you type L, to have the program display the data that you've entered, the display prompts with

```
Output device: P)rinter S)creen
```

After you've made your selection, probably by typing S, you're prompted with

```
Sort by C)ode N)ame U)nsorted
```

If you now type N, the program presents you with codes and names, in alphabetical order by last names.

To retrieve entire records, use **F)ind** from the display that was previously used to enter data. As before, an underline will appear after **Code:**. You have three possible choices of the keys to be used. You can use the code, the first and last names, or the last name only. If you want to use the last name, the most usual choice, simply press ENTER several times until the underline appears next to **Last Name:**. Type the last name of the person you want, and the program responds by displaying the entire record for that person.

You're now asked whether you want to see the next or previous record. If you select **N)ext**, you'll be shown the next record in alphabetical order, not the order in which records were originally entered. Similarly, if you select **P)revious**, then the alphabetically previous record will be displayed.

A MINOR MODIFICATION

Before attempting to make any modification of the existing program, you'll have to analyze the program and its various components to understand where, exactly, the changes will have to be made. One problem is that the source code that is shown on pages 44 through 57 of the documentation book does not match what we're looking at when we call up BTREE.PAS. Apparently, the program was modified after the book was printed, because the code reproduced in the book is identified as "version 1.0," written in 1984, while the code on the disk was modified in October of 1985.

In this section you'll make a very small change. It will alter the character of the database program from one that stores records of customers to one that handles a product inventory. For anyone other than an extremely experienced programmer, making major changes is likely to produce all manner of confusion because of the profusion of procedures and functions that must interact with one another. What you'll do is simply change the input prompts and leave everything else alone. This means, of course, that you must find the procedure that produces the record that is used for data input. Judging by the program listing in the book, that procedure is called OutForm and it appears on page 48. But is is certainly nowhere to be found in the BTREE.PAS source code (Fig. 3-30). That source code does include an {$I BTREE.INC} line just ahead of the main program, which should tip you off to the fact that OutForm is likely to be found in the BTREE.INC module. By listing the source code for that module, you'll find the procedure approximately 130 lines down from the top.

The trick is to change the prompts that make up the record form in such a way that retrieval of individual records is easy. Remember that the way the program is written, records may be retrieved by typing the code, the first and last name, or the last name only, but not the first name only. Also, the individual fields are limited in the number of characters that may be entered into each:

Code	15 characters
Date	8 characters
First name	15 characters
Last name	30 characters
Company	40 characters
Address 1	40 characters
Address 2	40 characters
Phone	15 characters
Extension	5 characters
Remarks 1	40 characters
Remarks 2	40 characters
Remarks 3	40 characters

The new entry prompts selected for this modification are Product (name of the product), Mfr. (manufacturer), Contact (name of the sales person to contact), Cost (wholesale price), Price (retail price), Reorder (minimum number to be kept in inventory), and On Hand (number on hand). There would seem to be no reason to change the Code, Date and Remarks prompts.

Replace First Name with Product, Last Name with Mfr., Company with Contact, Address 1 with Cost $, Address 2 with Price $, Phone with Reorder, and Extension with On Hand (Fig. 3-31). Code can be entered as before, but be aware that numerical codes are sorted by the first digit first, so that code numbers 300, 101, 2105, 50 would be sorted as 101, 2105, 300, 50. Decide

Fig. 3-30. The modification made in the OutForm procedure of the BTREE demonstration program changes it from a customer to a product inventory program.

```
procedure OutForm;
begin
  GotoXY(7,5);  Write('Code :');
  GotoXY(29,5); Write('Date :');
  GotoXY(1,7);  Write('Product     :');
  GotoXY(29,7); Write('Mfr.        :');
  GotoXY(2,9);  Write('Contact     :');
  GotoXY(2,10); Write('Cost        $');
  GotoXY(2,11); Write('Price       $');
  GotoXY(2,13); Write('Reorder     :');
  GotoXY(29,13);Write('On hand     :');
  GotoXY(2,15); Write('Remarks 1   :');
  GotoXY(2,16); Write('Remarks 2   :');
  GotoXY(2,17); Write('Remarks 3   :');
end;
```

Fig. 3-31. The initial version of the main program shows the structure of the personalized database program.

```
{Personalized Database main program}
{PGM.P    }

var CHOICE     : integer;

{$I VALUES.DB    }
{$I TYP.DB       }

{$I ACCESS.BOX   }
{$I ADDKEY.BOX   }
{$I GETKEY.BOX   }
{$I DELKEY.BOX   }

{$I GLBL.DB      }
{$I QUIT.DB      }
{$I OPNDTA.DB    }
{$I ENTREC.DB    }
{$I SETINDX.DB   }
{$I PRNTNG.DB    }
{$I SHOW.DB      }
{$I LIST.DB      }
{$I FIND.DB      }
{$I CHANGE.DB    }
{$I MENU.DB      }

begin
  OpenDataFile(PersFile,'PersFile.DAT',SizeOf(PersRec));
  OpenIndexFile(NameIndx,'NameFile.NDX',
                SizeOf(Person.PersCode)-1,Duplicates);
     repeat
     Selection;
     until CHOICE = 0;
     CloseFile(PersFile);
     CloseIndex(NameIndx);
{     CloseIndex(CompFile.NDX);
     CloseIndex(CityFile.NDX);
     CloseIndex(StIDFile.NDX);
     CloseIndex(ZipFile.NDX);
     CloseIndex(AreaFile.NDX);
     CloseIndex(MnthFile.NDX);      }
end.
```

on the number of digits to be used by estimating the number of different products that might be entered into the database (3 digits = 999 max, 4 digits = 9,999 max, 5 digits = 65,535 max). The date is entered as usual, and should always be reentered when changes are made in one of the fields. The product name or description is limited to 15 characters, that should be sufficient. The manufacturer may be up to 30 characters long, and the name of the contact at the supplier is limited to 40 characters. For cost and price entries, there is no need to worry about the character limit. The same is true of the reorder number. The number on hand is limited to five characters (99999 or 9,999) which should be more than enough. Remarks can be used for anything you like (up to 40 characters each), such as the supplier's address and phone number, or current credit balance. If the lines are always used for specific purposes, you might want to change the prompt from Remarks 1 to, say, Address 1.

As the modification now stands, records may be retrieved by the code, by typing the product name and the manufacturer, or by typing just the manufacturer. If the Mfr.: and Product: prompts are reversed, it would be possible to retrieve records by the product name alone, which, in certain cases, might be preferable.

This modification works perfectly without the need to touch anything else in the program. Beware of either adding or deleting any of the prompts that make up the record, or of attempting to change the keys by which records may be retrieved. If you do that, you'll find that you'll also have to make changes in the procedures ClearForm, InputCust, and OutCust. There might be other changes that would need to be made in BTREE.INC, as well as in BTREE.PAS. In other words, no matter what type of data you want to record, make do with the existing 12 input-prompt positions, leaving everything else untouched. For instance, if you wanted to use the program to keep a record of recipes, you could change the prompt descriptions to permit the entry of a list of ingredients in prompts 3 through 9, and use 10 through 12, the Remarks prompts, for a description of what must be done with the ingredients.

If you need a really sophisticated database program, one that not only stores information, but also produces comparison charts and all sorts of other gimmicks, then instead of spending $54.95 for the Turbo Database Toolbox, add roughly $100 and buy the Borland International program called Reflex.

CREATING A DATABASE PROGRAM

Having gotten this far, the next logical step would seem to be to go to work and try to write your own database program, using parameters of your choosing and, of course, the facilities and conveniences offered by the Turbo Database Toolbox routines.

This exercise, though useful in resulting in a degree of familiarity with the Database Toolbox routines, shows the difficulties involved in extensively modifying the code, because it in no way matched the hoped-for improvements.

The first step should be to write the main program, a catchall framework that is to be used with a large number of include files (Fig. 3-31). Thus, the main program is designed to do nothing more than call up the menu to give the user the opportunity to select a choice or exit the program. The **repeat . . . until** loop permits repeated use of the program without having to reactivate it each time. The loop will always return the user to the menu after the completion of a task. At this stage, the include files, with the exception of those with the extension .BOX, are, to some extent, guesswork. Those with that .BOX extension are the ones contained on the Turbo Database Toolbox distribution disk. Those with the extension DB are the ones that you have to write yourself.

Logically, the next step would be to write the menu, because the choices listed on it will determine the makeup of the rest of the database program. In keeping with the convention of using only include files, write it as MENU.DB (Fig. 3-32). Remember that Turbo Pascal assumes a three-letter extension. Therefore, if fewer than three letters are used, there must be at least three spaces between the period and the closing brace. Otherwise, the computer will assume that the closing brace is part of the extension. The four .BOX files must be copied from the distribution disk onto the disk you're working with. All of the .DB files, once they are written, must also be on that disk.

The menu is designed to eventually give the user nine choices, one to permit data entry and eight different methods by which records can be retrieved. The reason for these different retrieval options is that, for instance, you might remember an area code, but not the exact name of the person you're looking for. Therefore, the program should be able to display all records that conform to any of the keys. For the moment, as you'll notice by looking at the **case CHOICE of** section, I've enclosed selections three through eight in braces. I expect to encounter enough problems getting the program to compile and work, without, for the time being, worrying about those extra data and index files. Also, the procedure names for those selections are strictly tem-

Fig. 3-32. The include file MENU.DB contains the menu with its ten choices.

```
{This is the menu for the personalized database program}
{MENU.DB }

procedure Selection;
    begin
          clrscr;  gotoxy(1,4);
          writeln('                       MENU');
          writeln('                       ====');
          writeln;
          writeln('          1)    Enter new records');
          writeln('    ----------------------------------------');
          writeln('                Retrieve records by:');
          writeln('                --------------------');
          writeln('          2)    Last Name');
          writeln('          3)    Company');
          writeln('          4)    City');
          writeln('          5)    State ID');
          writeln('          6)    Zip code (first 2 digits)');
          writeln('          7)    Area code');
          writeln('          8)    Birth month');
          writeln('    ----------------------------------------');
          writeln('          9)    Display all records');
          writeln('    ----------------------------------------');
          writeln('          0)    Exit program');
          writeln('    ----------------------------------------');
          write('               Which?                    ');
          readln(CHOICE);
                         case CHOICE of
                         1 :  AddPerson(PersFile,NameIndx);
                         2 :  FindPerson(PersFile,NameIndx);
      {                   3 :  RetrieveCompany;
                         4 :  RetrieveCity;
                         5 :  RetrieveID;
                         6 :  RetrieveZip;
                         7 :  RetrieveArea;
                         8 :  RetrieveMonth;      }
                         9 :  ListPersons(PersFile);
                         0 :  end;

    end;
```

porary and might eventually have to be changed, once the appropriate include files have been written.

The first include file that must be written is one to declare the constants that are going to be used throughout program execution by the Toolbox modules and include files. This file is called VALUES.DB (Fig. 3-33). The values shown were derived by compiling and using the SET-CONST.PAS program from the distribution disk. The value for Max DataRecSize is the number of bytes shown by PC DOS when I wrote a record using the maximum number of characters for each line. I used the DIR command to get the number of bytes used by each file. The Turbo Pascal main menu will also display the number of bytes after you use the editing mode to write a temporary file that consists of the maximum number of characters allowed in a single record. (There is a SizeOf procedure available with Turbo Pascal that accomplished the same thing.) Notice that I declared the constant Duplicates as one, meaning that duplicate keys are allowed, because the program does not include a requirement for a unique code for each person, using last names and other criteria as keys, so there are bound to be duplicates.

Fig. 3-33. The include file VALUES.DB contains the constants needed by the program during execution.

```
{Declaration of constants to be used in the personalized database program}
{VALUES.DB }

Const
  MaxDataRecSize = 178;
  MaxKeyLen      =  30;
  PageSize       =  24;
  Order          =  12;
  PageStackSize  =  10;
  MaxHeight      =   3;
  Duplicates     =   1;
```

A second include file that will be used to handle the type declarations must be written. I've called it TYP.DB. It declares every field in the record as a string with a given maximum number of characters. The PersCode will eventually have to be changed to string[30], because that's the longest field that can be used as a key, but for the time being [15] will be fine (Fig. 3-34).

The next include file, GLBL.DB, (Fig. 3-35) simply declares three global variables. Its include directive in the main program must be placed after the four Toolbox include files, because the values represented by DataFile and IndexFile are established somewhere in those files, and PersRec was declared in the TYP.DB.

Any program needs a procedure that is called when the program is aborted for one reason or another. This include file, called QUIT.DB (Fig. 3-36), simply displays a line of text before responding to Halt, which is a procedure contained in the Toolbox routines.

ENTREC.DB (Fig. 3-37) is the next file to be written. It consists of two procedures. One is called EnterData, which declares a number of variables and uses a Repeat . . . Until loop to call the procedure that is used to enter the information into a record. Then it calls the other procedure, AddRec, which causes this data to be added to the data file. This routine continues for as many records as you wish to enter. This include file must be placed after one that opens the appropriate data file. Otherwise, it would not be possible to place the typed data into the file.

Fig. 3-34. The file TYP.DB performs the type definitions.

```
{Type declarations for personalized database program}
{TYP.DB }

type
    PersRec = record
            PersStatus     : integer;
            PersCode       : string[15];
            FirstName      : string[15];
            LastName       : string[15];
            Company        : string[25];
            City           : string[30];
            Addr           : string[40];
            StateID        : string[2];
            Zip            : string[10];
            Area           : string[3];
            Phone          : string[8];
            Ext            : string[3];
            BirthMonth     : string[2];
   end;

FilenameType = string[14];
```

Fig. 3-35. GLBL.DB contains the global variables.

```
{Global variables declared here}
{GLBL.DB  }

var PersFile  : DataFile;
NameIndx      : IndexFile;
Person        : PersRec;
```

Fig. 3-36. QUIT.DB terminates program execution.

```
{This procedure stops program execution}
{QUIT.DB }

procedure Stop;

begin
     clrscr;  gotoxy(1,10);
     writeln('                    Database program has been aborted.');
     writeln('                    ==================================');
     Halt;
end;
```

Fig. 3-37. ENTREC.DB is used to enter data for the individual records.

```
{Here information is entered into the data file}
{ENTREC.DB }

procedure InputInformation(var Person : PersRec);


     begin
          clrscr;  gotoxy(1,5);
       writeln('      Enter Customer Information');
       writeln('      ==========================');
       With Person do begin
       write('Enter First Name       (to 15 characters)   ');
       readln(FirstName);
       write('Enter Last Name        (to 15 characters)   ');
       readln(PersCode);
       write('Enter Company          (to 25 characters)   ');
       readln(Company);
       write('Enter Address          (to 40 characters)   ');
       readln(Addr);
       write('Enter City             (to 30 characters)   ');
       readln(City);
       write('Enter State ID         (2 characters)       ');
       readln(StateID);
       write('Enter Zip Code         (to 10 characters)   ');
       readln(Zip);
       write('Enter Area code        (3 digits)           ');
       readln(Area);
       write('Enter Phone number     (8 characters)       ');
       readln(Phone);
       write('Enter phone extension  (to 3 characters)    ');
       readln(Ext);
       write('Enter Month of Birth   (1 or 2 digits)      ');
       readln(BirthMonth);
       end;
```

```
end;

procedure EnterData;

var
  InputRec        : PersRec;
  RecordNumber    : integer;
  Response        : char;
  PersFile        : DataFile;

begin
  repeat
    InputInformation(InputRec);
    AddRec(PersFile,RecordNumber,InputRec);
    writeln;
    write(`Enter another record?  (Y/N)    ');
    read(KBD,Response);
    writeln(UpCase(Response));
  until UpCase(Response) <> 'Y';
end;
```

OPNDTA.DB (Fig. 3-38) is the file containing the procedure OpenDataFile, which calls the Toolbox routine OpenFile, which opens the data file called PersFile and prepares it to accept data. If this is the first run and that file does not yet exist, the procedure calls the alternate Toolbox routine MakeFile that creates the needed data file, opening it at the same time.

The next include file, SETINDX.DB (Fig. 3-39), deals with index files. It is a duplicate of the one that either opens or creates a data file, except that, in this case, it is an index file that is opened or created.

SHOW.DB (Fig. 3-40) is the include file that's used to display the data contained in the data

Fig. 3-38. OPNDTA.DB is used to open a data file, or to create one if it does not already exist.

```
{Open the data file called PersFile.DTA}
{OPNDTA.DB }

procedure OpenDataFile(var PersFile   :  DataFile;
                           Fname      :  FilenameType;
                           Size       :  integer);

var   create  :  char;

begin
     OpenFile(PersFile,Fname,Size);
     if not OK then
          begin
             clrscr; gotoxy(1,10);
             writeln('  The data file ',Fname,' does not yet exist.  ');
             writeln;
             write('  Do you want to create that file?  (Y/N)   ');
             read(KBD,create);
             writeln;
             if UpCase(create) = 'Y' then
                  MakeFile(PersFile,Fname,Size)
             else Stop;
           end;
           if not OK then Stop;
     end;
```

Fig. 3-39. SETINDX.DB opens or creates an index file.

```
{Open or create index file}
{SETINDX.DB }

  procedure OpenIndexFile(var NameIndx  : IndexFile;
                              Fname     : FilenameType;
                              KeySize   : integer;
                              Dups      : integer);

  var
    create : char;

  begin
    InitIndex;
    OpenIndex(NameIndx, Fname,KeySize,Dups);
    if not OK then
    begin
      writeln;
      writeln;
      writeln(' The index file: ',fname,' does not yet exist.');
      writeln;
      write(' Do you want to create it? ');
      read(KBD, create);
      if UpCase(create) = 'Y' then
        RebuildIndex(PersFile,NameIndx)
      else
        Stop;
    end;
    If not OK then Stop;
  end;
```

file, one record at a time. The 12 If . . . Then lines convert the numbers 1 to 12 to the names of months, which produces a better looking display. The last line asks whether the displayed record is to be printed, in which case the procedure PrintPerson is called (Fig. 3-40). That procedure is contained in the include file PRNTNG.DB (Fig. 3-41) which has yet to be written. In the main program, it must be placed ahead of SHOW.DB in order to be called without the need for some complicated Forward declaration.

LIST.DB (Fig. 3-42) is the include file that contains the procedure ListPersons, used to list all records sequentially without accessing any index files. After each record display a key must be pressed in order to go on to the next one.

FIND.DB (Fig. 3-43) is used to ask that a key be entered, in this case, the last name of the person in question. The procedure FindPerson then calls the Toolbox procedure FindKey to compare that name with the one stored in the index file as a key. When it's found, it causes the appropriate record(s) to be displayed.

ADD.DB (Fig. 3-44) uses the procedure AddPerson to call the Toolbox procedures AddRec and AddKey to add new records and keys to the data and index files.

CHANGE.DB (Fig. 3-45) is used to edit a record when changes are called for. It finds the record in question, deletes it, and then asks that you type in the corrected data. At this point, unfortunately, it is not possible to type only the changes, while retaining the unchanged portions of the record.

So far, so good. The compiler, after stopping a few times because of some missing semicolons or similar errors, compiles the program. As it's being run, it asks the appropriate questions about the creation of a data and index file, and then displays the prompts used to enter the data

Fig. 3-40. SHOW.DB displays a record on the screen, converting the number that represents the birth month into the name of the month.

```
{Display records}
{SHOW.DB }

procedure DisplayPerson(Person : PersRec);

var MONTH      : string[10];
    BIRTHMONTH : string[2];
    YN         : char;

begin
         if BirthMonth = '1' then MONTH := 'January';
         if BirthMonth = '2' then MONTH := 'February';
         if BirthMonth = '3' then MONTH := 'March';
         if BirthMonth = '4' then MONTH := 'April';
         if BirthMonth = '5' then MONTH := 'May';
         if BirthMonth = '6' then MONTH := 'June';
         if BirthMonth = '7' then MONTH := 'July';
         if BirthMonth = '8' then MONTH := 'August';
         if BirthMonth = '9' then MONTH := 'September';
         if BirthMonth = '10' then MONTH := 'October';
         if BirthMonth = '11' then MONTH := 'November';
         if BirthMonth = '12' then MONTH := 'December';

    with Person do
    begin
         clrscr;  gotoxy(1,8);
       writeln('Name:          ',FirstName,' ',PersCode);
       writeln('Company:       ',Company);
       writeln;
       writeln('Address:       ',Addr,', ',City,', ',StateID,' ',Zip);
       writeln;
       writeln('Phone:         (',Area,') ',Phone,' Ext: ',Ext);
       writeln;
       writeln('Birth Month: ',BirthMonth);
 {      writeln('-----------------------------------------------------');
       write('Do you want this record printed?  (Y/N)    ');
       readln(YN);
          if UpCase(YN) = 'Y' then PrintPerson(PersRec) else    }
       end;
  end;
```

Fig. 3-41. PRNTNG.DB is the same as SHOW.DB, except that the data are sent to the printer instead of being displayed on the screen.

```
{Procedure to have records printed}
{PRNTNG.DB }

procedure PrintPerson(Person : PersRec);

var MONTH      : string[10];
    BIRTHMONTH : string[2];

begin
         if BirthMonth = '1' then MONTH := 'January';
         if BirthMonth = '2' then MONTH := 'February';
         if BirthMonth = '3' then MONTH := 'March';
```

```
        if BirthMonth = '4' then MONTH := 'April';
        if BirthMonth = '5' then MONTH := 'May';
        if BirthMonth = '6' then MONTH := 'June';
        if BirthMonth = '7' then MONTH := 'July';
        if BirthMonth = '8' then MONTH := 'August';
        if BirthMonth = '9' then MONTH := 'September';
        if BirthMonth = '10' then MONTH := 'October';
        if BirthMonth = '11' then MONTH := 'November';
        if BirthMonth = '12' then MONTH := 'December';

  with Person do
  begin
        clrscr;  gotoxy(1,5);
     writeln(Lst,'Name:          ',FirstName,' ',LastName);
     writeln(Lst,'Company:       ',Company);
     writeln(Lst);
     writeln(Lst,'Address:       ',Addr,' ',City,', ',StateID,' ',Zip);
     writeln(Lst);
     writeln(Lst,'Phone:          (',Area,') ',Phone,' Ext: ',Ext);
     writeln(Lst);
     writeln(Lst,'Birth Month: ',Month);
     writeln(Lst);
     writeln(Lst);
     end;
end;
```

Fig. 3-42. LIST.DB causes records to be displayed sequentially in the order in which they were originally entered.

```
{List all records in sequence}
{LIST.DB}

procedure ListPersons(var PersFile: DataFile);

    var
      NumberOfRecords,
      RecordNumber     : integer;
      Pause            : char;

    begin
          clrscr; gotoxy(1,8);
      NumberOfRecords := FileLen(PersFile);
      for RecordNumber := 1 to NumberOfRecords - 1 do
      begin
        GetRec(PersFile,RecordNumber,Person);
        if Person.PersStatus = 0 then DisplayPerson(Person);
      end;
      writeln;
      write(` Press any key to continue      ');
      read(KBD,Pause);
      writeln;
    end;
```

Fig. 3-43. This file causes records to be displayed based on the last name of the person in question.

```
{Find all records by a given last name}
{FIND.DB}

procedure FindPerson(var PersFile : DataFile;
```

```
                    var NameIndx : IndexFile);

var
  NumberOfRecords,
  RecordNumber    : integer;
  Pause           : char;
  Name, PersCode  : string[15];
  X               : integer;

begin
       X := 1;
       clrscr; gotoxy(1,8);
  write('Enter last name  ');
  readln(Name);
  NumberOfRecords := FileLen(PersFile);
  for RecordNumber := X to NumberOfRecords - 1 do
  begin
    SearchKey(NameIndx,RecordNumber,PersCode);
    if OK then
    begin
    GetRec(PersFile,RecordNumber,Person);
    DisplayPerson(Person);
    end;
       gotoxy(1,20);
  write('Press any key to continue      ');
  read(KBD,Pause);
       X := X + 1;
  end;
  writeln;
end;
```

Fig. 3-44. ADD.DB is used to add new records to the file.

```
{Add new records}
{ADD.DB }

  procedure AddPerson(var PersFile : DataFile;
                      var NameIndx : IndexFile);

  var
    RecordNumber    : integer;
    Response        : char;

  begin
    repeat
      InputInformation(Person);
      begin
        AddRec(PersFile,RecordNumber,Person);
        AddKey(NameIndx,RecordNumber,Person.PersCode);
        write('Add another record? ');
      end;
    until UpCase(Response) <> 'Y';
  end;
```

Fig. 3-45. CHANGE.DB is used to edit data in existing records.

```
{Procedure to edit records}
{CHANGE.DB }
```

```
procedure UpdatePerson(var  PersFile : DataFile;
                       var  NameIndx : IndexFile);

  var
    RecordNumber      : integer;
    Response          : char;
    PersonCode        : string[15];

  begin
    repeat
      write('Enter last name of person to be updated: ');
      readln(PersonCode);
      FindKey(NameIndx,RecordNumber,PersonCode);
      if OK then
      begin
        GetRec(PersFile,RecordNumber,Person);
        DisplayPerson(Person);
        InputInformation(Person);
        PutRec(PersFile,RecordNumber,Person);
        if PersonCode <> Person.PersCode then
        begin
          DeleteKey(NameIndx,RecordNumber,PersonCode);
          AddKey(NameIndx,RecordNumber,Person.PersCode);
        end;
        write('Update another record?  (Y/N)   ');
      end
      else
        write('That last name was not found. Try another name?  (Y/N)   ');
        read(KBD,Response);
        writeln(UpCase(Response));
    until UpCase(Response) <> 'Y';
end;
```

that make up a record. Trouble! After all data are typed and ENTER is pressed, the display adds:

```
TURBO-access I/O error 145
File Record 26633
Program aborted
```

Thanks heaps. Well, nowhere, absolutely nowhere, is there an explanation for what a TURBO-access I/O error 145 is supposed to represent. I tried to find out what was wrong by trial and error, knowing that, if worse comes to worst, I'd have to call the technical assistance people at Borland, because presumably they'd know what that error stands for.

It took a while, but I found what was wrong. The procedure EnterData in the include file ENTREC.DB was the culprit. I got rid of it and replaced it with the file contained in the include file ADD.DB, getting rid of ADD.DB altogether (Fig. 3-46). Having done that, the error message no longer appeared. After entering some data into the files, I tried to list these records, using selection number nine from the menu, but nothing happened.

A closer look at the procedure ListPersons in the include file LIST.DB (Fig. 347) made me suspicious of the line reading

```
if Person.PersStatus = 0 then DisplayPerson(Person);
```

I added a temporary line reading

```
writeln('Person.PersStatus:   ',Person.PersStatus);
```

Fig. 3-46. ENTREC.DB is used to key in the data to be stored in the data file.

```
{Here information is entered into the data file}
{ENTREC.DB }

procedure InputInformation(var Person : PersRec);

var PersStatus : integer;

     begin
       PersStatus := 0;
           clrscr;  gotoxy(1,5);
       writeln('       Enter Customer Information');
       writeln('       ==========================');
       With Person do begin
       write('Enter First Name       (to 15 characters)  ');
       readln(FirstName);
       write('Enter Last Name        (to 15 characters)  ');
       readln(PersCode);
       write('Enter Company          (to 25 characters)  ');
       readln(Company);
       write('Enter Address          (to 40 characters)  ');
       readln(Addr);
       write('Enter City             (to 30 characters)  ');
       readln(City);
       write('Enter State ID         (2 characters)      ');
       readln(StateID);
       write('Enter Zip Code         (to 10 characters)  ');
       readln(Zip);
       write('Enter Area code        (3 digits)          ');
       readln(Area);
       write('Enter Phone number     (8 characters)      ');
       readln(Phone);
       write('Enter phone extension  (to 3 characters)   ');
       readln(Ext);
       write('Enter Month of Birth   (1 or 2 digits)     ');
       readln(BirthMonth);
       end;
  end;

  procedure AddPerson(var PersFile : DataFile;
                      var NameIndx : IndexFile);

  var
    RecordNumber    : integer;
    Response        : char;

  begin
    repeat
      InputInformation(Person);
      begin
        AddRec(PersFile,RecordNumber,Person);
        AddKey(NameIndx,RecordNumber,Person.PersCode);
        write('Add another record? ');
      end;
    until UpCase(Response) <> 'Y';
  end;
```

Fig. 3-47. This file is a modification of LIST.DB that lists all records in sequence.

```
{List all records in sequence}
{LIST.DB}

procedure ListPersons(var PersFile: DataFile);

    var
      NumberOfRecords,
      RecordNumber      : integer;
      Pause             : char;

    begin
           clrscr; gotoxy(1,8);
      NumberOfRecords := FileLen(PersFile);
      for RecordNumber := 1 to NumberOfRecords - 1 do
      begin
        GetRec(PersFile,RecordNumber,Person);
        if Person.PersStatus >= 0 then DisplayPerson(Person);
           gotoxy(1,20);
      write('Press any key to continue      ');
      read(KBD,Pause);
      end;
      writeln;
    end;
```

and I found that the number was anything but zero. I changed the equal sign (=) in that line to greater or equal (> =), compiled and ran the program again, and this time it listed each record sequentially, the way it is supposed to. Having solved this problem, let's go on to the next.

It appears that I was overly ambitious when I wrote the menu for this program, because, if there is more than one record with the same key, it is impossible to cause the program to display all of those records. The Toolbox procedures FindKey and SearchKey both insist on displaying only the first record that corresponds to the typed-in key, and no matter how hard I tried, the program stubbornly refused to do what I had envisioned it to do.

AN EXERCISE IN SORTING FILES

The Turbo Database Toolbox includes two demonstration programs that sort several files included on the distribution disk, thus saving you the trouble of having to write some lengthy data files.

The first program, the simpler of the two, is called SortAFile. It is on the disk in source code as SORT1.PAS. If you compile and run it, you'll see 100 records scroll past you on the screen at a speed that's much too fast to read, except for the last few lines that remain on the screen when all records have been sorted. In this form the program is of no value to anyone unless you send the sorted list to the printer, or modify the program to stop each time the screen is nearly full, requiring that some key be pressed to place the next screenful into display. To accomplish this, I've modified the program (Fig. 3-48) just slightly. The only changes were made in the procedure OutP, where a **clrscr** was added, followed by **for i := 1 to 20 do begin**, which limits the number of lines in display at one time to 20. Then, at the end of the loop, I've added a prompt that asks that ENTER be pressed in order to continue program execution. When you compile and run the program, only 20 lines appear at a time, enabling you to read what's on the screen.

The program sorts records by an integer number. Unless that integer number is something like a zip code, it's fairly meaningless because you're not too likely to enter data with code

Fig. 3-48. This sorting program is used to sort records by an identification code number.

```
{SORTF.P    }


{$C-}
program SortAFile;

type
  NameString = string[25];
  CustRec = record
              Number: integer;
              Name:   NameString;
              Addr:   string[20];
              City:   string[12];
              State:  string[3];
              Zip:    string[5];
            end;
  CustFileType = file of CustRec;

var
  CustFile : CustFileType;
  Customer : CustRec;
  Results  : integer;

{$I SORT.BOX }

procedure OpenFile(var f : CustFileType; Name : NameString);

begin
  ClrScr;
  Writeln('TURBO-SORT DEMONSTRATION PROGRAM');
  Writeln;
  Writeln('Opening data file');
  Assign(f, Name);
  {$I-}
  Reset(f);
  {$I+}
  if IOresult <> 0 then
  begin
    Writeln(^G, '  -- Cannot find ', Name);
    Halt;
  end;
end;

procedure Inp;

var
  rec : integer;
begin
  rec := 0;
  Writeln;
  Writeln('Input routine -- sending ', FileSize(CustFile),
          ' records to sort:');
  repeat
    rec := rec + 1;
    Write(#13, rec:6);
    Read(CustFile,Customer);
```

```
    SortRelease(Customer);
  until EOF(CustFIle);
  Writeln;
  Writeln;
  Writeln('Done with input -- sorting ',
           FileSize(CustFile), ' records . . .');
end;
  Writeln('Done with input -- sorting ',
           FileSize(CustFile), ' records . . .');
end;

function Less;

var
  FirstCust:  CustRec absolute X;
  SecondCust: CustRec absolute Y;
begin
  Less := FirstCust.Number < SecondCust.Number;
end;

procedure OutP;

var
  i  : integer;
  GO : char;
begin

  repeat
      clrscr;
    for i := 1 to 20 do begin
    SortReturn(Customer);
      with Customer do begin
      Write(Name,' ');
      for i := Length(Name) to 25 do Write(' ');
      Write(Addr);
      for i := Length(Addr) to 20 do Write(' ');
      Write(City);
      for i := Length(City) to 12 do Write(' ');
      Writeln(State,' ', Zip);
      end;
      end;
      writeln;
      write('Press ENTER to continue   ');
      readln(GO);
  until SortEOS;
  end;

procedure DisplayResults(results : integer);
begin
  Writeln;
  Writeln;
  case Results of
     0 : Writeln('Done with sort and display.');
     3 : Writeln('Error:  not enough memory to sort');
     8 : Writeln('Error:  illegal item length.');
     9 : Writeln('Error:  can only sort ', MaxInt, ' records.');
    10 : Writeln('Error:  disk full or disk write error.');
    11 : Writeln('Error:  disk error during read.');
```

```
    12 : Writeln('Error:  directory full or invalid path name');
  end;
end;

begin
  OpenFile(CustFile, 'CUSTOMER.DTA');
  Results := TurboSort(SizeOf(CustRec));
  DisplayResults(Results);
end.
```

numbers. A more intelligent way of sorting would be by alphabetical order. Let's see if the program can be modified to accomplish that. I wrote a little program to try comparing two strings based on alphabetical preferences (Fig. 3-49). I typed in various company names, and each time the program displayed them in the correct alphabetical order.

What would be needed to make the program do the same thing? Actually, it turns out to be very simple. All you have to do is change, in **function Less**, the line reading

Less := FirstCust.Number < SecondCust.Number

to another variable:

Less := FirstCust.Name < SecondCust.Name

(Fig. 3-50). Once compiled, the program now displays all those 100 records in alphabetical order by company name. Take it one step further, changing the variable to State, which results in the records being displayed alphabetically by state IDs. Then change it once more to Zip and this time the 100 records are sorted numerically by zip codes. You can, in fact, use any variable under which data are stored as the key.

The distribution disk also includes a program, SortMultipleFiles (SORT2.PAS), which the manual claims is a better and more sophisticated version of SORT1.PAS. Frankly, I find it to be unnecessarily cumbersome. It, too, scrolls the data across the screen at 90 miles an hour, making

Fig. 3-49. This little program determines the best way to sort data alphabetically.

```
{SORT.TST }

program SortAlphaTest;

var NAME1, NAME2 : string[15];

begin
     clrscr;  gotoxy(1,10);
     write('Enter one company name       ');
     readln(NAME1);
     writeln;
     write('Enter another company name   ');
     readln(NAME2);
     writeln;
     writeln;
     writeln(NAME1,'     ',NAME2);
     writeln;
     writeln;
     if NAME1 > NAME2 then
     writeln(NAME2,'     ',NAME1)
     else
     writeln(NAME1,'     ',NAME2);
end.
```

Fig. 3-50. The sorting program has been changed to sort records alphabetically by last name.

```
{Modified to sort alphabetically}
{SORTA.P    }


{$C-}
program SortAFileAlphabetically;

type
  NameString = string[25];
  CustRec = record
              Number: integer;
              Name:   NameString;
              Addr:   string[20];
              City:   string[12];
              State:  string[3];
              Zip:    string[5];
            end;
  CustFileType = file of CustRec;

var
  CustFile : CustFileType;
  Customer : CustRec;
  Results  : integer;

{$I SORT.BOX }

procedure OpenFile(var f : CustFileType; Name : NameString);

begin
  ClrScr;
  Writeln('TURBO-SORT DEMONSTRATION PROGRAM');
  Writeln;
  Writeln('Opening data file');
  Assign(f, Name);
  {$I-}
  Reset(f);
  {$I+}
  if IOresult <> 0 then
  begin
    Writeln(^G, '  -- Cannot find ', Name);
    Halt;
  end;
end;

procedure Inp;

var
  rec : integer;
begin
  rec := 0;
  Writeln;
  Writeln('Input routine -- sending ', FileSize(CustFile),
          ' records to sort:');
  repeat
    rec := rec + 1;
    Write(#13, rec:6);
    Read(CustFile,Customer);
```

```
    SortRelease(Customer);
  until EOF(CustFIle);
  Writeln;
  Writeln;
  Writeln('Done with input -- sorting ',
           FileSize(CustFile), ' records . . .');
end;

function Less;

var
  FirstCust:  CustRec absolute X;
  SecondCust: CustRec absolute Y;
begin
  Less := FirstCust.Name < SecondCust.Name;
end;

procedure OutP;

var
  i  : integer;
  GO : char;
begin

  repeat
      clrscr;
    for i := 1 to 20 do begin
    SortReturn(Customer);
      with Customer do begin
      Write(Name,' ');
      for i := Length(Name) to 25 do Write(' ');
      Write(Addr);
      for i := Length(Addr) to 20 do Write(' ');
      Write(City);
      for i := Length(City) to 12 do Write(' ');
      Writeln(State,' ', Zip);
      end;
      end;
      writeln;
      write('Press ENTER to continue    ');
      readln(GO);
  until SortEOS;
  end;

procedure DisplayResults(results : integer);
begin
  Writeln;
  Writeln;
  case Results of
     0 : Writeln('Done with sort and display.');
     3 : Writeln('Error:  not enough memory to sort');
     8 : Writeln('Error:  illegal item length.');
     9 : Writeln('Error:  can only sort ', MaxInt, ' records.');
    10 : Writeln('Error:  disk full or disk write error.');
    11 : Writeln('Error:  disk error during read.');
    12 : Writeln('Error:  directory full or invalid path name');
  end;
end;
```

```
begin
  OpenFile(CustFile, 'CUSTOMER.DTA');
  Results := TurboSort(SizeOf(CustRec));
  DisplayResults(Results);
end.
```

it impossible to read. Attempting to change that by adding the same loop that worked so well with SORT1.PAS was only partially successful—that heading line seems to create problems.

Still smarting from my lack of success with the multiple choice database program, it occurred to me that I might be able to achieve the desired result using the sorting routine. I added a line in the new program DisplaySelectData (SELECT.P) (Fig. 3-51) that asks for the name of the companies to be displayed. Then, an **if . . . then** statement compares the typed-in data with that in the data file, displaying one matching record after another, but ignoring those that don't match.

Fig. 3-51. This program is used to display only selected data, such as the names of persons working for a specific company.

```
{Displaying only selected data}
{SELECT.P    }

{$C-}
program DisplaySelectedData;

type
  NameString = string[25];
  CustRec = record
              Number: integer;
              Name:   NameString;
              Addr:   string[20];
              City:   string[12];
              State:  string[3];
              Zip:    string[5];
            end;
  CustFileType = file of CustRec;

var
  CustFile : CustFileType;
  Customer : CustRec;
  Results  : integer;

{$I SORT.BOX }

procedure OpenFile(var f : CustFileType; Name : NameString);

begin
  ClrScr;
  Writeln('SELECTIVE DISPLAY PROGRAM');
  Writeln;
  Writeln('Opening data file');
  Assign(f, Name);
  {$I-}
  Reset(f);
  {$I+}
  if IOresult <> 0 then
  begin
    Writeln(^G, '  -- Cannot find ', Name);
    Halt;
```

```
  end;
end;

procedure Inp;

var
  rec : integer;
begin
  rec := 0;
  Writeln;
  Writeln('Input routine -- sending ', FileSize(CustFile),
          ' records to sort:');
  repeat
    rec := rec + 1;
    Write(#13, rec:6);
    Read(CustFile,Customer);
    SortRelease(Customer);
  until EOF(CustFIle);
  Writeln;
  Writeln;
  Writeln('Done with input -- sorting ',
           FileSize(CustFile), ' records . . .');
end;
function Less;

var
  FirstCust:  CustRec absolute X;
  SecondCust: CustRec absolute Y;
begin
  Less := FirstCust.Name < SecondCust.Name;
end;

procedure OutP;

var
  i         : integer;
  CO, Name  : string[25];
  X         : char;
begin
     clrscr; gotoxy(1,10);
     write('Enter name of company to be displayed     ');
     readln(CO);
  repeat
      clrscr;
    SortReturn(Customer);
      with Customer do begin
      if Name = CO then begin
      Write(Name,' ');
      for i := Length(Name) to 25 do Write(' ');
      Write(Addr);
      for i := Length(Addr) to 20 do Write(' ');
      Write(City);
      for i := Length(City) to 12 do Write(' ');
      Writeln(State,' ', Zip);
      writeln;
      write('Press ENTER   ');
      readln(X);
      end
 else
```

```
      end;
  until SortEOS;
  end;

procedure DisplayResults(results : integer);
begin
  Writeln;
  Writeln;
  case Results of
     0 : Writeln('Done with sort and display.');
     3 : Writeln('Error:  not enough memory to sort');
     8 : Writeln('Error:  illegal item length.');
     9 : Writeln('Error:  can only sort ', MaxInt, ' records.');
    10 : Writeln('Error:  disk full or disk write error.');
    11 : Writeln('Error:  disk error during read.');
    12 : Writeln('Error:  directory full or invalid path name');
  end;
end;

begin
  OpenFile(CustFile, 'CUSTOMER.DTA');
  Results := TurboSort(SizeOf(CustRec));
  DisplayResults(Results);
end.
```

In SELECT.P, I've used the name of the company or person. The Name in the line **if Name = CO then begin** can be changed to City, State, Zip, or anything else that might be included in the data file that's being used. If the selected sorting routine matches the key being used, the procedure is quite fast because all of the records to be displayed will have been sorted into a single group. If you want to use the zip code as a key, it would probably be advisable to type only the first two digits, then use the **copy(CO,1,2)** statement in the comparison line to compare only those digits. Figures 3-52 and 3-53 are variations on the original modification that are designed to sort data by two-letter state IDs or by zip codes.

Fig. 3-52. This version of the sorting program sorts records by zip codes.

```
{Modified to sort by state Zip codes}
{SORTZ.P    }


{$C-}
program SortAFileByZipCodes;

type
  NameString = string[25];
  CustRec = record
              Number: integer;
              Name:   NameString;
              Addr:   string[20];
              City:   string[12];
              State:  string[3];
              Zip:    string[5];
            end;
  CustFileType = file of CustRec;

var
```

```
  CustFile : CustFileType;
  Customer : CustRec;
  Results  : integer;
  CHOICE   : char;
  LIST     : file;

{$I SORT.BOX }

procedure OpenFile(var f : CustFileType; Name : NameString);

begin
  ClrScr;
  Writeln('TURBO-SORT DEMONSTRATION PROGRAM');
  Writeln;
  Writeln('Opening data file');
  Assign(f, Name);
  {$I-}
  Reset(f);
  {$I+}
  if IOresult <> 0 then
  begin
    Writeln(^G, '  -- Cannot find ', Name);
    Halt;
  end;
end;

procedure Inp;

var
  rec : integer;
begin
  rec := 0;
  Writeln;
  Writeln('Input routine -- sending ', FileSize(CustFile),
          ' records to sort:');
  repeat
    rec := rec + 1;
    Write(#13, rec:6);
    Read(CustFile,Customer);
    SortRelease(Customer);
  until EOF(CustFIle);
  Writeln;
  Writeln;
  Writeln('Done with input -- sorting ',
           FileSize(CustFile), ' records . . .');
end;

function Less;

var
  FirstCust:  CustRec absolute X;
  SecondCust: CustRec absolute Y;
begin
  Less := FirstCust.Zip < SecondCust.Zip;
end;

procedure OutP;

var
```

```
  i  : integer;
  GO : char;
begin

  repeat
      clrscr;
    for i := 1 to 20 do begin
    SortReturn(Customer);
      with Customer do begin
      Write(Name,' ');
      for i := Length(Name) to 25 do Write(' ');
      Write(Addr);
      for i := Length(Addr) to 20 do Write(' ');
      Write(City);
      for i := Length(City) to 12 do Write(' ');
      Writeln(State,' ', Zip);
      end;
      end;
      writeln;
      write('Press ENTER to continue   ');
      readln(GO);
  until SortEOS;
  end;

procedure DisplayResults(results : integer);
begin
  Writeln;
  Writeln;
  case Results of
     0 : Writeln('Done with sort and display.');
     3 : Writeln('Error:  not enough memory to sort');
     8 : Writeln('Error:  illegal item length.');
     9 : Writeln('Error:  can only sort ', MaxInt, ' records.');
    10 : Writeln('Error:  disk full or disk write error.');
    11 : Writeln('Error:  disk error during read.');
    12 : Writeln('Error:  directory full or invalid path name');
  end;
end;

begin
  OpenFile(CustFile, 'CUSTOMER.DTA');
  Results := TurboSort(SizeOf(CustRec));
  DisplayResults(Results);
end.
```

Fig. 3-53. This version of the sorting program sorts records by two-letter state abbreviations.

```
{Modified to sort by state IDs}
{SORTS.P    }


{$C-}
program SortAFileByStateIDs;

type
  NameString = string[25];
  CustRec = record
              Number: integer;
```

```
              Name:   NameString;
              Addr:   string[20];
              City:   string[12];
              State:  string[3];
              Zip:    string[5];
            end;
  CustFileType = file of CustRec;

var
  CustFile : CustFileType;
  Customer : CustRec;
  Results  : integer;
  CHOICE   : char;
  LIST     : file;

{$I SORT.BOX }

procedure OpenFile(var f : CustFileType; Name : NameString);

begin
  ClrScr;
  Writeln('TURBO-SORT DEMONSTRATION PROGRAM');
  Writeln;
  Writeln('Opening data file');
  Assign(f, Name);
  {$I-}
  Reset(f);
  {$I+}
  if IOresult <> 0 then
  begin
    Writeln(^G, '  -- Cannot find ', Name);
    Halt;
  end;
end;

procedure Inp;

var
  rec : integer;
begin
  rec := 0;
  Writeln;
  Writeln('Input routine -- sending ', FileSize(CustFile),
          ' records to sort:');
  repeat
    rec := rcc + 1;
    Write(#13, rec:6);
    Read(CustFile,Customer);
    SortRelease(Customer);
  until EOF(CustFIle);
  Writeln;
  Writeln;
  Writeln('Done with input -- sorting ',
           FileSize(CustFile), ' records . . .');
end;

function Less;

var
```

```
  FirstCust:  CustRec absolute X;
  SecondCust: CustRec absolute Y;
begin
  Less := FirstCust.State < SecondCust.State;
end;

procedure OutP;

var
  i  : integer;
  GO : char;
begin

  repeat
     clrscr;
    for i := 1 to 20 do begin
    SortReturn(Customer);
      with Customer do begin
      Write(Name,' ');
      for i := Length(Name) to 25 do Write(' ');
      Write(Addr);
      for i := Length(Addr) to 20 do Write(' ');
      Write(City);
      for i := Length(City) to 12 do Write(' ');
      Writeln(State,' ', Zip);
      end;
      end;
      writeln;
      write('Press ENTER to continue    ');
      readln(GO);
  until SortEOS;
  end;

procedure DisplayResults(results : integer);
begin
  Writeln;
  Writeln;
  case Results of
     0 : Writeln('Done with sort and display.');
     3 : Writeln('Error:  not enough memory to sort');
     8 : Writeln('Error:  illegal item length.');
     9 : Writeln('Error:  can only sort ', MaxInt, ' records.');
    10 : Writeln('Error:  disk full or disk write error.');
    11 : Writeln('Error:  disk error during read.');
    12 : Writeln('Error:  directory full or invalid path name');
  end;
end;

begin
  OpenFile(CustFile, 'CUSTOMER.DTA');
  Results := TurboSort(SizeOf(CustRec));
  DisplayResults(Results);
end.
```

In the previous examples, I have limited the use of the program to the data file CUSTOMER.DTA included on the distribution disk. To demonstrate that any other type of data file would do just as well, I rewrote the program, calling the new version SLCTSTK.P. The other data file on the distribution disk, STOCK.DTA, will be the one used to display items whose price is equal to or less than the amount typed in.

With these few modifications, this relatively simple sorting program can be used for a multitude of applications. Chapter 7 contains another version of a sorting program.

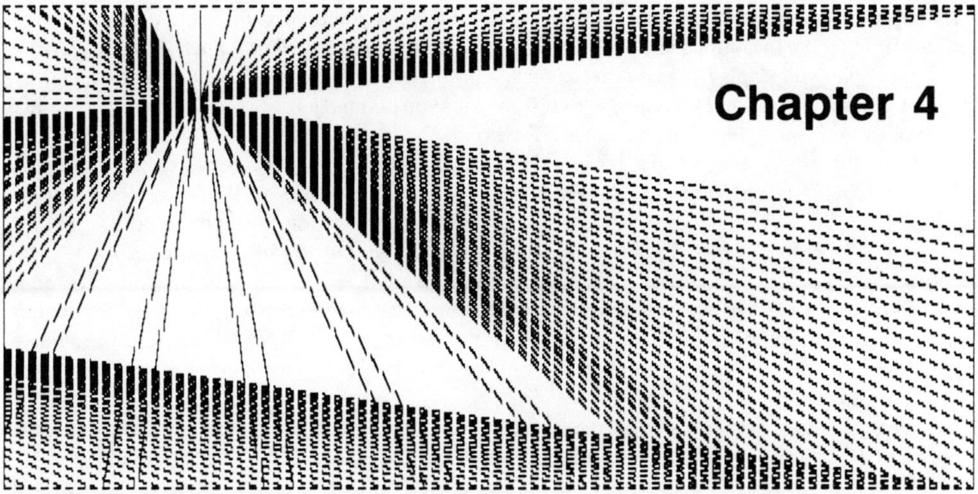

Chapter 4

The Turbo Graphix Toolbox

The Turbo Graphix Toolbox is a collection of procedures and functions designed to simplify the task of producing graphic images. It consists primarily of 119 procedures and functions contained in 19 system files recorded on the 5.25-inch distribution disk, with 27 sample programs and a 256-page documentation book.

The sample programs in this toolbox, unlike those in the others, are of little practical value other than to demonstrate some of the capabilities of this software package; you've got to do a great deal of studying before you'll be able to use what is being offered.

When you understand all those procedures and functions, you can use them by including them in programs of your own. You can draw points, lines, labeled pie charts, bar charts with programmable shading, a variety of curves using different line styles with optional smoothing, a full range of geometric shapes, and animated images. You can, in addition, include full graphics window management, meaning that you can display several images at the same time.

This sounds very exciting, but this package is definitely not easy to use until a reasonable amount of time has been spent familiarizing yourself with it. This is, in fact, simply a bunch of building blocks, and it is up to you to put them together to produce the desired results. The documentation, while quite thorough, does assume a considerable amount of programming expertise, plus a fair degree of familiarity with computer functions in general and Turbo Pascal in particular.

The minimum hardware and software requirements are 128K RAM, and a computer that runs Turbo Pascal 2.0 or greater, PC DOS 1.0 or greater, or MS DOS 1.0 or greater. It must be equipped with at least one disk drive, with an IBM-compatible graphics adapter or Hercules Graphics Card. A monochrome monitor can be used, but a color monitor is greatly preferred because of the wide range of colors available with the Turbo Graphix Toolbox.

GETTING STARTED WITH THE GRAPHIX TOOLBOX

The distribution disk of the Turbo Graphix Toolbox includes an enormous number of demonstration programs (those with a .PAS extension) that, once compiled, will produce a variety of graphics. If you try to compile one of them (using the routine described in Appendix B) the Turbo Pascal compiler will display an error message, asking that you press ESC. This produces a lengthy piece of information, telling you that certain steps must be taken in order to configure the Graphix Toolbox to your particular hardware specifications.

Depending on the type of graphics adapter, you're asked to type a certain combination of letters that will cause some adjustments to be written into one of the program modules (GRAPHIX.SYS). The trouble is that the displayed instructions don't tell you what to do next. ESC or ENTER don't work. In fact, since we're still in the Turbo Pascal compiler mode, you have to type ^K^D, which returns you to the compiler prompt. Type Q to quit the compiler, and, with the copy of your Turbo Graphix distribution disk in the logged drive, type the letter combination in accordance with the instructions. In my case that was TGINST IBM. This produces a question that you can ignore. Simply press any key and the required conversion will take place automatically.

When you again try to compile one of the .PAS programs, it'll work without a hitch. But remember that the compiler includes all of those {$I FILENAME.EXT} files that are used by the different programs. The compiled versions, therefore, tend to be extremely long—several thousand lines—adding up to tens of thousands of bytes. With this in mind, it's a good idea to copy the compiled versions onto other disks, or very soon, there will not be any space left on the distribution disk. Then, when you try to run the programs that you have copied onto other disks, you'll be greeted by two error messages: Error #0 and Error #1. To avoid this, always copy ERROR.MSG, 4X6.FON, 8X8.FON, and 14X9.FON from the copy of the distribution disk onto the disks to which you'll be copying the .COM programs. That will take care of the problem.

The Turbo Graphix Toolbox really does not include demonstration programs that would be of practical use. For instance, one of the demonstration programs creates a shaded bar chart, but the program does not include input lines that would permit you to enter parameters to control the dimension of each of the bars. The program must be modified to eventually serve a practical purpose. Similarly, there is a program that shows a pie chart along with a graph, including all manner of text. That's very nice, but not very useful unless the program is rewritten to permit the user to determine the sizes of the pie-chart segments and the graph bars, and add explanatory text in predetermined locations.

In the meantime, compile all of the .PAS programs and run each one, to see what they do and how you might be able to convert some of them to your own use. There is a total of 53 files on the distribution disk, 27 of which are .PAS files that you can compile and run. They are:

TGDEMO.PAS	DRWPNT.PAS	DRWPNTS.PAS
DRWLIN.PAS	DRWLINS.PAS	WDRWPNTS.PAS
DRWSQ.PAS	ONEHIST.PAS	DRWCIR.PAS
DRWHCH.PAS	DRWSTXT.PAS	DRWATXT.PAS
SIMPWIND.PAS	MULTWIND.PAS	FLOWDEMO.PAS
ONEPIE.PAS	PIEHISTO.PAS	ONEAXIS.PAS
ONEPOLY.PAS	POLYAXIS.PAS	MOVEPOLY.PAS
INTERP.PAS	FINDWRLD.PAS	BEZIDEMO.PAS
SCREENIO.PAS	SCRNPRINT.PAS	SAMPLE.PAS

A CLOSER LOOK AT SOME SIMPLE PROGRAMS

The first program shown in the manual, called ExamplePoint simply draws one lonely dot on the left side of the screen, half way down. The position is identified by setting both the horizontal and vertical coordinates to 100 in the line that reads:

```
DrawPoint(100,100);
```

DrawPoint is one of the standard procedures buried in one of the include files. If you're interested in knowing where it is located, the include file is KERNEL.SYS.

A program that simply draws a point is not of much use to anyone, but it illustrates the system of horizontal and vertical coordinates. To make the program slightly more interesting, you can give the user an opportunity to determine the position where the point is to be drawn. Add some text lines that ask the user to key in the horizontal and vertical coordinates, assigning each to a variable (Fig. 4-1). In the modified version reproduced here, HC and VC are the declared variables of the type integer. We then use three lines of text AHEAD of the line that reads: **InitGraphic;**, which initializes the graphics system. When the revised program is compiled and run, enter the coordinate values that you're interested in, and the program will draw a point in accordance with those coordinates. Any key stroke will terminate the program and return you to the DOS prompt.

To modify the program a bit more, a second **repeat . . . until** loop (Fig. 4-2) will return the user to the input line prompt each time a key is pressed with the graphics screen in display, providing a chance to move the point around on the screen. This is a useful exercise, because it can be used to familiarize yourself with the results obtained by a nearly unlimited number of coordinate combinations. In this rather primitive modification, you're asked to type 0 for both coordinates in order to exit the program. (By the way, (0,0) produces an invisible point on the border, as does (639,199) because the 640-by-200 grid involves coordinates 0 through 639 and 0 through 199.)

The second program, the one called DrawPoints (DRWPNTS.PAS), draws 1,000 points. A logical modification would be an input prompt that would control the number of random points being drawn. Add a second variable of the type integer and a few lines of code that cause the input prompt to be repeated until 0 is pressed (Fig. 4-3).

Although all of this might seem awfully basic and simple, going through these preliminary

Fig. 4-1. The modified version of the demonstration program that draws a single point allows input of the desired coordinates.

```
program ExamplePoint;

var  HC, VC  :  integer;

{$I typedef.sys}
{$I graphix.sys}
{$I kernel.sys }

begin
     clrscr;
     writeln('To draw a point enter the coordinates');
     writeln;
     write('Enter the horizontal coordinate (1 to 639)    ');
     readln(HC);
     write('Enter the vertical coordinate   (1 to 199)    ');
     readln(VC);

   InitGraphic;
   DrawBorder;

   DrawPoint(HC,VC);

   repeat until Keypressed;
   LeaveGraphic;

end.
```

Fig. 4-2. In this modification of the point-drawing program, different coordinates can be entered over and over again.

```
program ExamplePoint;

var  HC, VC  :  integer;

{$I typedef.sys}
{$I graphix.sys}
{$I kernel.sys }

begin
               repeat
     clrscr;
     writeln('To draw a point enter the coordinates');
     writeln;
     writeln('(To exit program type zero for both)');
     writeln;
     write('Enter the horizontal coordinate (1 to 639)     ');
     readln(HC);
     write('Enter the vertical coordinate   (1 to 199)     ');
     readln(VC);

  InitGraphic;
  DrawBorder;

  DrawPoint(HC,VC);

  repeat until Keypressed;
  LeaveGraphic;

             until (HC = 0) and (VC = 0);
end.
```

Fig. 4-3. The program that produces a profusion of random points has been modified to permit input of the number of points desired.

```
{DRWPNTS.P   }

program DrawPoints;

{$I typedef.sys}
{$I graphix.sys}
{$I kernel.sys }

var i, x : integer;

begin
            repeat
            clrscr;
  write('How many random points?  (1 to 1000) (0 to exit) ');
            readln(x);
  InitGraphic;
  DrawBorder;

  for  i:= 1 to x do
     DrawPoint(random(639),random(199));
```

```
    repeat until keypressed;
    LeaveGraphic;
                until x = 0;
  end.
```

routines is useful in helping demonstrate the more advanced capabilities of the Turbo Graphix Toolbox. Therefore, let's continue to take it one step at a time.

On page 23 of the manual, there is a program that draws a single diagonal line. In the process, it introduces a couple of new concepts that represent something called the World Coordinate System. The foregoing programs have used the Screen Coordinate System, in which the horizontaland vertical coordinates are based on the number of pixels. The numbers used in the World Coordinate System have no relationship whatever to the number of pixels. Playing around a bit with the program DrawLine (DRWLIN.PAS) will show how this works.

The world coordinate system requires five parameters in parentheses:

DefineWorld(NUM,ULH,ULV,LRH,LRV)

NUM represents the number of such worlds used, something that will be discussed further in section four, about the windowing business. ULH represents the horizontal coordinate for the upper left-hand corner, ULV the vertical coordinate for that corner, LRH the horizontal coordinate for the lower right-hand corner, and LRV the vertical coordinate for that corner. In the program, as shown on page 23 of the documentation book, ULH and LRV are 0, and ULV and LRH are 1000.

By editing the source code (Fig. 4-4) to permit entry of new coordinates, absolutely nothing has changed. You can enter such entirely different values as, say, (1,300,600,600,300), and the resulting display is exactly as it was when the numbers were (1,0,1000,1000,0). Here, again, the window section will explain what this is all about.

Fig. 4-4. The DrawLine program has been changed to allow for data input.

```
{LINDRW.P   }

program DrawLine;

{$I typedef.sys}
{$I graphix.sys}
{$I kernel.sys }

var i, ULH, ULV, LRH, LRV : integer;

begin
     repeat
     clrscr;
     writeln('Enter four values, two for the upper left-hand corner');
     writeln('and two for the lower right-hand corner'); writeln;
     writeln('Enter all zeros to exit'); writeln;
     write('Upper left horizontal coordinate?   ');
     readln(ULH);
     write('Upper left vertical coordinate?     ');
     readln(ULV);
     write('Lower right horizontal coordinate?  ');
     readln(LRH);
     write('Lower right vertical coordinate?    ');
```

```
    readln(LRV);

  InitGraphic;
  DrawBorder;

  DefineWorld(1,ULH,ULV,LRH,LRV);
  SelectWorld(1);
  SelectWindow(1);

  DrawLine(ULH,ULV,LRH,LRV);

  repeat until KeyPressed;
  LeaveGraphic;

    until (ULH = 0) and (ULV = 0) and (LRH = 0) and (LRV = 0);
end.
```

There is a way to benefit from the four input prompts. By reinstating the DefineWorld line to its former values:

```
DefineWorld(1,0,1000,1000,0) ;
```

but retaining the use of the variables in the DrawLine line:

```
DrawLine(ULH,ULV,LRH,LRV) ;
```

(Fig. 4-5), the input values will affect only the line being drawn. It is good practice to experiment with different input values, to learn which coordinate combinations produce what results.

The next program, called DrawLines (DRWLINS.PAS) draws what is described as a "walking line." As shown, it uses a loop to draw 20 lines in progressing positions, producing what looks like a partial spider web. In Fig. 4-6 an input prompt has been added, and the DrawLine parameters have been changed to use that input value. Here, again, it's interesting to experiment with different values, anything from very small to quite large, and to observe the different effects that result. In addition to the input prompt, I've added Delay(500) to slow down the rate at which lines are displayed, for easier observation. For a bit of additional experimentation with that same program, you could add a second input line:

```
write('Number of lines to be displayed? ');
readln(B) ;
```

Then, replace the 20 in the loop and change it to:

```
for i := 1 to B do begin
```

This would enable the user to increase or decrease the number of steps through the loops and, in turn, the number of lines being drawn.

The last two programs to be looked at in this section are called DrawSquare (DRWSQ.PAS) and DrawHatch (DRWHCH.PAS). The first, when compiled and run will fill the screen with rectangles (not squares). Here, once more, adding some input prompts and a refinement or two helps demonstrate what is taking place. The second program produces five rectangles of random shapes, shading each with a density derived at random.

In DrawSquare, two input prompts have been added that determine the number of rectangles to be drawn and the distance between the lines. A Delay(500) line has also been added to

Fig. 4-5. The DrawLine program has been modified once more to permit any number of lines to be drawn.

```
{DRWLIN.P   }

program DrawLine;

{$I typedef.sys}
{$I graphix.sys}
{$I kernel.sys }

var i, ULH, ULV, LRH, LRV : integer;

begin
     repeat
     clrscr;
     writeln('Enter four values, two for the upper left-hand corner');
     writeln('and two for the lower right-hand corner'); writeln;
     writeln('Enter all zeros to exit'); writeln;
     write('Upper left horizontal coordinate?    ');
     readln(ULH);
     write('Upper left vertical coordinate?      ');
     readln(ULV);
     write('Lower right horizontal coordinate?   ');
     readln(LRH);
     write('Lower right vertical coordinate?     ');
     readln(LRV);

  InitGraphic;
  DrawBorder;

  DefineWorld(1,0,1000,1000,0);
  SelectWorld(1);
  SelectWindow(1);

  DrawLine(ULH,ULV,LRH,LRV);

  repeat until KeyPressed;
  LeaveGraphic;

     until (ULH = 0) and (ULV = 0) and (LRH = 0) and (LRV = 0);
end.
```

Fig. 4-6. This version draws a profusion of lines in accordance with user input.

```
{DRWLINS.P   }

program  DrawLines;

{$I typedef.sys}
{$I graphix.sys}
{$I kernel.sys }

var i, A : integer;

begin
     repeat
     clrscr;
     writeln('Enter a value to determine line positions');
     writeln;
```

```
    writeln('Enter 0 to exit');
    writeln;
    write('Enter value      ');
    readln(A);

  InitGraphic;

  DefineWorld(1,0,1000,1000,0);
  SelectWorld(1);
  SelectWindow(1);

  SetBackground(0);
  DrawBorder;

  for i := 1 to 20 do begin
      Delay(500);
      DrawLine(i * A,0,1000 - i * A,i * A);
      end;

  repeat until KeyPressed;
  LeaveGraphic;

    until A = 0;

end.
```

slow down the action for better observation (Fig. 4-7). If you enter a very small value for the variable B, and a large one for A, you'll find that the screen will turn white or nearly white. Playing around with different values is quite instructive.

DrawHatch doesn't lend itself to the kind of editing that was done with the others because all values used are created at random. The only modification added is a prompt (Fig. 4-8) that asks the user to enter the number of repeat displays that the program should produce before exiting to the system. A **repeat . . . until** loop uses that input to control the number of repeat displays. It is quite interesting to watch this program produce different images during each run through the loop. The shapes of the rectangles and the density of the shading change with each display.

THE NEXT GROUP OF PROGRAMS

The program called DrawCirc (DRWCIR.PAS) draws curved lines, eventually forming a circular design that gives the impression of being three dimensional.

Once more, input prompts and an additional loop were added to make it possible to vary some of the values that control the graphic image produced by the program. The first input prompt asks for the number of circles to be drawn, assigning the value to the variable A. The second determines the distance between the individual lines, assigning that value to the variable B. The 15 in the **for i := 1 to 15 do** line was replaced with the variable A, and the 10 in the **SetAspect(0.2+i/10);** line with the variable B.

When this edited version (Fig. 4-9) is compiled and run, you can enter different values for the two variables each time you're prompted to do so. You can then watch the effect of the different values on the graphic image on the screen.

If you want to go some steps further, you could add three more input prompts. One replaces the two 500s with a variable C in the **DrawCircle(500,500,rad);** line, which controls the position of the graphic image on the screen. The second replaces the .2 with a variable D in **SetAspect (0.2+i/B);**. The third replaces the .05 with the variable E in **rad:=rad-0.05;**.

Fig. 4-7. This modification permits data input to the program that draws a succession of rectangles.

```
{DRWSQ.P  }

program DrawSquares;

{$I typedef.sys}
{$I graphix.sys}
{$I kernel.sys }

var i, A, B : integer;

begin
  repeat
  clrscr;
  writeln('Enter two values (all 0s to quit)      ');
  writeln;
  write('Number of steps through the loop?       ');
  readln(A);
  write('Coordinate value?                       ');
  readln(B);

  InitGraphic;

  DefineWorld(1,0,1000,1000,0);
  SelectWorld(1);
  SelectWindow(1);
  DrawBorder;

  for i := 1 to A do begin
  Delay(500);
  DrawSquare(500 - i * B,500 - i * B,500 + i * B,500 + i * B,false);
  end;

  repeat until KeyPressed;
  LeaveGraphic;

     until (A = 0) and (B = 0);

end.
```

Fig. 4-8. Input prompts have been added to the DrawHatch program.

```
{DRWHCH.P  }

program DrawHatch;

{$I typedef.sys}
{$I graphix.sys}
{$I kernel.sys }
{$I hatch.hgh  }

var i, A, B                   : integer;
    x1, x2, y1, y2, temp : real;

begin
  clrscr;
  write('Enter number of repetitions         ');
  readln(A);
```

```
 B := 0;
 repeat
 B := B + 1;
 InitGraphic;

 DefineWorld(1,0,1000,1000,0);
 SelectWorld(1);
 SelectWindow(1);
 DrawBorder;

 for i := 1 to 5 do
 begin
   x1 := 100 + random(800);
   x2 := 100 + random(800);
   y1 := 100 + random(800);
   y2 := 100 + random(800);

   if x1 > x2 then
    begin
     temp := x1;
     x1   := x2;
     x2   := temp;
    end;

   if y1 > y2 then
    begin
     temp := y1;
     y1   := y2;
     y2   := temp;
    end;

   DrawSquare(x1,y1,x2,y2,false);
   hatch(x1,y1,x2,y2,random(22) - 11);
 end;

 repeat until KeyPressed;
 LeaveGraphic;

 until B = A;

end.
```

Fig. 4-9. This program draws a series of circular lines, in response to input prompts.

```
program DrawCirc;

{$I typedef.sys}
{$I graphix.sys}
{$I kernel.sys }

var i, A, B         : integer;
    AspectLoc,rad : real;

begin
  repeat
  clrscr;
  write(`Enter the number of circles to draw (0 to exit)    ');
  readln(A);
  writeln;
```

```
  write(`Enter size value                                   ');
  readln(B);

  InitGraphic;

  DefineWorld(1,0,1000,1000,0);
  SelectWorld(1);
  SelectWindow(1);
  DrawBorder;

  rad := 1.5;
  AspectLoc := GetAspect;
  SetAspect(0.2);

  for i := 1 to A do
  begin
    DrawCircle(500,500,rad);
    SetAspect(0.2 + i / B);
    rad := rad - 0.05;
  end;

  SetAspect(AspectLoc);

  repeat until KeyPressed;
  LeaveGraphic;

  until A = 0;

end.
```

If you enter different values for each of the five variables, it'll be easy to watch the effects produced by the variations. Remember, though, that the variables identified here as D and E must be declared as type Real.

The next two programs deal with the important subject of combining graphic images with text.

The first called DrawStandardText (DRWSTXT.PAS), produces what is described as machine-dependent text, meaning that it is identical to the text produced by the Turbo Pascal text editor. In this version of using text while in the graphic mode, the screen is divided into 25 lines and 80 columns and the placement of text is controlled by using the Turbo Pascal procedures **gotoxy(X,Y), writeln('text') ;** and **write ('text') ;.** The program places machine-dependent text into three different positions on the screen, drawing a box around one of the text blocks. The two variables Charwidth and CharHeight are used to compute the width and height of the characters. This is not necessary for the text itself, but must be available when any other graphic image is used in conjunction with machine-dependent text.

No practical purpose would be served by modifying this demonstration program, though you could vary the parameters in parentheses in the line

```
DrawSquare(9*CharWidth,7*CharHeight, (22*CharWidth) +2, (8*CharHeight) +2, true) ;
```

This will change the size of the box that's being drawn around that one text block.

The next program, DrawAlternateText (DRWATXT.PAS) produces four-by-six pixel characters that are used whenever text that is either larger or smaller than machine-dependent text is needed. The example program displays the complete ASCII character set in the smallest possible size in the upper left-hand corner of the screen. Then, a group of characters, the size and placement of which are selected at random, appears all over the screen.

The use of text in conjunction with graphics is extremely important. Therefore, in addition to studying these two programs, let's write another to demonstrate the various text options a little better. It is called DrawTextDemo (DRWTXTD.P   ), and uses a number of newly created include files to make it as easy as possible to understand.

The main module of DrawTextDemo (Fig. 4-10) consists of only three lines that repeatedly call the procedure Menu until the variable WHICH has the value of zero. The procedure Menu offers two choices, plus the exit-program choice, sending the computer to one of two procedures called MachineDep or PixelTxt. Both are contained in separate include files. In addition, DrawTextDemo has a constant and variable declaration portion and five include directives. The first three directives contain the usual toolbox routines. The last two are written specifically for this program.

The include file MACHINE.BOX (Fig. 4-11) consists of the procedure MachineDep and starts with a variable declaration block. That is followed by a series of input prompts that are self-explanatory. Next, a routine initializes the graphic mode. Finally, you come to the portion of the procedure that causes the text, with a graphic box, to be displayed on the screen.

The four lines ahead of DrawSquare convert Screen Coordinates to World Coordinates, because DrawSquare requires World Coordinates. This makes it possible to enter Screen Coordinates in reply to the last input prompts.

The include file PIXEL.BOX (Fig. 4-12) consists of the procedure PixelText. It is much shorter because it is designed to display just one character at a time. After the variable declaration lines there are four input prompts. The first asks for the character to be displayed. It will accept any character represented by an ASCII code because the typed character, represented by the variable LET, is converted to its ASCII equivalent, represented by the integer variable Letter. The second prompt asks for the size. The integer one is the smallest possible, two is twice as large as one, three is twice as large as two, and so on. The other two prompts ask for the world coordinates that will represent the upper left-hand corner of the displayed character (0 to 639 horizontally, and 0 to 199 vertically).

When you look at different sizes for the various characters, you'll find that the larger the character, the less realistic it looks, except for such letters as E, T, and H, which consist exclusively of vertical and horizontal lines. In other words, the text that is generated by the graphic system should be used rather sparingly, because it's much harder to read than machine-dependent text.

With this kind of experimentation, you can gain sufficient experience to make the design of more complicated graphics programs somewhat less daunting.

Fig. 4-10. This program is used to enter either machine-dependent text or 4 × 6 pixel text.

```
{DRWTXTD.P   }

program DrawTextDemo;

const MaxWorldX : real = 1000.0;
      MaxWorldY : real = 1000.0;

var   CharHeight, CharWidth : real;
      WHICH                 : integer;

{$I TYPEDEF.SYS }
{$I GRAPHIX.SYS }
{$I KERNEL.SYS  }
{$I MACHINE.BOX }
{$I PIXEL.BOX   }
```

```
procedure Menu;
begin
     clrscr;  gotoxy(1,10);
     writeln('                         MENU');
     writeln('                         ====');
     writeln;
     writeln('           1) Machine-Dependent Text');
     writeln('           2) 4x6 Pixel Text         ');
     writeln('           -------------------------');
     writeln('           0) Exit program           ');
     writeln('           -------------------------');
     write('         Which?     ');
     readln(WHICH);
                    case WHICH of
                    1 : MachineDep;
                    2 : PixelTxt;
                    end;
end;

begin
     repeat
     Menu;
     until WHICH = 0;
end.
```

Fig. 4-11. MACHINE.BOX is the include file that produces machine-dependent text.

```
{MACHINE.BOX }

procedure MachineDep;

var CoordX1, CoordY1     : integer;
    CoordX2, CoordY2     : integer;
    CoordX3, CoordY3     : integer;
    CoordX4, CoordY4     : real;
    CoordX5, CoordY5     : real;
    LINE1, LINE2, LINE3 : array[1..75] of char;

begin
    clrscr;  gotoxy(1,8);
    write('Text (1st line)   ');
    readln(LINE1);
    write('Enter horizontal coordinate (1 to 80)   ');
    readln(CoordX1);
    write('Enter vertical coordinate   (1 to 25)   ');
    readln(CoordY1);
    write('Text (2nd line)   ');
    readln(LINE2);
    write('Enter horizontal coordinate (1 to 80)   ');
    readln(CoordX2);
    write('Enter vertical coordinate   (1 to 25)   ');
    readln(CoordY2);
    write('Text (3rd line)   ');
    readln(LINE3);
    write('Enter horizontal coordinate (1 to 80)   ');
    readln(CoordX3);
    write('Enter vertical coordinate   (1 to 25)   ');
    readln(CoordY3);
    writeln;
```

```
    write('Enter 1st horizontal coordinate for box ');
    readln(CoordX4);
    write('Enter 1st vertical coordinate for box   ');
    readln(CoordY4);
    write('Enter 2nd horizontal coordinate for box ');
    readln(CoordX5);
    write('Enter 2nd vertical coordinate for box   ');
    readln(CoordY5);

    InitGraphic;
    DefineWorld(1,0,MaxWorldY,MaxWorldX,0);
    SelectWorld(1);
    SelectWindow(1);
    DrawBorder;

    gotoxy(CoordX1,CoordY1);
    write(LINE1);
    gotoxy(CoordX2,CoordY2);
    write(LINE2);
    gotoxy(CoordX3,CoordY3);
    write(LINE3);
    CoordX4 := MaxWorldX / 80 * CoordX4;
    CoordY4 := MaxWorldY / 25 * CoordY4;
    CoordX5 := MaxWorldX / 80 * CoordX5;
    CoordY5 := MaxWorldY / 25 * CoordY5;
    DrawSquare(CoordX4,CoordY4,CoordX5,CoordY5,false);

    repeat until KeyPressed;
    LeaveGraphic;
end;
```

Fig. 4-12. PIXEL.BOX is used to produce 4 x 6 pixel text.

```
{PIXEL.BOX  }

procedure PixelTxt;

var  CoordX, CoordY, Size, Letter : integer;
     LET                          : char;

begin
     clrscr; gotoxy(1,10);
     write('Enter character to be displayed    ');
     readln(LET);
     Letter := integer(LET);
     write('Enter character size               ');
     readln(Size);
     write('Horizontal world coordinate?       ');
     readln(CoordX);
     write('Vertical world coordinate?         ');
     readln(CoordY);

     InitGraphic;
     DefineWorld(1,0,MaxWorldY,MaxWorldX,0);
     SelectWorld(1);
     SelectWindow(1);
     DrawBorder;

     DrawAscii(CoordX,CoordY,Size,Letter);
```

```
    repeat until KeyPressed;
    LeaveGraphic;

end;
```

ALL ABOUT WINDOWS

The use of windows is something that's made its appearance fairly recently. It refers to the ability to have several blocks of data, graphics, or whatever on the screen at the same time. You are able to manipulate not only the window sizes and positions, but also the information contained in a given window, independent of any other.

In this section you'll become conversant with the various routines that control the different aspects of "windowing," starting with very simple programs and progressing to the more advanced. Here, again, the demonstration programs that are provided with the Turbo Graphix Toolbox will be edited to permit data input for more meaningful experimentation. Simply looking at a program that uses predetermined values is of little practical use in most cases.

The first program in this group, SimpleWindow (SIMPWIND.PAS) produces a single window that is somewhat smaller than the full screen. Before making any modification, compile and run SIMPWIND.PAS. Having done that, you can change the program to include a group of input prompts that will make it possible to change the size of the window and its location on the screen (Fig. 4-13).

The input prompts ask for the horizontal and vertical coordinates for the upper left-hand and the lower right-hand corners. That gets a bit tricky, because each point represents eight pixel positions. Thus, if you enter 10, you're actually moving the position on the screen 80 pixels to the right. With the vertical coordinates, on the other hand, each single value represents a single pixel. Play around with different inputs to see the window change size and position.

The XMaxGlb and YMaxGlb variables have been done away with for the moment. They are, in fact, not variables but constants, defined in some of the include files, representing the maximum allowable horizontal and vertical positions for your particular system. If you're not sure about the values represented by those two constants, there's a short program that will cause those values to be displayed (Fig. 4-14).

The next program, MultipleWindows (MULTWIND.PAS), not only teaches how to display more than one window at a time, but also causes graphic displays to be shown in each of three windows. Before going on, compile the program and run it.

The program source code is quite well annotated, and by studying the remarks and the associated procedures, you can determine what takes place in each section. To provide a chance to observe the effects of using different values, I've modified the program to accept a number of inputs (Fig. 4-15). The first three input prompts produce values that control the World Coordinate system for each of the three windows. The values used in the original version of the program were 2000 for the first window, 1000 for the second and 500 for the third. By using different numbers, you'll be able to observe how the images inside the windows are affected while the actual dimensions of the windows themselves do not change. The copy for the headers is changed, because the original copy is no longer applicable.

The fourth input prompt is used to control the attitude of the "walking line" in the same way as in the DrawLines program. The value used in the original program is 50. You can observe what takes place if you use larger or smaller numbers.

The next program, MoveWindows (MOVEWIND.PAS) deals with the method of moving windows from one position to another on the screen. The demonstration program is designed to display two windows, one of which is fixed, while the other can be moved about by using the arrow keys. Before going any further, compile the program, run it, and then move the window that's located in the right bottom quarter of the screen by using the four arrow keys (Do not use Home, PgUp, End or PgDn. They don't work.)

Fig. 4-13. This is the file that creates a single window, with input prompts added.

```
{Simple window with input prompots}

program SimpleWindow;

{$I typedef.sys}
{$I graphix.sys}
{$I kernel.sys}
{$I windows.sys}

var HC1, HC2, VC1, VC2  : integer;

begin
     clrscr;  gotoxy(1,10);
     write('       Enter the first horizontal coordinate    ');
     readln(HC1);
     write('       Enter the second horizontal coordinate    ');
     readln(HC2);
     write('       Enter the first vertical coordinate    ');
     readln(VC1);
     write('       Enter the second horizontal coordinate    ');
     readln(VC2);

InitGraphic;

DrawBorder;
DefineWindow(1,HC1,VC1,HC2,VC2);
DefineHeader(1,'THIS IS ANOTHER EXAMPLE WINDOW');
SetHeaderOn;
DefineWorld(1,0,1000,1000,0);
SelectWindow(1);
SelectWorld(1);
SetBackground(85);
DrawBorder;

repeat until keypressed;

LeaveGraphic;

end.
```

Fig. 4-14. This little program displays the values assigned to the constants XMaxGlb and YMaxGlb contained in some of the include modules.

```
{SHOW.BOX }

program DisplayValue;

{$I TYPEDEF.SYS }
{$I GRAPHIX.SYS }
{$I KERNEL.SYS  }

begin
     clrscr; gotoxy(1,10);
     writeln('Screen width: ',XMaxGlb,' positions and ',XMaxGLB*8+7,' pixels');
     writeln;
     writeln('Screen height: ',YMaxGlb,' pixels');
     Repeat until KeyPressed;
end.
```

Fig. 4-15. This is the modified version of the demonstration program that creates and draws three windows.

```
{Multiple windows with input prompts}

program MultipleWindows;

{$I typedef.sys}
{$I graphix.sys}
{$I kernel.sys}
{$I windows.sys}

var I : integer;
    HC11, HC12, VC11, VC12  : integer;
    HC21, HC22, VC21, VC22  : integer;
    HC31, HC32, VC31, VC32  : integer;

procedure DrawLines;
var I : integer;
begin
  for I := 1 to 20 do DrawLine(I * 50,0,1000 - I * 50,I * 50);
end;

begin
     clrscr;  gotoxy(1,10);
     writeln('     Coordinates for window #1:');
     writeln;
     write('       Enter the first horizontal coordinate    ');
     readln(HC11);
     write('       Enter the second horizontal coordinate    ');
     readln(HC12);
     write('       Enter the first vertical coordinate    ');
     readln(VC11);
     write('       Enter the second horizontal coordinate    ');
     readln(VC12);
     clrscr;  gotoxy(1,10);
     writeln('     Coordinates for window #2:');
     writeln;
     write('       Enter the first horizontal coordinate    ');
     readln(HC21);
     write('       Enter the second horizontal coordinate    ');
     readln(HC22);
     write('       Enter the first vertical coordinate    ');
     readln(VC21);
     write('       Enter the second horizontal coordinate    ');
     readln(VC22);
     clrscr;  gotoxy(1,10);
     writeln('     Coordinates for window #3:');
     writeln;
     write('       Enter the first horizontal coordinate    ');
     readln(HC31);
     write('       Enter the second horizontal coordinate    ');
     readln(HC32);
     write('       Enter the first vertical coordinate    ');
     readln(VC31);
     write('       Enter the second horizontal coordinate    ');
     readln(VC32);

InitGraphic;
DrawBorder;
```

```
DefineWindow(1,HC11,VC11,HC12,VC12);
DefineHeader(1,'THIS IS THE FIRST WINDOW');
DefineWorld(1,0,2000,2000,0);
DefineWindow(2,HC21,VC21,HC22,VC22);
DefineHeader(2,'THIS IS THE SECOND WINDOW');
DefineWorld(2,0,1000,1000,0);
DefineWindow(3,HC31,VC31,HC32,VC32);
DefineHeader(3,'THIS IS THE THIRD WINDOW');
DefineWorld(3,0,500,500,0);
for I := 1 to 3 do begin
   SelectWindow(I);
   SetHeaderOn;
   SelectWorld(I);
   SetBackground(0);
   DrawBorder;
   DrawLines;
  end;

repeat until keypressed;
LeaveGraphic;

end.
```

Close scrutiny and considerable study of the text and the annotations in the source code is required to understand how this program functions. To illustrate it a little more, I've modified the program a bit (Fig. 4-16), calling it MoveWindowsSelectively (MVWND.P), and adding two variables and an input line that asks which window you'd like to move. The ones and twos in parentheses, associated with DefineWindow, DefineWorld, SelectWindow and SelectWorld in the bottom portion of the program, have been replaced with the two variables W1 and W2. The top left window becomes movable if you type one and the bottom right one responds to two. A zero causes the program to quit. Everything else is unchanged, because the variable replacements were all that was needed to produce the desired effect.

The last demonstration program in this section uses a flow chart placed into a movable window to demonstrate how window moving can be used to animate a graphic design for a specific purpose. The source code for the program, called FlowDemo (FLOWDEMO.PAS), is quite long (over three and a half pages). Underlining the procedure names FlowChartDemo, DrawArrowHor, DrawArrowVer, Blink, and the "begin" following that last procedure, in red, will simplify the task of studying what goes on here.

When the program is run, a window containing the legend I = 1 keeps running around a certain path. The I is incremented by one during each pass through the loop, until I = 5, at which point it goes to the END block and stops.

There is no modification that I can think of that would make this program any easier to decipher. It must simply be studied. If you examine the comments in the source code, and study the explanations given along with the descriptions of the various Toolbox procedures on pages

Fig. 4-16. This is the modified version of the program that is used to move individual windows selectively.

```
{MVWND.P }

program MoveWindowsSelectively;

{$I typedef.sys  }
{$I graphix.sys  }
{$I kernel.sys   }
```

```
{$I windows.sys  }

var i, W1, W2 : integer;
   Ch         : char;

procedure DrawLines;
var i : integer;
begin
  for i := 1 to 20 do DrawLine(i * 50,0,1000 - i * 50,i * 50);
end;


begin
     repeat
     clrscr; gotoxy(1,10);
     writeln('Window #1: Upper left.  Window #2: Lower right');
     writeln('----------------------------------------------');
     write('Select window to move (type 1 or 2) (0 to exit)   ');
     readln(W1);
     if W1 = 1 then W2 := 2 else W2 := 1;

InitGraphic;
DrawBorder;
DefineWindow(1,trunc(XMaxGlb / 10),trunc(YMaxGlb / 10),
               trunc(XMaxGlb / 2),trunc(YMaxGlb / 2));
DefineHeader(1,'THIS IS WINDOW NUMBER 1');
DefineWorld(1,0,1000,1000,0);
DefineWindow(2,trunc(XMaxGlb / 2),trunc(YMaxGlb / 2),
               trunc((XMaxGlb * 9) / 10),trunc((YMaxGlb * 9) / 10));
DefineHeader(2,'THIS IS WINDOW NUMBER 2');
DefineWorld(2,0,1000,1000,0);
SelectWindow(W2);
SetHeaderOn;
SelectWorld(W2);
SetBackground(0);
DrawBorder;
DrawLines;
CopyScreen;
       SetBreakOff;
       SetMessageOff;
SelectWindow(W1);
SetHeaderOn;
SelectWorld(W1);
SetBackground(0);
DrawBorder;
DrawLines;

       repeat
  read(Kbd,Ch);
  case ord(Ch) of
      72 : MoveVer(-4,true);
      75 : MoveHor(-1,true);
      77 : MoveHor(1,true);
      80 : MoveVer(4,true);
  end;
until Ch = ' ';
LeaveGraphic;
      until W1 = 0;
end.
```

107 through 235 of the manual, you'll get a fair idea of how all of this works and how to make it work for you.

ALL ABOUT CHARTS AND GRAPHS

There are three demonstration programs that use some of the toolbox routines that produce pie charts and bar graphs in the documentation book. We'll be looking at, and then editing, all three of them.

The first program produces one pie chart. It is called, appropriately, OnePieDemo (ONEPIE.PAS). When it is compiled and run it produces a five-segment pie chart with the first segment moved outward. Each segment is labeled with its size and description, giving a demonstration of what the program can be used for.

Such a program is of practical value only if the pie-segment sizes can vary, as well as the associated text. To accomplish this, the program (Fig. 4-17) has been edited by first declaring a group of global variables after the program identification. Next 11 input prompts were added. One asked the number of segments to be drawn, in this case limiting the number to five. There are five input prompts for the size of each segment, and five for the associated text to be used. The text is limited to five characters. Finally, the original values in the program section described in the comments as {the number of pie segments} and {initialize the pie array} were replaced with the previously declared global variables.

When the program is once more complied and run, it displays the input prompts, one after another, along with a line that explains how to exit the program. The values entered for the pie-segment sizes may be integers, or numbers with decimal fractions. They will always be displayed with the integer portion followed by a decimal point and two decimal places. The total of the aggregate values associated with the pie segments makes no difference. Whatever it may be, the program automatically divides the pie in such a way that each segment is correctly proportioned. For the text portion, you may enter any type of character, but the numbers representing segment sizes will be butted directly to the last character. Thus, it might be advisable to use only four characters followed by a blank space, a colon, or an equal sign.

If you opt for less than five segments, enter sizes and text for only the number desired. Press ENTER for the rest, and the program will produce a pie chart with the specified number of segments in the correct proportion. If you want to be able to use a larger number of segments, you'll have to add and declare the appropriate number of additional variables, add input prompts, and, in the section where fixed values were replaced by the global variables, add the necessary extra lines (Fig. 4-18). If you want to be able to move sections of the pie outward other than section number 1, add an input prompt that asks which section is to be moved out, and add another global variable of the type integer. Replace the ones in the line that reads:

```
a[1].area: = – a[1].area;
```

with the new global variable. In that way, you can select the segment to be emphasized by being separated from the rest.

The demonstration program that produces bar graphs is called OneHist (ONEHIST.PAS). The Hist part of the name refers to the fact that bar charts are also called "histograms" by those who want to be fancy. The demonstration program, with the source code included on the copy of the distribution disk, is a bit impractical because it produces a bar graph with ten bars of random heights. It's the random part that's a nuisance, because it makes it unnecessarily difficult to figure out how the height of each bar is arrived at. If you compile and run it several times, you'll see that the height of the various bars changes with each run. A close scrutiny of the source code shows that this time the editing will be a bit more involved. In the edited version (Fig. 4-19) three new global variables have been declared. An input prompt asking for the number of bars

Fig. 4-17. This program uses data input to create a pie chart with up to five segments.

```
program OnePieDemo;

var  A1, A2, A3, A4, A5 : real;
     T1, T2, T3, T4, T5 : string[5];
     P                  : integer;

{$I typedef.sys }
{$I graphix.sys }
{$I kernel.sys  }
{$I windows.sys }
{$I circsegm.hgh}
{$I pie.hgh     }

procedure OnePieDem;

var sum, x1, y1, Radius, Theta, InRadius, OutRadius : real;
    n, Mode, Size                                   : integer;
    a                                               : PieArray;
    back                                            : byte;
    ch                                              : char;

begin
  ClearScreen;
  SetColorWhite;

  DefineWindow(1,0,0,XMaxGlb,YMaxGlb);
  DefineHeader(1,'A SINGLE PIE CHART');
  DefineWorld(1,0,1000,1000,0);
  SelectWorld(1);
  SelectWindow(1);
  SetHeaderOn;
  SetBackground(0);
  DrawBorder;

  n          := P;
  a[1].area := A1;
  a[2].area := A2;
  a[3].area := A3;
  a[4].area := A4;
  a[5].area := A5;
  a[1].text := T1;
  a[2].text := T2;
  a[3].text := T3;
  a[4].text := T4;
  a[5].text := T5;

  a[1].area := -a[1].area;

  x1 := 500;
  y1 := 500;

  Radius := 200;
  Theta  := 60;

  SetAspect(1.0);

  InRadius   := 0.7;
```

```
  OutRadius  := 1.25;

  Mode := 2;
  Size := 2;

  DrawPolarPie(x1,y1,Radius,Theta,InRadius,OutRadius,a,n,Mode,Size);

end;

begin
     repeat
     clrscr; gotoxy(1,8);
     writeln('To exit program type one 0, then ENTERs');
     writeln('----------------------------------------');
     write('Enter number of segments (max: 5)      ');
     readln(P);
     write('Enter segment #1, size                 ');
     readln(A1);
     write('Enter segment #2, size                 ');
     readln(A2);
     write('Enter segment #3, size                 ');
     readln(A3);
     write('Enter segment #4, size                 ');
     readln(A4);
     write('Enter segment #5, size                 ');
     readln(A5);
     write('Enter segment #1, text (to 5 char''s)                  ');
     readln(T1);
     write('Enter segment #2, text (to 5 char''s)                  ');
     readln(T2);
     write('Enter segment #3, text (to 5 char''s)                  ');
     readln(T3);
     write('Enter segment #4, text (to 5 char''s)                  ');
     readln(T4);
     write('Enter segment #5, text (to 5 char''s)                  ');
     readln(T5);

InitGraphic;
OnePieDem;
repeat until KeyPressed;
LeaveGraphic;
     until A1 = 0;
end.
```

Fig. 4-18. This version of the pie-chart program permits selection of up to ten segments for the chart.

```
program OnePieDemo;

var  A    : array [1..10] of real;
     T    : array [1..10] of string[5];
     P, N : integer;

{$I typedef.sys }
{$I graphix.sys }
{$I kernel.sys  }
{$I windows.sys }
{$I circsegm.hgh}
{$I pie.hgh     }

procedure OnePieDem;
```

```
var sum, x1, y1, Radius, Theta, InRadius, OutRadius : real;
    n, Mode, Size                                   : integer;
    a                                               : PieArray;
    back                                            : byte;
    ch                                              : char;

begin
  ClearScreen;
  SetColorWhite;

  DefineWindow(1,0,0,XMaxGlb,YMaxGlb);
  DefineHeader(1,'A SINGLE PIE CHART');
  DefineWorld(1,0,1000,1000,0);
  SelectWorld(1);
  SelectWindow(1);
  SetHeaderOn;
  SetBackground(0);
  DrawBorder;

  n          := P;
  a[1].area := A[1];
  a[2].area := A[2];
  a[3].area := A[3];
  a[4].area := A[4];
  a[5].area := A[5];
  a[6].area := A[6];
  a[7].area := A[7];
  a[8].area := A[8];
  a[9].area := A[9];
  a[10].area := A[10];
  a[1].text := T[1];
  a[2].text := T[2];
  a[3].text := T[3];
  a[4].text := T[4];
  a[5].text := T[5];
  a[6].text := T[6];
  a[7].text := T[7];
  a[8].text := T[8];
  a[9].text := T[9];
  a[10].text := T[10];

  a[1].area := -a[1].area;

  x1 := 500;
  y1 := 500;

  Radius := 200;
  Theta  :=  60;

  SetAspect(1.0);

  InRadius  := 0.7;
  OutRadius := 1.25;

  Mode := 2;
  Size := 2;

  DrawPolarPie(x1,y1,Radius,Theta,InRadius,OutRadius,a,n,Mode,Size);
```

```
end;

begin
     repeat
     clrscr; gotoxy(1,8);
     writeln('To exit program type one 0, then ENTERs');
     writeln('---------------------------------------');
     write('Enter number of segments (max: 10)      ');
     readln(P);
               for N := 1 to P do begin
     write('Enter segment #',P,', size                    ');
     readln(A[N]);
               end;
               for N := 1 to P do begin
     write('Enter segment #',N,', text (to 5 char''s)                ');
     readln(T[N]);
               end;

InitGraphic;
OnePieDem;
repeat until KeyPressed;
LeaveGraphic;
     until A1 = 0;
end.
```

Fig. 4-19. This modification draws a bar chart.

```
program OneHist;

var L, N : integer;
    H    : array[1..20] of integer;

{$I typedef.sys }
{$I graphix.sys }
{$I kernel.sys  }
{$I windows.sys }
{$I hatch.hgh   }
{$I histogrm.hgh}


procedure HistoDem;
var i, DisplyLen, HatchDen : integer;
    a                      : PlotArray;
    r                      : real;
    ch                     : char;
    Hatch                  : boolean;

begin
  DisplyLen := L;

  for i := 0 to DisplyLen do
    begin
      a[i + 1,2] := H[i];
    end;

  SetColorWhite;
  SetBackground(0);
```

```
  SetHeaderOn;
  DefineWindow(1,0,0,XMaxGlb,YMaxGlb);
  DefineHeader(1,'A BAR CHART WITH HATCHING');
  DefineWorld(1,-DisplyLen,1000,1000,0);
  SelectWorld(1);
  SelectWindow(1);

  DrawBorder;

  Hatch:=true;
  HatchDen:=7;

  DrawHistogram(a,-DisplyLen,Hatch,HatchDen);

end;

begin
     repeat
     clrscr; gotoxy(1,8);
     writeln('Type 0 once, the ENTERs to exit program');
     writeln('---------------------------------------');
     write('Enter number of bars                    ');
     readln(L);
              for N := 1 to L do begin
     write('Enter height of bar #',N,'              ');
     readln(H[N]);
              end;

InitGraphic;
HistoDem;
repeat until KeyPressed;
LeaveGraphic;
     until L = 0;
end.
```

to be used has been added, and a loop of input prompts asks that you enter the height for each bar. In addition, the World Coordinate system was changed to accept heights from 1 to 1000, because charts of this type usually represent monetary or other values involving up to three-digit figures. If larger values are to be represented, you must change the 1000 in the DefineWorld line to the appropriate figure, say, 10000. Also, in the loop, **random** was replaced by H[i], and DisplyLen now equals L instead of 10. When the program is compiled and run, it explains how to exit it and then displays the various input prompts. After that, it displays the bar graph with as many bars of a given height as determined by the typed-in values.

The last demonstration program in this group, called PieHisto (PIEHISTO.PAS), produces a combination of pie chart and bar graph in two separate windows, with some descriptive text. The source code for the program specifies that the text and values to be used are the same as those in the OnePieDemo program. When you compile and run the program, it displays the text plus values in a text plus values in a text block, and then draws a pie chart followed by a bar graph, each in its separate window.

To edit the program to permit data input and, thus, experimentation, all you have to do is duplicate the exact modification that was performed with the OnePieDemo program (Fig. 4-20). When those additions and changes have been made, the program, after having been compiled, works just fine with different values, different text, and a different number of pie segments and bars. Furthermore, additional editing possibilities exist here as they do with OnePieDemo.

Fig. 4-20. This version produces a pie chart and a bar chart, and includes the necessary input prompts.

```
program PieHisto;

var A1, A2, A3, A4, A5 : real;
    T1, T2, T3, T4, T5 : string[5];
    P                  : integer;

{$I typedef.sys   }
{$I graphix.sys   }
{$I kernel.sys    }
{$I windows.sys   }
{$I circsegm.hgh  }
{$I pie.hgh       }
{$I hatch.hgh     }
{$I histogrm.hgh  }


procedure PieHistoDem;

var sum, x1, y1, x2, y2, InRadius, OutRadius : real;
    i, n                                     : integer;
    a                                        : PieArray;
    b                                        : PlotArray;
    ch                                       : char;
    NumText                                  : WrkString;

begin

  n          := P;
  a[1].area := A1;
  a[2].area := A2;
  a[3].area := A3;
  a[4].area := A4;
  a[5].area := A5;
  a[1].text := T1;
  a[2].text := T2;
  a[3].text := T3;
  a[4].text := T4;
  a[5].text := T5;


  for i := 1 to n do
    b[i,2] := a[i].area;

  ClearScreen;
  SetColorWhite;

  DefineWindow(1,0,0,XMaxGlb,YMaxGlb);
  DefineHeader(1,'BOTH A PIE AND A BAR CHART');
  SelectWindow(1);
  SetHeaderOn;
  SetBackground(0);
  DrawBorder;

  for i := 1 to n do
   begin
    GotoXY(60,4 + i);
    write(a[i].text,'=');
```

```
   str(a[i].area:6:2,NumText);
   write(NumText);
  end;

 DefineWindow(2,trunc(XMaxGlb / 10),trunc(YMaxGlb / 10),
                trunc(XMaxGlb * 6 / 10),trunc(YMaxGlb * 7 / 10));
 DefineHeader(2,'A PIE CHART');
 DefineWorld(2,0,1000,1000,0);
 SelectWorld(2);
 SelectWindow(2);
 SetHeaderOn;
 SetBackground(0);
 DrawBorder;

 a[1].area := -a[1].area;
 SetAspect(1.0);

 x1 := 500;
 y1 := 500;

 x2 := 600;
 y2 := 350;

   InRadius  := 0.7;
   OutRadius := 1.25;

   DrawCartPie(x1,y1,x2,y2,InRadius,OutRadius,a,n,2,1);

   a[1].area := -a[1].area;

   DefineWindow(3,trunc(XMaxGlb / 2),trunc(YMaxGlb / 2),
                  trunc(XMaxGlb * 9 / 10),trunc(YMaxGlb * 9 / 10));
   DefineHeader(3,'A BAR CHART');
   DefineWorld(3,0,60,10,0);
   SelectWorld(3);
   SelectWindow(3);
   SetHeaderOn;
   SetBackground(0);
   DrawBorder;

   DrawHistogram(b,n,true,5);

 for i := 1 to n do
  begin
   DrawTextW((10 / n) * (i - 1),10,1,'    '+ a[i].text);
   str(a[i].area:6:2,NumText);
   DrawTextW((10 / n) * (i - 1),16,1,' '+ NumText);
  end;

 end;

 begin
      repeat
      clrscr; gotoxy(1,8);
      writeln('To exit program type one 0, then ENTERs');
      writeln('---------------------------------------');
      write('Enter number of segments (max: 5)      ');
      readln(P);
      write('Enter segment #1, size                 ');
```

```
     readln(A1);
     write('Enter segment #2, size                    ');
     readln(A2);
     write('Enter segment #3, size                    ');
     readln(A3);
     write('Enter segment #4, size                    ');
     readln(A4);
     write('Enter segment #5, size                    ');
     readln(A5);
     write('Enter segment #1, text (to 5 char''s)                 ');
     readln(T1);
     write('Enter segment #2, text (to 5 char''s)                 ');
     readln(T2);
     write('Enter segment #3, text (to 5 char''s)                 ');
     readln(T3);
     write('Enter segment #4, text (to 5 char''s)                 ');
     readln(T4);
     write('Enter segment #5, text (to 5 char''s)                 ');
     readln(T5);

InitGraphic;
PieHistoDem;
repeat until KeyPressed;
LeaveGraphic;

     until A1 = 0;

end.
```

THROWING CURVES

In this section things tend to get a bit involved. It deals with plotting curves that are actually series of points connected by line segments, also known as polygons.

The first demonstration program in this section is called OnePolygon (ONEPOLY.PAS). It draws what is known as a sine curve. The problem is that the program uses a loop to plot the curve. Non-mathematicians, like myself, find it difficult to figure out what is represented by the equations in the procedure GenerateFunction, which is the one that actually causes the curve to be drawn. In fact, the only way to experiment with this particular program is to change the value assigned to the variable n, which controls the number of segments used to make up the curve. To do this, add an input prompt and the usual **repeat . . . until** loop (Fig. 4-21). This gives a chance to observe the effect of using smaller and larger numbers of segments, an effect that may vary among different computer systems.

The edited version left nearly all of the original source code undisturbed. All that was done was to add a global variable NN, to change **n := 30;** to **n := NN;**, and add the usual input prompt in the main program ahead of InitGraphic. When you compile and run the edited version, you can experiment to your heart's content. You'll find that the smaller then number, the rougher the curve and, conversely, the larger the number, the smoother the curve.

Let's design an entirely new program that creates a different type of curved line. This program is as simple as possible to demonstrate the routines that are used.

There are, actually, two versions of the same program. The short version, named Polygon (POLYTST.P) (Fig. 4-22), simply draws one straight diagonal line from the left bottom, slanting to the right. The prompts ask that you key in the number of segments, the character code, and answer a question about drawing lines. The character code determines what symbols, if any, appear at each of the segment endings (for the code numbers, see page 147 of the documentation book, where the procedure DrawPolygon is described in detail).

Fig. 4-21. Some input prompts have been added to the program that draws a predetermined curve.

```
program OnePolygon;

var NN : integer;

{$I typedef.sys }
{$I graphix.sys }
{$I kernel.sys  }
{$I windows.sys }
{$I polygon.hgh }

procedure PolygonDem;
var n      : integer;
    b,a    : PlotArray;
    ch     : char;
    x1,x2  : integer;

procedure GenerateFunction(var a,b : PlotArray; n : integer);

var i     : integer;
    delta : real;

begin
  delta := 2 * pi / (n - 1);
  for i := 1 to n do
    begin
      a[i,1] := (i-1) * delta - pi;
      a[i,2] := sin(a[i,1]);
    end;
end;

begin
  ClearScreen;
  n := NN;
  GenerateFunction(a,b,n);

  DefineWindow(1,0,0,XMaxGlb,YMaxGlb);
  DefineHeader(1,'SINE CURVE AS A POLYGON');
  DefineWorld(1,-pi,1,pi,-1);
  SelectWorld(1);
  SelectWindow(1);
  SetBackground(0);
  SetHeaderOn;
  DrawBorder;
  DrawPolygon(a,1,n,0,0,0);
end;

begin
     repeat
     clrscr; gotoxy(1,10);
     writeln('Type 0 to exit the program');
     writeln('--------------------------');
     write('Enter number of segments  ');
     readln(NN);

InitGraphic;
PolygonDem;
repeat until KeyPressed;
```

```
LeaveGraphic;

     until NN = 0;

end.
```

Fig. 4-22. In this modification of the polygon program, other input prompts have been added.

```
program TestPolygonWithLoop;

{$I typedef.sys }
{$I graphix.sys }
{$I kernel.sys  }
{$I windows.sys }
{$I polygon.hgh }

var PA            : PlotArray;
    CD, N, Z, L : integer;
    CH            : char;

procedure CurveLoop;
begin
     for Z := 1 to N do
     begin
       PA[Z,1] := 20 * Z;
       PA[Z,2] := 20 * Z;
       writeln(PA[Z,1]:3:1,' ',PA[Z,2]:3:1);
     end;
       readln(CH);

  DefineWindow(1,0,0,XMaxGlb,YMaxGlb);
  DefineHeader(1,'THIS IS A POLYGON TEST');
  DefineWorld(1,0,1000,1000,0);
  SelectWorld(1);
  SelectWindow(1);
  SetBackground(0);
  SetHeaderOn;
  DrawBorder;
  DrawPolygon(PA,1,N,CD,4,L);
end;

begin
     repeat
     clrscr; gotoxy(1,10);
     writeln('Type 0 to exit the program');
     writeln('--------------------------');
     write('Enter number of segments  ');
     readln(N);
     write('Enter character code      ');
     readln(CD);
     write('Draw lines? (0 or 1)      ');
     readln(L);
InitGraphic;
CurveLoop;
repeat until KeyPressed;
LeaveGraphic;

     until N = 0;

end.
```

If you enter 50 for the number of segments, you'll get a diagonal line all the way across the screen. In the **for Z := 1 to N do** loop each segment is given a length value of 20, so the World Coordinate system is set up for 1000 units (20 * 50 = 1000).**Draw Lines? (0 or 1)** asks whether you want lines drawn from the bottom of the screen to each of the segment end points. If you type 0, no lines are drawn. If you type any number greater than 0, vertical lines are drawn. In the **DrawPolygon(PA,1,N,CD,4,L);** line, PA is the value of the PlotArray, 1 is the number of the first segment to be drawn, N is the number of the last segment to be drawn, CD is the character code, 4 is the size those characters will appear, and L determines whether vertical lines will be drawn.

In this, as in the next version, I have included a display of the numbers that are associated with each segment point, which requires pressing ENTER to continue program execution. If and when that becomes a nuisance, simply delete the **writeln(PA[. . .** line and the **readln(CH);** line. Compile and run the program and experiment with different segment numbers (up to 50), with their different codes from 1 through 9, and with the line command on and off. It helps to understand the program.

The second version, TestPolygon (TSTPOLY.P) (Fig. 4-23), differs from the first in the values assigned to the PA array (PlotArray). They are written as part of the program for each segment. To keep the program from getting too long, the number of segments is limited to 10. This produces a very rough zigzag type of line, but does effectively illustrate how the DrawPolygon procedure reacts to the values assigned to the PlotArray. The other difference is that, in answer to the question about the number of segments, you can enter any number up to and including 10, but not greater.

In practice it would probably be better to create an input loop, to permit varying the resulting polygon. Another version of the same program gives that option. That version is called TestPolygonWithLoop (TESTPOLY.P) (Fig. 4-24). Depending on your patience, and the desired smoothness of the resulting curve, you can enter any number of curve segments up to 100. Most of the time something like 30 would be sufficient. All those lines that determined the values used for the X and Y coordinates have been deleted. Instead, a **for Z:= 1 to N do begin** loop permits inputs for those X and Y coordinates, determined when you enter a value representing the number of segments. Each entry is assigned to the PlotArray in **PA[Z,1]:= /CX; PA[Z,2] := CY;** before the next pass through the loop.

When using this version of the program, it would be a good idea to draw an approximation of the desired curve on some graph paper in to determine the most likely coordinates in advance, instead of guessing while running the program.

The next demonstration program in this group produces labeled axes that can be used with polygons or almost anything else. It's called OneAxisDemo (ONEAXIS.PAS). When compiled and run, it produces a horizontal and a vertical line, centered in the display area with ruler-like labels along the left and bottom sides. In order to simplify experimentation, Fig. 4-25 shows a modified version in which the parameters affecting DrawAxis are replaced by variables, and a group of eight input prompts has been added. A bit of playing around with different input values helps you become familiar with the effects that are produced by these values.

POLYAXIX.PAS, the next demonstration program on the copy of the distribution disk, is a combination of the two previous ones. It draws a sine curve inside axes. This demonstration program has been combined with two previous programs, TestPolygonWithLoop and OneAxisModified, into a new one called PolygonWithRulers (AXP.P, Fig. 4-26). It includes all of the input prompts and added variables from the two previous programs, producing a polygon with rulers along the left and bottom edges, based on data that are keyed in during the run of the program.

The next demonstration program, MovePolygon, demonstrates the availability of routines that can be used to move things on the screen, to animate whatever design you've drawn. When compiled and run it shows an arrowhead, pointing up, center screen. Using the arrow keys, you

Fig. 4-23. This program can be used to draw a variety of different polygons.

```
program TestPolygon;

{$I typedef.sys }
{$I graphix.sys }
{$I kernel.sys  }
{$I windows.sys }
{$I polygon.hgh }

var PA           : PlotArray;
    CD, N, Z, L : integer;
    CH           : char;

procedure CurveLoop;
begin
      PA[1,1] := 100;
      PA[1,2] := 100;
      writeln(PA[1,1]:3:1,' ',PA[1,2]:3:1);
      PA[2,1] := 200;
      PA[2,2] := 150;
      writeln(PA[2,1]:3:1,' ',PA[2,2]:3:1);
      PA[3,1] := 300;
      PA[3,2] := 175;
      writeln(PA[3,1]:3:1,' ',PA[3,2]:3:1);
      PA[4,1] := 400;
      PA[4,2] := 400;
      writeln(PA[4,1]:3:1,' ',PA[4,2]:3:1);
      PA[5,1] := 500;
      PA[5,2] := 100;
      writeln(PA[5,1]:3:1,' ',PA[5,2]:3:1);
      PA[6,1] := 600;
      PA[6,2] := 300;
      writeln(PA[6,1]:3:1,' ',PA[6,2]:3:1);
      PA[7,1] := 700;
      PA[7,2] := 600;
      writeln(PA[7,1]:3:1,' ',PA[7,2]:3:1);
      PA[8,1] := 800;
      PA[8,2] := 800;
      writeln(PA[8,1]:3:1,' ',PA[8,2]:3:1);
      PA[9,1] := 900;
      PA[9,2] := 500;
      writeln(PA[9,1]:3:1,' ',PA[9,2]:3:1);
      PA[10,1] := 1000;
      PA[10,2] := 300;
      writeln(PA[10,1]:3:1,' ',PA[10,2]:3:1);
      readln(CH);

  DefineWindow(1,0,0,XMaxGlb,YMaxGlb);
  DefineHeader(1,'THIS IS A POLYGON TEST');
  DefineWorld(1,0,1000,1000,0);
  SelectWorld(1);
  SelectWindow(1);
  SetBackground(0);
  SetHeaderOn;
  DrawBorder;
  DrawPolygon(PA,1,N,CD,4,L);
end;

begin
```

```
      repeat
      clrscr; gotoxy(1,10);
      writeln('Type 0 to exit the program');
      writeln('--------------------------');
      write('Enter number of segments  ');
      readln(N);
      write('Enter character code      ');
      readln(CD);
      write('Draw lines? (0 or 1)      ');
      readln(L);

InitGraphic;
CurveLoop;
repeat until KeyPressed;
LeaveGraphic;

      until N = 0;

end.
```

Fig. 4-24. This program also draws polygons, but it uses a loop for the inputs, which makes it neater.

```
program TestPolygonWithLoop;

{$I typedef.sys }
{$I graphix.sys }
{$I kernel.sys  }
{$I windows.sys }
{$I polygon.hgh }

var PA           : PlotArray;
    CD, N, Z, L  : integer;
    CX, CY       : integer;
    CH           : char;

procedure CurveLoop;
begin

  DefineWindow(1,0,0,XMaxGlb,YMaxGlb);
  DefineHeader(1,'THIS IS A POLYGON TEST');
  DefineWorld(1,0,1000,1000,0);
  SelectWorld(1);
  SelectWindow(1);
  SetBackground(0);
  SetHeaderOn;
  DrawBorder;
  DrawPolygon(PA,1,N,CD,4,L);

end;

begin
      repeat
      clrscr; gotoxy(1,10);
      writeln('Type 0 first plus ENTER to exit the program');
      writeln('-------------------------------------------');
      write('Enter number of segments  ');
      readln(N);
            for Z := 1 to N do begin
      write('Segment #',Z,', enter X coordinate (1 to 1000)  ');
```

```
     readln(CX);
     write('Segment #',Z,', enter Y coordinate (1 to 1000)  ');
     readln(CY);
     writeln('------------------------------------------------------');
     PA[Z,1] := CX;
     PA[Z,2] := CY;
          end;
     write('Enter character code       ');
     readln(CD);
     write('Draw lines? (0 or 1)       ');
     readln(L);

InitGraphic;
CurveLoop;
repeat until KeyPressed;
LeaveGraphic;

     until N = 0;

end.
```

Fig. 4-25. The OneAxis program has been modified to include input prompts.

```
program OneAxisModified;

{$I typedef.sys }
{$I graphix.sys }
{$I kernel.sys  }
{$I windows.sys }
{$I axis.hgh    }

var  Q1, Q2, Q3, Q4, Q5, Q6, Q7, Q8 : integer;
     CH                             : integer;

procedure OneAxisDem;

begin
  ClearScreen;
  SetColorWhite;
  SetBackground(0);

  DefineHeader(1,'LABELED AXES');
  SetHeaderOn;
  DefineWorld(1,-10,10,10,-10);
  SelectWindow(1);
  SelectWorld(1);

  DrawBorder;

  DrawAxis(Q1,Q2,Q3,Q4,Q5,Q6,Q7,Q8,true);

end;


procedure EnterData;
begin
     clrscr; gotoxy(1,5);
     write('Enter horizontal axis density      ');
     readln(Q1);
```

```
        write('Enter vertical axis density        ');
        readln(Q2);
        write('Enter distance from left edge      ');
        readln(Q3);
        write('Enter distance from top edge       ');
        readln(Q4);
        write('Enter distance from right edge     ');
        readln(Q5);
        write('Enter distance from bottom edge    ');
        readln(Q6);
        write('Enter line style, horizontal axis ');
        readln(Q7);
        write('Enter line style, vertical axis    ');
        readln(Q8);

    InitGraphic;
    OneAxisDem;
    repeat until KeyPressed;
    LeaveGraphic;
    end;

    procedure Menu;
    begin
        clrscr; gotoxy(1,10);
        writeln('            Menu');
        writeln('            ====');
        writeln('1)          Enter Data');
        writeln('2)         Exit program');
        writeln('--------------------------------------');
        write('Which?                   ');
        readln(CH);

                case CH of
                1: EnterData;
                2: end;
    end;

    begin
        repeat
        Menu;
        until CH = 2;
    end.
```

Fig. 4-26. Another modification of the OneAxis program produces a polygon with rulers.

```
    program PolygonWithRulers;

    {$I typedef.sys  }
    {$I graphix.sys  }
    {$I kernel.sys   }
    {$I windows.sys  }
    {$I axis.hgh     }
    {$I polygon.hgh  }

    var PA                        : PlotArray;
        CD, N, Z, L               : integer;
        CX, CY                    : integer;
```

```
     Q1,Q2,Q3,Q4,Q5,Q6,Q7,Q8 : integer;
     CH                      : char;

procedure CurveLoop;
begin

  DefineWindow(1,0,0,XMaxGlb,YMaxGlb);
  DefineHeader(1,'THIS IS A POLYGON PLUS AXES TEST');
  DefineWorld(1,0,1000,1000,0);
  SelectWorld(1);
  SelectWindow(1);
  SetBackground(0);
  SetHeaderOn;
  DrawBorder;
  DrawAxis(Q1,Q2,Q3,Q4,Q5,Q6,Q7,Q8,false);
  DrawPolygon(PA,1,N,CD,4,L);

end;

begin
     repeat
     clrscr; gotoxy(1,8);
     writeln('To exit program type 0 once, then ENTERs');
     writeln('----------------------------------------');
     write('Enter number of segments                 ');
     readln(N);
           for Z := 1 to N do begin
     write('Segment #',Z,', enter X coordinate     ');
     readln(CX);
     write('Segment #',Z,', enter Y coordinate     ');
     readln(CY);
     writeln('----------------------------------------');
     PA[Z,1] := CX;
     PA[Z,2] := CY;
           end;
     write('Enter character code                   ');
     readln(CD);
     write('Draw lines? (0 or 1)                   ');
     readln(L);
     writeln('----------------------------------------');
     write('Enter horizontal axis density          ');
     readln(Q1);
     write('Enter vertical axis density            ');
     readln(Q2);
     write('Enter distance from left edge          ');
     readln(Q3);
     write('Enter distance from top edge           ');
     readln(Q4);
     write('Enter distance from right edge         ');
     readln(Q5);
     write('Enter distance from bottom edge        ');
     readln(Q6);
     write('Enter horizontal axis line style       ');
     readln(Q7);
     write('Enter vertical axis line style         ');
     readln(Q8);

InitGraphic;
CurveLoop;
```

```
repeat until KeyPressed;
LeaveGraphic;

    until N = 0;
end.
```

can move that arrowhead to any position on the screen, turn it to point in any direction, and so on. You might want to change the image of that arrowhead to something else. The procedure MakeArrow is used for that purpose. Leave the variable and array names unchanged, varying only the values to the right of the colons. Otherwise, inconsistencies might cause the program to cease to function properly.

The polygon that makes up the arrowhead consists of five segments. You can increase or decrease the number of segments by adding or deleting **Arrow[x,x]:** lines. In Fig. 4-27 the entire procedure MakeArrow has been deleted and replaced with an input-prompt loop. This makes it easy to experiment with different numbers of segments and different values for the X and Y coordinates at each segment's beginning and end.

FindWorld (FINDWRLD.PAS), the next demonstration program, creates a window that fits the dimensions of a given polygon. In this demonstration program the polygon is created using random values, so that each run the polygon will change shape. FindWorldModification (FDWD.P), Fig. 4-28, is a modification of that program. The random values, and many of the previously fixed values, are replaced by data entered by the user in reply to a series of input prompts.

The last two demonstration programs in this group deal with something referred to as "curve fitting," the problem of creating a smooth curve based on a series of points, such as those used previously to create polygons.

The first of the two programs uses a Spline procedure to round out the jagged edges of a polygon. The program is nearly identical to the one called Findworld, as you'll see when you compile and run it. The procedure Spline(. . .), contained in the include file SPLINE.HGH, creates a number of additional points between those used in creating the original polygon. In the demonstration program, the variable M is used to determine the number of points to be created, and a value of 50 is assigned to it. In other words, if you started with a polygon consisting of 10 segments, the Spline procedure creates a total of 50 points, in order to draw a smooth curve. Figure 4-29 is a modified version of the program, in which the variable names are replaced by others used in some of the earlier modifications. A block of input prompts asks that you key in the parameters for the original polygon, as well as the number of Spline points you want the program to use.

The last demonstration program in this section uses a different method to produce a smooth curve. Known as the Bezier method, it is contained in the Bezier procedure that can be found in the BEZIER.HGH include file. The program is called BeziDemo (BEZIDEMO.PAS, page 76 of the manual) and, at first glance, it's rather obscure. Most of it, however, consists of procedures that you have already become familiar with in earlier programs. Therefore, compile and run it in order to see what happens. When the program is run you'll find that it includes some input prompts that ask that the X and Y coordinates for a selected point be changed to some other values. This can be repeated over and over again, producing new and different curves based on the changing positions of one polygon point or another. To exit the program, press ENTER. In order to understand the various steps taken by the program, study the annotations in the source code and the procedure descriptions in the Technical Reference section of the documentation book.

COLOR ME PURPLE

So far, everything you've done has been in "living black and white," meaning that all our designs have been white on black. Depending on the color adapter used in your system, you might have as many as 16 colors available for the graphic images and also for the backgrounds. With

Fig. 4-27. This version of the MovePolygon program enables the user to design any kind of shape which can be moved in any direction.

```
program MovePolygonTest;

{$I typedef.sys }
{$I graphix.sys }
{$I kernel.sys  }
{$I windows.sys }
{$I polygon.hgh }
{$I modpoly.hgh }

var ArrowAngle, N, NS                          : integer;
    Ch                                         : char;
    Arrow                                      : PlotArray;
    CurrX,CurrY,IncrX,IncrY,Size,Speed         : real;
    ArrowIncr                                  : array[0..7,1..2] of real;
    A, B                                       : array[1..10] of integer;

procedure MakeMoveTable;
begin
  ArrowIncr[0,1]:=0;
  ArrowIncr[0,2]:=1;
  ArrowIncr[1,1]:=-1;
  ArrowIncr[1,2]:=1;
  ArrowIncr[2,1]:=-1;
  ArrowIncr[2,2]:=0;
  ArrowIncr[3,1]:=-1;
  ArrowIncr[3,2]:=-1;
  ArrowIncr[4,1]:=0;
  ArrowIncr[4,2]:=-1;
  ArrowIncr[5,1]:=1;
  ArrowIncr[5,2]:=-1;
  ArrowIncr[6,1]:=1;
  ArrowIncr[6,2]:=0;
  ArrowIncr[7,1]:=1;
  ArrowIncr[7,2]:=1;
end;

procedure MoveForward;
begin
  SetColorBlack;
  DrawPolygon(Arrow,1,-5,0,0,0);
  CurrX:=CurrX+IncrX;
  CurrY:=CurrY+IncrY;
  TranslatePolygon(Arrow,5,IncrX,IncrY);
  SetColorWhite;
  DrawPolygon(Arrow,1,-5,0,0,0);
end;

procedure MoveBack;
begin
  SetColorBlack;
  DrawPolygon(Arrow,1,-5,0,0,0);
  CurrX:=CurrX-IncrX;
  CurrY:=CurrY-IncrY;
  TranslatePolygon(Arrow,5,-IncrX,-IncrY);
  SetColorWhite;
  DrawPolygon(Arrow,1,-5,0,0,0);
```

```
end;

procedure TurnLeft;
begin
  SetColorBlack;
  DrawPolygon(Arrow,1,-5,0,0,0);
  RotatePolygon(Arrow,5,45);
  ArrowAngle:=ArrowAngle+1;
  if ArrowAngle>7 then ArrowAngle:=0;
  IncrX:=Speed * ArrowIncr[ArrowAngle,1];
  Incry:=Speed * ArrowIncr[ArrowAngle,2];
  SetColorWhite;
  DrawPolygon(Arrow,1,-5,0,0,0);
end;

procedure TurnRight;
begin
  SetColorBlack;
  DrawPolygon(Arrow,1,-5,0,0,0);
  RotatePolygon(Arrow,5,-45);
  ArrowAngle:=ArrowAngle-1;
  if ArrowAngle<0 then ArrowAngle:=7;
  IncrX:=Speed * ArrowIncr[ArrowAngle,1];
  Incry:=Speed * ArrowIncr[ArrowAngle,2];
  SetColorWhite;
  DrawPolygon(Arrow,1,-5,0,0,0);
end;

begin
  repeat
  clrscr; gotoxy(1,10);
  writeln('To exit program type first 0 then ENTERs');
  writeln('----------------------------------------');
  write('Enter number of segments              ');
  readln(NS);
  writeln('----------------------------------------');
       for N := 1 to NS do begin
  write('Enter X value for segment #',N,'     ');
  readln(A[N]);
  write('Enter Y value for segment #',N,'     ');
  readln(B[N]);
  Arrow[N,1] := A[N];
  Arrow[N,2] := B[N];
  writeln('----------------------------------------');
       end;

InitGraphic;
DefineWindow(1,0,0,XMaxGlb,YMaxGlb);
DefineWorld(1,-1000,1000,1000,-1000);

SelectWorld(1);
SelectWindow(1);
SetBackground(0);

Size:=100;
Speed:=30;
CurrX:=0;
CurrY:=0;
ArrowAngle:=0;
```

```
IncrX:=0;
IncrY:=Speed;

MakeMoveTable;
DrawPolygon(Arrow,1,5,0,0,0);

repeat
  read(Kbd,Ch);
  case ord(Ch) of
      72 : MoveForward;
      75 : TurnLeft;
      77 : TurnRight;
      80 : MoveBack;
  end;
until Ch = ' ';
LeaveGraphic;

   until NS = 0;

end.
```

Fig. 4-28. Input prompts have been added to the FindWorld program.

```
program FindWorldModification;

{$I typedef.sys   }
{$I graphix.sys   }
{$I kernel.sys    }
{$I windows.sys   }
{$I findwrld.hgh }
{$I axis.hgh      }
{$I polygon.hgh   }
{$I spline.hgh    }

var x:real;
    PA                      :PlotArray;
    Q1,Q2,Q3,Q4,Q5,Q6,Q7,Q8 : integer;
    Q, Z, CX, CY, CD, L     : integer;

procedure FindWorldMod;
begin

  DefineWindow(1,0,0,XMaxGlb,YMaxGlb);
  DefineWindow(2,0,0,XMaxGlb,YMaxGlb);
  DefineWorld(1,0,1000,1000,0);

  DefineHeader(2,'ANOTHER FOUND WORLD');
  SelectWindow(2);
  SetHeaderOn;

  FindWorld(2,PA,Q,1,1.08);

  SelectWindow(2);
  DrawBorder;

  DrawAxis(Q1,Q2,Q3,Q4,Q5,Q6,Q7,Q8,false);
  DrawPolygon(PA,1,Q,CD,4,L);

  SelectWorld(1);
```

```
  SelectWindow(1);

  DrawTextW(730,450,1,^['7@2   The data');
  DrawTextW(730,550,1,'--  The curve');

end;

begin
     repeat
     clrscr; gotoxy(1,8);
     writeln('To exit program type 0 once, then ENTERs');
     writeln('----------------------------------------');
     write('Enter number of polygon segments       ');
     readln(Q);
     writeln('----------------------------------------');
           for Z := 1 to Q do begin
     write('Segment #',Z,', enter X coordinate     ');
     readln(CX);
     write('Segment #',Z,', enter Y coordinate     ');
     readln(CY);
     writeln('----------------------------------------');
     PA[Z,1] := CX;
     PA[Z,2] := CY;
           end;
     write('Enter character code                   ');
     readln(CD);
     write('Draw lines? (0 or 1)                   ');
     readln(L);
     writeln('----------------------------------------');
     write('Enter horizontal axis density          ');
     readln(Q1);
     write('Enter vertical axis density            ');
     readln(Q2);
     write('Enter distance from left edge          ');
     readln(Q3);
     write('Enter distance from top edge           ');
     readln(Q4);
     write('Enter distance from right edge         ');
     readln(Q5);
     write('Enter distance from bottom edge        ');
     readln(Q6);
     write('Enter horizontal axis line style       ');
     readln(Q7);
     write('Enter vertical axis line style         ');
     readln(Q8);

InitGraphic;
FindWorldMod;
repeat until KeyPressed;
LeaveGraphic;

     until Q = 0;
end.
```

Fig. 4-29. This program draws a smooth curve, with added input prompts.

```
program Interpolate;

{$I typedef.sys  }
```

```
{$I graphix.sys  }
{$I kernel.sys   }
{$I windows.sys  }
{$I findwrld.hgh }
{$I axis.hgh     }
{$I polygon.hgh  }
{$I spline.hgh   }

var x,                                 : real;
    PA, PB                             : PlotArray;
    Q1, Q2, Q3, Q4, Q5, Q6, Q7, Q8 : integer;
    Q, Z, CX, CY, CD, L, M, TMP       : integer;

procedure SplineMod;

begin

  DefineWindow(1,0,0,XMaxGlb,YMaxGlb);
  DefineWindow(2,0,0,XMaxGlb,YMaxGlb);
  DefineWorld(1,0,1000,1000,0);

  DefineHeader(2,'A CURVE FITTING EXAMPLE');
  SetHeaderOn;

  spline(PA,Q,PA[2,1],PA[Q - 1,1],PB,M);
  FindWorld(2,PB,M,1,1.08);

  with world[2] do
   begin
    TMP := Q4;
    Q4  := Q6;
    Q6  := TMP;
   end;

  SelectWindow(2);
  DrawBorder;

  DrawAxis(Q1,Q2,Q3,Q4,Q5,Q6,Q7,Q8,false);
  DrawPolygon(PA,2,Q-1,CD,4,L);

  SetLineStyle(0);
  DrawAxis(0,0,Q3,Q4,Q5,Q6,0,0,false);
  DrawPolygon(PB,1,-M,0,0,0);

  SelectWorld(1);
  SelectWindow(1);

  DrawTextW(730,400,1,^['7@2   The data');
  DrawTextW(730,500,1,'..  The initial polygon');
  DrawTextW(730,600,1,'__  The interpolated values');

 end;

 begin
     repeat
     clrscr; gotoxy(1,8);
     writeln('To exit program type 0 once, then ENTERs');
     writeln('----------------------------------------');
     write('Enter number of polygon segments       ');
```

```
        readln(Q);
        write('Enter number of spline points           ');
        readln(M);
        writeln('----------------------------------------');
              for Z := 1 to Q do begin
        write('Segment #',Z,', enter X coordinate     ');
        readln(CX);
        write('Segment #',Z,', enter Y coordinate     ');
        readln(CY);
        writeln('----------------------------------------');
        PA[Z,1] := CX;
        PA[Z,2] := CY;
              end;
        write('Enter character code                    ');
        readln(CD);
        write('Draw lines? (0 or 1)                    ');
        readln(L);
        writeln('----------------------------------------');
        write('Enter horizontal axis density           ');
        readln(Q1);
        write('Enter vertical axis density             ');
        readln(Q2);
        write('Enter distance from left edge           ');
        readln(Q3);
        write('Enter distance from top edge            ');
        readln(Q4);
        write('Enter distance from right edge          ');
        readln(Q5);
        write('Enter distance from bottom edge         ');
        readln(Q6);
        write('Enter horizontal axis line style        ');
        readln(Q7);
        write('Enter vertical axis line style          ');
        readln(Q8);

InitGraphic;
SplineMod;
repeat until keypressed;
LeaveGraphic;

   until Q = 0;

end.
```

mine, I can vary the colors of any image, but the background is always black because the constants MinBackground and MaxBackground, contained in the GRAPHIX.SYS module, are both set to 0. The book warns that those values are system dependent and should not be changed.

The documentation book gives no examples of the use of color, except for the brief descriptions in the Technical Reference portion of the few procedures associated with the use of color. If you want to do things in color, it requires considerable experimenting to achieve some of the effects that you might want to create. In the following examples some of the demonstration programs contained in the documentation book have been modified using the procedures SetForegroundColor(X), SetBackgroundColor(X) and InvertScreen; and InvertWindow; to create certain effects. Four programs have been used as demonstrations of the colors that are available with my system. Not all systems respond in the same way to the different numbers, so you should experiment especially with the first program in the group, COLOR.P (Fig. 4-30), that uses a loop

Fig. 4-30. This program demonstrates the colors that are available with the graphics card that is being used.

```
{A program demonstrating the use of available colors}

{COLOR.P  }

{$I TYPEDEF.SYS  }
{$I GRAPHIX.SYS  }
{$I KERNEL.SYS   }

var  X, I             : integer;
     AspectLoc, rad : real;

begin
     InitGraphic;
     DefineWorld(1,0,1000,1000,0);
     SelectWorld(1);
     SelectWindow(1);

     repeat
           for X := 1 to 15 do begin
           ClearScreen;
           SetForegroundColor(X);
           DrawBorder;
           gotoxy(2,2);
           writeln(X);
           Delay(100);
           rad        := 1.5;
           AspectLoc := GetAspect;
           SetAspect(0.2);
           for I := 1 to 15 do begin
           Delay(50);
           DrawCircle(500,500,rad);
           SetAspect(0.2+I/10);
           rad := rad - 0.05;
           end;
           end;
     until KeyPressed;
     SetAspect(AspectLoc);
     LeaveGraphic;
end.
```

to run through all the colors from 1 to 15, indicating the color number in the upper left-hand corner of the screen.

COLOR.P is a variation of the DrawCirc demonstration program that is included on the distribution disk. Modified for color, it will continue to run indefinitely, always starting with color #1 (dark blue), continuing to color #15 (white), and then starting all over again. Press any key, and the program will terminate the next time color #15 (white) is reached.

Earlier I said that, with my system, it's impossible to use backgrounds other than black. But the procedures InvertScreen and InvertWindow can be used to reverse the foreground and background colors. If I asked for the foreground color to be, say, yellow, and then used one of those two procedures, the background would be yellow and the foreground black. The program identified as BGCOLOR.P (Fig. 4-31) is the same as the previous one except that InvertWindow; has been added just ahead of the SetForegroundColor(X) ; line. When this version of the program is run, it keeps changing back and forth between black and colored backgrounds, creating a fairly odd, pulsating effect.

Fig. 4-31. This program demonstrates the background colors that are available with the InvertWindow function.

```
{A program demonstrating the use of available background colors}

{BGCOLOR.P  }

{$I TYPEDEF.SYS   }
{$I GRAPHIX.SYS   }
{$I KERNEL.SYS    }
{$I WINDOWS.SYS   }

var  X, I           : integer;
     AspectLoc, rad : real;

begin
     InitGraphic;
     DefineWorld(1,0,1000,1000,0);
     SelectWorld(1);
     SelectWindow(1);

     repeat
          for X := 1 to 15 do begin
          InvertWindow;
          SetForegroundColor(X);
          DrawBorder;
          gotoxy(2,2);
          writeln(X);
          Delay(100);
          rad        := 1.5;
          AspectLoc := GetAspect;
          SetAspect(0.2);
          for I := 1 to 15 do begin
          Delay(50);
          DrawCircle(500,500,rad);
          SetAspect(0.2+I/10);
          rad := rad - 0.05;
          end;
          end;
     until KeyPressed;
     SetAspect(AspectLoc);
     LeaveGraphic;
end.
```

The third program in this group, shown in Fig. 4-32, is a variation of the demonstration program DrawSquares in the manual. It uses InvertScreen after drawing all rectangles in the **for i := 1 to 20 do** loop, followed by the procedure setting the foreground color, **read(CH);**, and then another **InvertScreen** command. The entire routine is set up as a **repeat . . . until** loop that makes 15 passes to display each of the colors (excluding black). The effect is that each color, in turn, colors the background, with the rectangles in black against those colored backgrounds. This image is held on the screen by the read(CH) statement until you press ENTER, causing the next color to appear. The program continues until all colors have been displayed, then it terminates automatically.

In the final program in the group, MultiplewindowsColor (Fig. 4-33), I tried something else with rather disappointing results. I thought that it would be logical for each window to be colored independently of each other window. I started by using the SetForegroundColor procedure three times, once for each window, using different color values. Well, no such luck. The first

Fig. 4-32. Color has been added to the program that draws a series of rectangles.

```
program DrawSquaresWithColorBackgrounds;

{$I typedef.sys }                    {include the graphics system code}
{$I graphix.sys }
{$I kernel.sys  }

var i, Z : integer;
    CH   : char;

begin
  InitGraphic;
  Z := 0;
  repeat
  Z := Z + 1;
  DefineWorld(1,0,1000,1000,0);
  SelectWorld(1);
  SelectWindow(1);
  DrawBorder;
  for i:=1 to 20 do DrawSquare(500-i*25,500-i*25,500+i*25,500+i*25,false);
  InvertScreen;
  SetForegroundColor(Z);
  read(CH);
  InvertScreen;
  until Z = 15;
  LeaveGraphic;
end.
```

Fig. 4-33. This version of the MultipleWindows program has color added.

```
program MultipleWindowsInColor;

{$I typedef.sys  }
{$I graphix.sys  }
{$I kernel.sys   }
{$I windows.sys  }

var i: integer;

procedure DrawLines;
var i:integer;
begin
  for i:=1 to 20 do DrawLine(i*50,0,1000-i*50,i*50);
end;


begin

InitGraphic;

DrawBorder;

DefineWindow(1,trunc(XMaxGlb/10),trunc(YMaxGlb/10),
               trunc(XMaxGlb/2),trunc(YMaxGlb/2));
            SetForegroundColor(13);
DefineHeader(1,'THIS IS A LARGER WORLD');
DefineWorld(1,0,2000,2000,0);
   SelectWindow(1);
```

```
    SetHeaderOn;
    SelectWorld(1);
    DrawBorder;
    DrawLines;
DefineWindow(2,trunc(XMaxGlb/3),trunc(YMaxGlb/3),
              trunc((XMaxGlb*2)/3),trunc((YMaxGlb*2)/3));
           SetForegroundColor(10);
DefineHeader(2,'THIS IS A CORRECT WORLD');
DefineWorld(2,0,1000,1000,0);
    SelectWindow(2);
    SetHeaderOn;
    SelectWorld(2);
    DrawBorder;
    DrawLines;
DefineWindow(3,trunc(XMaxGlb/2),trunc(YMaxGlb/2),
              trunc((XMaxGlb*9)/10),trunc((YMaxGlb*9)/10));
            InvertWindow;
DefineHeader(3,'THIS IS A SMALLER WORLD');
DefineWorld(3,0,500,500,0); {give it a smaller world coordinate system}
    SelectWindow(3);
    SetHeaderOn;
    SelectWorld(3);
    DrawBorder;
    DrawLines;

repeat until keypressed;       {wait until a key is pressed}
LeaveGraphic;                  {leave the graphics system}

end.
```

window appeared with the selected color, but the whole thing then changed to the second color and finally to the third. So that it shouldn't be a total loss, I changed the last SetForegroundColor to InvertWindow. This inverted not the third, but the second window, causing the first and third to be light green lines on a black background and the second window showing a light green background with black lines.

COLORS AND GRAPHICS WITH TURBO PASCAL

If you study the section of the Turbo Pascal version 3.0 manual that deals with color and graphics (Chapter 19, IBM PC Goodies, pages 159 through 186), you'll find that there are procedures and functions that, in many ways, duplicate what is being offered by the Turbo Graphix Toolbox, although the Toolbox does offer a great many things that are not easily available with Turbo Pascal alone. What follows is a few very short programs that illustrate a few of the color and graphics routines available with Turbo Pascal. Going any further into greater detail is beyond the scope of this book.

The program TurboPascalColor (Fig. 4-34) uses the procedure TextColor(X); to simply print the alphabet across the center of the screen, fifteen times, each time in a different color. The colors and the associated numbers used here are identical to those dealt with in the previous section.

The next program, TurboPascalMultipleColors (Fig. 4-35), uses the same procedure to print the letters of the alphabet across the center of the screen, but this time each letter is a different color than the next. In this mode it is possible to have up to 15 colors, plus black, on the screen at the same time.

The third program, TurboPascalColorWithBlink (Fig. 4-36), is identical to the first, except that the function Blink has been added in the **TextColor(A + Blink);** line, causing the line

Fig. 4-34. This program demonstrates the colors that are available with Turbo Pascal alone.

```
{Color Test #1 using Turbo Pascal}
{TBC.P}

program TurboPascalColor;

var X, A   : integer;
    CH     : char;

begin
     X := 0;
     repeat
     X := X + 1;
     clrscr;  gotoxy(1,10);
     for A := 65 to 90 do begin
     TextColor(X);
     write('   ',chr(A));
     end;
     Delay(2000);
     until X = 15;
end.
```

Fig. 4-35. This program is used to show that it is possible with Turbo Pascal to have different colors on the same screen at the same time.

```
{Color Test #2 using Turbo Pascal}
{TMULTC.P}

program TurboPascalMultipleColors;

var X, A   : integer;
    CH     : char;

begin
     clrscr;  gotoxy(1,10);
     TextColor(1);
     write('  A');
     TextColor(2);
     write('  B');
     TextColor(3);
     write('  C');
     TextColor(4);
     write('  D');
     TextColor(5);
     write('  E');
     TextColor(6);
     write('  F');
     TextColor(7);
     write('  G');
     TextColor(8);
     write('  H');
     TextColor(9);
     write('  I');
     TextColor(10);
     write('  J');
     TextColor(11);
```

```
     write('  K');
     TextColor(12);
     write('  L');
     TextColor(13);
     write('  M');
     TextColor(14);
     write('  N');
     TextColor(15);
     write('  O');
     TextColor(1);
     write('  P');
     TextColor(2);
     write('  Q');
     TextColor(3);
     write('  R');
     TextColor(4);
     write('  S');
     TextColor(5);
     write('  T');
     TextColor(6);
     write('  U');
     TextColor(7);
     write('  V');
     TextColor(8);
     write('  W');
     TextColor(9);
     write('  X');
     TextColor(10);
     write('  Y');
     TextColor(11);
     write('  Z');
     TextColor(12);
end.
```

Fig. 4-36. This little program demonstrates the BLINK function.

```
{Color Test #3 adding Turbo Pascal's BLINK procedure}
{BLINKC.P}

program TurboPascalColorWithBlink;

var X, A  : integer;
    CH    : char;

begin
     X := 0;
     repeat
     X := X + 1;
     clrscr;  gotoxy(1,10);
     for A := 65 to 90 do begin
     TextColor(X + Blink);
     write('  ',chr(A));
     end;
     Delay(2000);
     until X = 15;
     clrscr;
end.
```

Fig. 4-37. This program demonstrates the different background color effects.

```
{Program changing textand background colors}
{TXTBG.P}

program TextBackgroundColors;

var A, B : integer;

begin
     A := 0;   B := -1;
     repeat
     A := A + 1;
     B := B + 1;
     clrscr; gotoxy(30,10);
     TextColor(A);
     TextBackground(B);
     write('HHHHHHHHHHHHHHHHHHHH');
     Delay(1000);
     until A = 8;
end.
```

of letters in the center of the screen to blink on and off. Don't look at it too long. It's likely to give you a headache.

TurboPascal includes a procedure called TextBackground(X), which colors the small rectangular area occupied by a letter, in other words, the immediate background. There are eight colors available for this function (0 through 7). The program TextBackgroundColors (Fig. 4-37) prints Hs in the center of the screen, and the background colors change as the program runs.

So far you've only changed the colors of the text. Now let's look at some simple graphics. The program HiResColorGraphics (Fig. 4-38) produces successive burst of lines from the left upper corner to the right side of the screen. It uses the procedures HiRes, HiResColor(B), DRAW(......), and TextMode. HiRes activates the high-resolution graphics mode, and HiResColor(B) controls the color in which the graphics image will be drawn. Draw(parameters) draws a line that is controlled by the parameters given, and TextMode returns the computer to the text mode before exiting the program. The first **repeat . . . until** loop creates the graphic image. The second one, nearly identical to the first, causes the image to be erased by repeating action in black before starting a new color. The whole thing is included in a **for . . . to . . . do begin** loop that causes all colors (except black) to be displayed.

Fig. 4-38. This program demonstrates the Turbo Pascal high-resolution graphics mode.

```
{Using the Turbo Pascal High Resolution Color Graphics Mode}
{GRPH.P}

program HiResColorGraphics;

var  A, B : integer;

begin
          A := 10; B := 1;
     HiRes;
     for B := 1 to 15 do begin
          A := 10;
          repeat
          A := A + 10;
     HiResColor(B);
```

```
     Draw(20,20,630,A,15);
          until A = 190;
     HiResColor(B);
          A := 10;
               repeat
          A := A + 10;
     HiResColor(0);
     Draw(20,20,630,A,0);
          until A = 190;
     end;
     TextMode;
end.
```

The last program in this chapter, TurboPascalTurtle (Fig. 4-39), uses the Turtle Graphics capabilities available exclusively for the IBM PC (and compatibles). It uses a few of the commands to cause the turtle to draw a square in whatever color you choose in reply to the input prompt. Turtle Graphics, as well as what is referred to in the manual as Extended Graphics, requires that the external files GRAPH.P and GRAPH.BIN are on the disk along with your programs, because you must request the include file by adding the line {$I GRAPH.P }. That module, in turn, calls up the external file GRAPH.BIN. The Forward(50) ; and TurnRight(90) ; commands cause the turtle to move a given number of spaces (50 vertically and 100 horizontally in this program) in the direction in which the arrow points. It then makes a 90-degree turn to the right and continues on its way until the square is completed.

The Turtle Graphics capabilities include a large number of additional commands. You can have a great deal of fun causing the turtle to execute some really wild gyrations.

Fig. 4-39. TurboPascalTurtle is used to demonstrate the Turbo Pascal version of turtle graphics.

```
{A program demonstrating turtle graphics with colors}
{TURT.P}

program TurboPascalTurtle;

{$I GRAPH.P   }

var A : integer;

begin
         repeat
  clrscr;  gotoxy(1,10);
TextColor(11);
  writeln('Type 0 to exit program');
  writeln('----------------------');
  write('Enter Turtle color (1 through 15)    ');
  readln(A);
     HiRes;
     ClearScreen;
     HiResColor(A);
     ShowTurtle;
     TurtleDelay(1000);
     Forwd(50);
     TurnRight(90);
     SetPenColor(1);
     Forwd(100);
     TurnRight(90);
     SetPenColor(1);
```

```
        Forwd(50);
        TurnRight(90);
        SetPenColor(1);
        Forwd(100);
            until A = 0;
        repeat until KeyPressed;
    end.
```

SAVING, LOADING, AND PRINTING

After you've created a graphic image to serve some purpose you'll probably want to preserve it on disk, as a hard copy on paper, or both. The Turbo Graphix Toolbox does include cedures that will accomplish those jobs. The demonstration program called Screen1O (SCREEN-IO.PAS) creates a graphic image, saves it on disk under the file name DEMO.PIC, and then reloads it to once more display it on the screen.

This is one of the worst demonstration programs in the book, because the three pages of recursive procedures that create what is described as a Sierpinski curve tend to obscure the only important portion of the program—the very end, where the saving and loading takes place. Compile and run the program and you'll see what I mean.

To demonstrate a different approach to the subject, the program called ScreenIOModified (Fig. 4-40) uses the procedure GraphicImage to create a simple polygon. After it has been displayed on the screen, you are asked whether you want that graphic image saved on disk. If you answer in the affirmative, it is saved under the file name SCREEN.PIC. Otherwise, the program simply terminates without saving the image. A companion program, LoadGraphicScreen, is used to retrieve and display previously saved graphic images (Fig. 4-41). It is very short and uncomplicated, simply asking that you enter the name of the file that contains the graphic image to be retrieved. It assigns that file name to the variable LD, which is an array of up to 12 characters, allowing for an eight-character name with a period and a three-character extension. It then loads the graphic image into RAM and displays it on the screen.

In the ScreenIOModified program, the procedure GraphicImage is used to create a graphic image for the purpose of demonstration. For practical use, the best method is to include the "Save

Fig. 4-40. This program demonstrates how graphic images can be saved on disk.

```
program ScreenIOModified;

{$I typedef.sys  }
{$I graphix.sys  }
{$I kernel.sys   }
{$I windows.sys  }
{$I polygon.hgh  }

var  CH, YN : char;
     X      : integer;
     PA     : PlotArray;

procedure GraphicImage;
begin
      PA[1,1] := 100;
      PA[1,2] := 100;
      writeln(PA[1,1]:3:1,'  ',PA[1,2]:3:1);
      PA[2,1] := 200;
      PA[2,2] := 150;
      writeln(PA[2,1]:3:1,'  ',PA[2,2]:3:1);
      PA[3,1] := 300;
```

```
      PA[3,2] := 175;
      writeln(PA[3,1]:3:1,' ',PA[3,2]:3:1);
      PA[4,1] := 400;
      PA[4,2] := 400;
      writeln(PA[4,1]:3:1,' ',PA[4,2]:3:1);
      PA[5,1] := 500;
      PA[5,2] := 100;
      writeln(PA[5,1]:3:1,' ',PA[5,2]:3:1);
      PA[6,1] := 600;
      PA[6,2] := 300;
      writeln(PA[6,1]:3:1,' ',PA[6,2]:3:1);
      PA[7,1] := 700;
      PA[7,2] := 600;
      writeln(PA[7,1]:3:1,' ',PA[7,2]:3:1);
      PA[8,1] := 800;
      PA[8,2] := 800;
      writeln(PA[8,1]:3:1,' ',PA[8,2]:3:1);
      PA[9,1] := 900;
      PA[9,2] := 500;
      writeln(PA[9,1]:3:1,' ',PA[9,2]:3:1);
      PA[10,1] := 1000;
      PA[10,2] := 300;
  DefineWindow(1,0,0,XMaxGlb,YMaxGlb);
  SetHeaderOn;
  DefineWorld(1,0,1000,1000,0);
  SelectWorld(1);
  SelectWindow(1);
  DrawBorder;
  DrawPolygon(PA,1,10,4,4,1);                 {draw the polygon}
end;

begin
     clrscr; gotoxy(1,10);
     writeln('A DEMONSTRATION OF SAVING A GRAPHIC IMAGE');
     writeln('-----------------------------------------');
     write('Press ENTER     ');
     readln(CH);

InitGraphic;
DefineHeader(1,'DEMONSTRATE SCREEN SAVE AND READ TO/FROM DISK ON COMMAND');
SetHeaderOn;
GraphicImage;
     repeat until KeyPressed;
LeaveGraphic;
     clrscr; gotoxy(1,10);
     write('Save the image?  (Y/N)     ');
     readln(YN);
             case YN of
             'Y','y' :  begin
InitGraphic;
DefineHeader(1,'DEMONSTRATE SCREEN SAVE AND READ TO/FROM DISK ON COMMAND');
SetHeaderOn;
GraphicImage;
SaveScreen('SCREEN.PIC');
LeaveGraphic;
             end;
             'N','n' :  end;

end.
```

Fig. 4-41. This is the companion program to ScreenIOModified that loads graphic images from disk into RAM.

```
program LoadGraphicScreen;

{$I typedef.sys  }
{$I graphix.sys  }
{$I kernel.sys   }
{$I windows.sys  }
{$I polygon.hgh  }

var   LD : array[1..12] of char;

procedure LdScreen;
begin
InitGraphic;
  DefineWindow(1,0,0,XMaxGlb,YMaxGlb);
  SetHeaderOn;
  DefineWorld(1,0,1000,1000,0);
  SelectWorld(1);
  SelectWindow(1);
  DrawBorder;
  LoadScreen(LD);
  repeat until KeyPressed;
LeaveGraphic;
end;

begin
     clrscr; gotoxy(1,10);
     writeln('A DEMONSTRATION OF SAVING A GRAPHIC IMAGE');
     writeln('-----------------------------------------');
     write('Enter name of graphic image to be loaded   ');
     readln(LD);
     LdScreen;
end.
```

Fig. 4-42. This include file might be used with any graphics program, to ask if the image is to be saved on disk.

```
{SAVING.PG}
procedure SaveFile;

var  YN  : char;
     NME : array[1..12] of char;

begin
     clrscr; gotoxy(1,10);
     write('Save the image?  (Y/N)    ');
     readln(YN);
                case YN of
                'Y','y' :  begin
                           write('Enter file name for saved image  ');
                           readln(NME);
                           GraphicImage;
                           repeat until KeyPressed;
                           SaveScreen(NME);
                           LeaveGraphic;
                           end;
                'N','n' :  end;
end.
```

Image?" question and the **case YN of** routine in an appropriate place in any graphics program (Fig. 4-42) if there is a chance that you might want to save the graphic image. You can, if you like, write a boiler-plate routine that can simply be read into the source code of any program, requiring a minimum of editing. The program SaveGraphicImage is an example of this (Fig. 4-43).

Whether or not you can have your graphic images printed by the printer depends to some

Fig. 4-43. The procedure used in SaveFile has been incorporated into another program that saves graphic images.

```
program SaveGraphicImage;

{$I typedef.sys }
{$I graphix.sys }
{$I kernel.sys  }
{$I windows.sys }
{$I polygon.hgh }

var PA            : PlotArray;
    CD, N, Z, L : integer;
    CH, YN        : char;
    CX, CY        : integer;

procedure CurveLoop;
begin
  DefineWindow(1,0,0,XMaxGlb,YMaxGlb);
  DefineHeader(1,'THIS POLYGON CAN BE SAVED ON DISK');
  DefineWorld(1,0,1000,1000,0);
  SelectWorld(1);
  SelectWindow(1);
  SetBackground(0);
  SetHeaderOn;
  DrawBorder;
  DrawPolygon(PA,1,N,CD,4,L);
end;

begin
     repeat
     clrscr; gotoxy(1,10);
     writeln('Type 0 to exit the program');
     writeln('--------------------------');
     write('Enter number of segments  ');
     readln(N);
     writeln('-----------------------------------------------------');
               for Z := 1 to N do begin
     write('Segment #',Z,', enter X coordinate (0 to 1000)    ');
     readln(CX);
     write('Segment #',Z,', enter Y coordinate (0 to 1000)    ');
     readln(CY);
     writeln('-----------------------------------------------------');
     PA[Z,1] := CX;
     PA[Z,2] := CY;
               end;
     write('Enter character code       ');
     readln(CD);
     write('Draw lines? (0 or 1)       ');
     readln(L);
InitGraphic;
CurveLoop;
```

```
repeat until keypressed;
LeaveGraphic;
     clrscr;  gotoxy(1,10);
     write('Print this image?  (Y/N)     ');
     readln(YN);
          case YN of
          'Y','y' : begin
                    InitGraphic;
                    CurveLoop;
                    HardCopy(false,1);
                    LeaveGraphic;
                    end;
          'N','n' : end;

     until N = 0;

end.
```

extent on the type of printer you're using. The documentation book states that the package will work only with "Epson-like" printers, and it gives a number of alternative routines with which you might want to experiment. I've tried the Turbo Graphic Toolbox procedure called HardCopy on both of my printers. My favorite printer is an NEC PC-8023 dot matrix printer, and it didn't work at all (it prints beautiful graphics when working with my Apple II+ with the Grappler interface card from Orange Micro). The other, though identified as a TI 99/4 Impact Printer,

Fig. 4-44. This is a printout produced by the PrintGraphicImage program.

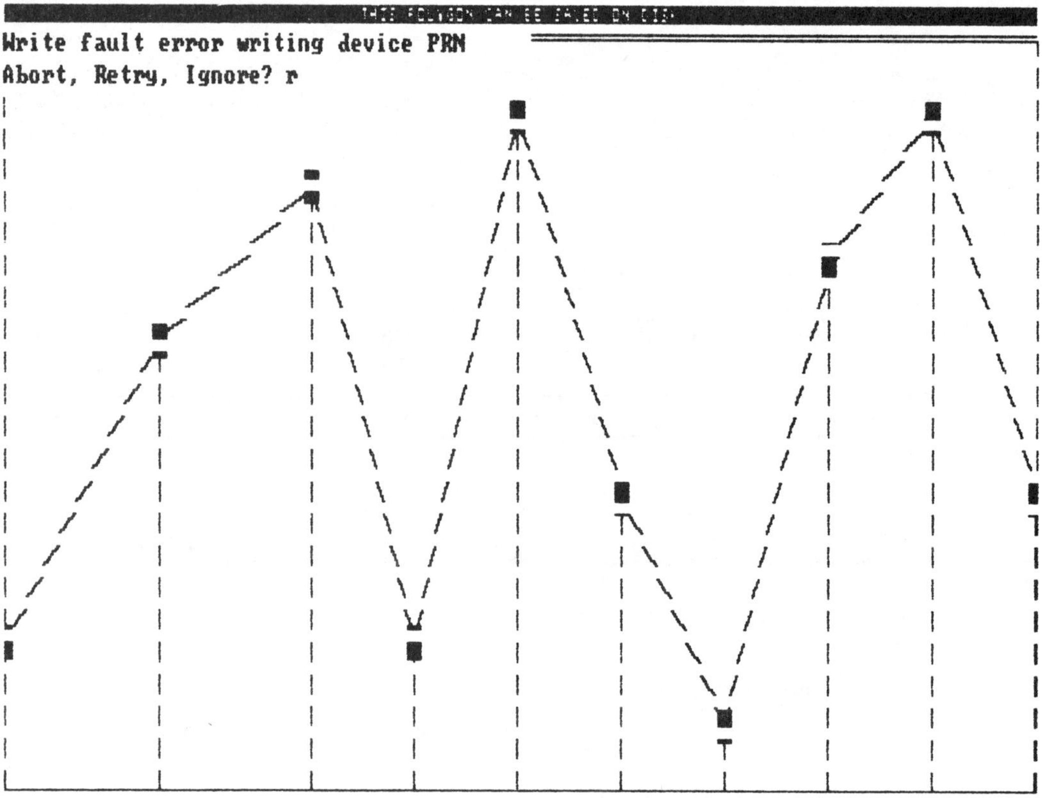

Fig. 4-45. This is a printout with the background and foreground colors reversed.

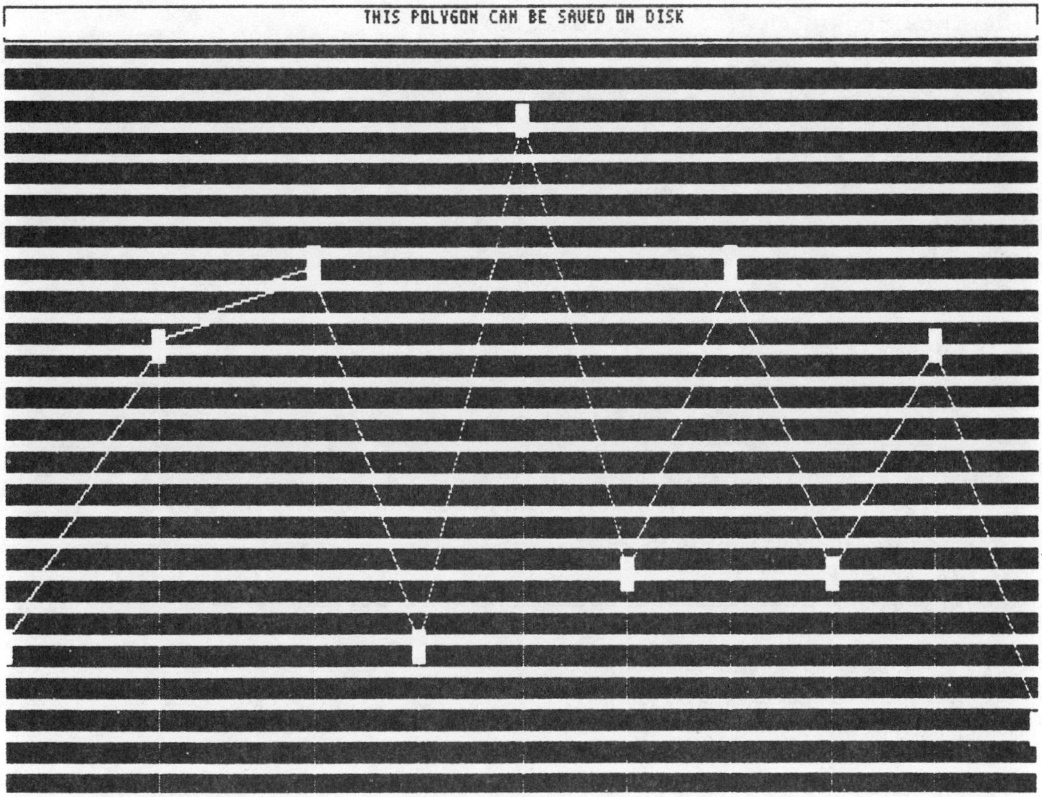

is, in fact, made by Epson. It produced the printouts shown in Figs. 4-44 and 4-45 using the program called PrintGraphicImage (Fig. 4-46). This program is very nearly identical to SaveGraphicImage, except for the two **if . . . then** routines, which offer the choice of having the image printed black on white or white on black.

Fig. 4-46. This program uses the HardCopy function to have an image sent to the printer.

```
program PrintGraphicImage;

label NEXT;

{$I typedef.sys }
{$I graphix.sys }
{$I kernel.sys  }
{$I windows.sys }
{$I polygon.hgh }

var PA           : PlotArray;
    CD, N, Z, L  : integer;
    CH, YN, BW   : char;
    CX, CY       : integer;
     until N = 0;

end.
```

```
procedure CurveLoop;
begin
  DefineWindow(1,0,0,XMaxGlb,YMaxGlb);
  DefineHeader(1,'THIS POLYGON CAN BE SAVED ON DISK');
  DefineWorld(1,0,1000,1000,0);
  SelectWorld(1);
  SelectWindow(1);
  SetBackground(0);
  SetHeaderOn;
  DrawBorder;
  end;

begin
     repeat
     clrscr; gotoxy(1,10);
     writeln('Type 0 to exit the program');
     writeln('-------------------------');
     write('Enter number of segments  ');
     readln(N);
     writeln('---------------------------------------------------');
               for Z := 1 to N do begin
     write('Segment #',Z,', enter X coordinate (0 to 1000)    ');
     readln(CX);
     write('Segment #',Z,', enter Y coordinate (0 to 1000)    ');
     readln(CY);
     writeln('---------------------------------------------------');
     PA[Z,1] := CX;
     PA[Z,2] := CY;
               end;
     write('Enter character code       ');
     readln(CD);
     write('Draw lines? (0 or 1)       ');
     readln(L);
InitGraphic;                              {initialize the graphics system}
CurveLoop;                                {do the demo}
repeat until keypressed;                  {wait until a key is pressed}
LeaveGraphic;                             {leave the graphics system}
     clrscr;  gotoxy(1,10);
     write('Print this image?  (Y/N)                   ');
     readln(YN);
          if (YN = 'N') or (YN = 'n') then goto NEXT else
     writeln;
     write('Black on white (B) or white on black (W)  ');
     readln(BW);
          if (BW = 'B') or (BW = 'b') then begin
                    InitGraphic;
                    CurveLoop;
                    HardCopy(false,1);
                    LeaveGraphic;
                    end
          else
                    begin
                    InitGraphic;
                    CurveLoop;
                    HardCopy(true,1);
                    LeaveGraphic;
                    end;
NEXT :
```

Fig. 4-47. This is a reduction of a printout produced in the DOS graphics mode by pressing the SHIFT and PrtSc * Keys simultaneously.

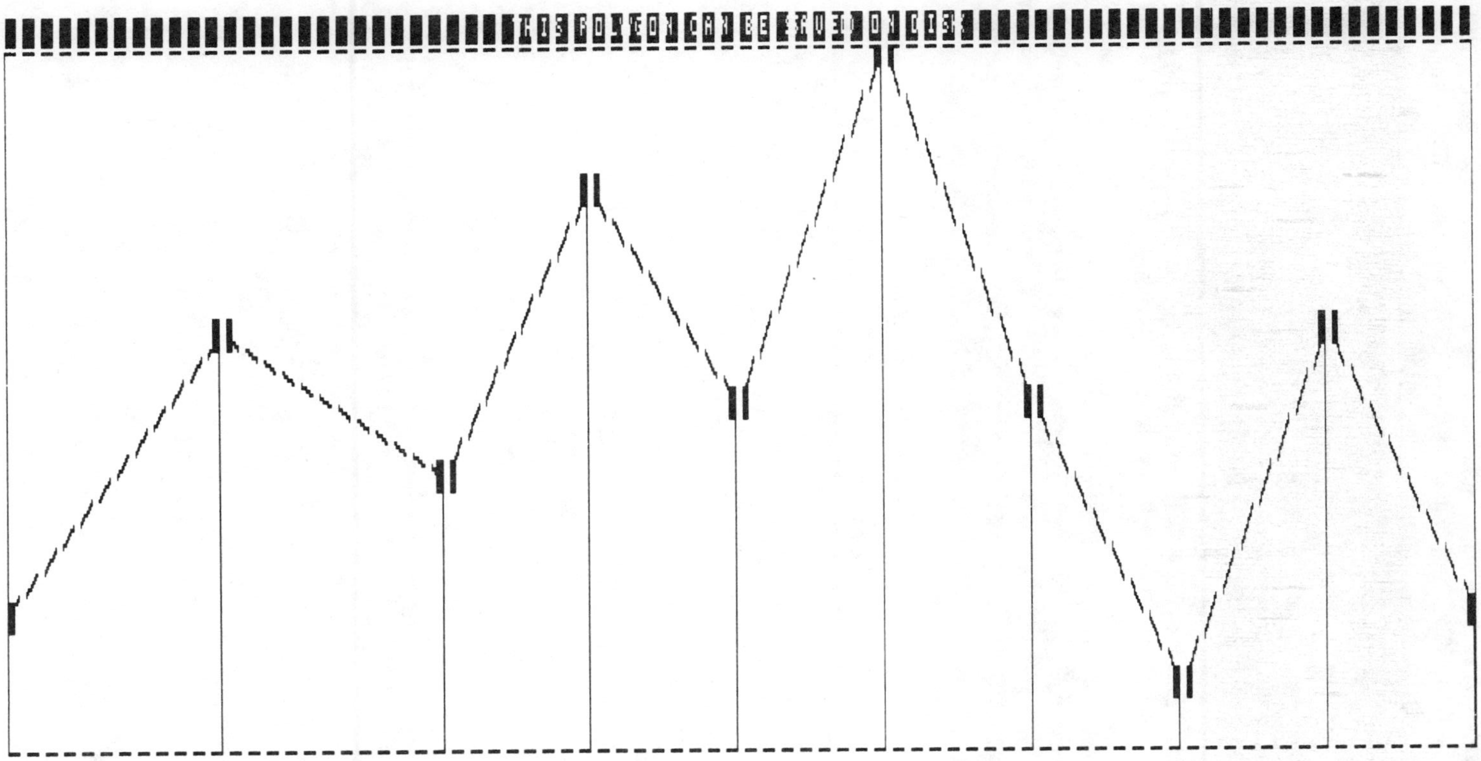

An alternative method of printing your graphic images is to use the GRAPHICS.COM program that is on the DOS disk. Simply type GRAPHICS and ENTER, and then go through whatever steps are necessary to produce the desired graphics image on the screen. Once the image is on the screen, type SHIFT Prt Sc (some keyboards don't require that SHIFT be pressed) and the image will be printed (again, only on an Epson-type printer). This time it's being printed sideways, producing a truly enormous image, occupying more than one average 11-inch page length (Fig. 4-47).

Both methods are exasperatingly slow. To print a single screen seems to take forever. But, maybe that's only because we're spoiled by the speed with which most things happen when dealing with computers and their accessories.

By now you've looked at all the demonstration programs that are part of the Turbo Graphix Toolbox. They're really of minor importance in the long run. What is important is to become familiar with the various routines, the procedures and functions that make up the different include files. That doesn't mean that you need to actually look at the source code or even know how it accomplishes what it does. What you do need to know is how to make use of them, by including them in the programs you write yourself.

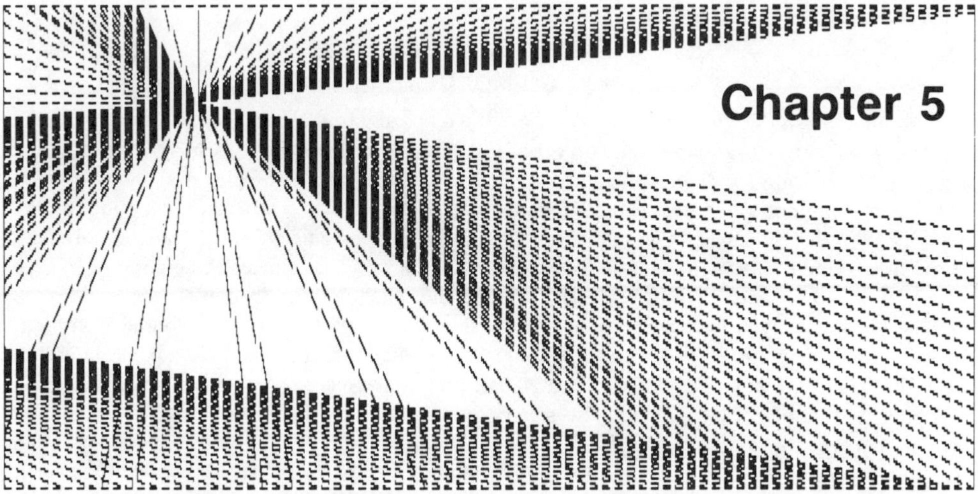

Chapter 5

The Turbo Gameworks

This is the only one of the four toolboxes that is purely recreational, with few practical applications. Some of the algorithms used in the programs that comprise this package, however, are designed to be used in other applications, such as business and professional programs that involve decision-making procedures. If such alternate applications are of interest or importance to you, I suggest that you produce a printout of the very lengthy source code for these games. That might simplify the task of determining which procedures might be useful, and how they will have to be modified to serve your purpose.

The package consists of two 5.25-inch disks and a 148-page documentation book. The disks contain three ready-to-play games: chess, go-moku, and bridge, plus the usual collection of procedures and functions that are used by those programs. For those who might be unfamiliar with the rules of any of these games, several appendices in the documentation book explain the rules in some detail.

The three game programs are extremely well designed, and playing them is an exciting challenge. Furthermore, if you don't already know how to play bridge, chess, or go-moku, or you've forgotten, this is an ideal way to learn or relearn.

By the way, bridge and chess don't work with all monochrome displays, because a large percentage of the graphic information that is needed to play these games disappears. If yours is a monochrome system and you're planning to purchase the Turbo Gameworks, be sure to get a demonstration before you pay.

If you just want to play or learn to play the games, trying to beat the computer, then familiarity with Turbo Pascal (or any other programming language) is quite unnecessary. On the other hand, if you want to use the algorithms and programming techniques to create other programs, you'll need to be reasonably conversant with Turbo Pascal and a fairly experienced programmer to start with. The thoroughly annotated source code reveals many of the tricks that are said to be important to any aspiring game designer.

The minimum system configuration calls for an IBM PC, XT, AT, Portable, 3270, PCjr, or any true compatible with at least 192K RAM, running PC DOS or MS DOS 2.0 or later, plus

Turbo Pascal 3.0 for IBM PC and compatibles.

GO-MOKU

Go-moku is a fancy version of Tic-Tac-Toe. It's a board game using a board with a 19-by-19 grid line, producing 361 squares. The object of the game is to place five of your pieces in a row, horizontally, vertically, or diagonally. The "pieces" are Xs, which are the player's, and Os, which belong to the computer. On the surface it would appear that this is a fairly simple game to play and win. Well, let me assure you, it's not. I played it for over half an hour, and the only way I was able to win at all was to use the function of the program that causes the computer to give me a hint, in other words, to let the computer tell me what my next move should be.

The game is played by moving the cursor (using the arrow keys for horizontal or vertical moves and the Home, Pg Up, End, and PG Dn keys for diagonal moves), to any position on the board that is not already occupied. Press ENTER and your piece, represented by the letter X, will appear in that position. The opponent's piece, represented by the letter O, will automatically appear wherever the computer thinks it'll prevent you from winning the game. If you have the time and patience, you should be able to become relatively expert, and the documentation book includes a number of strategy rules that should make it easier to beat the computer at this game. Nevertheless, don't expect to become a winner in a hurry.

Most of the other programs in the various toolboxes consist of a large number of independent modules, in the form of separate include files, that are incorporated into the programs during compilation as the result of the {$I FILENAME.EXT} statements. The go-moku program, however, is simply one long program, with each of the required actions represented by procedures. If you're going to use the program only to play the game, don't worry about what functions are performed by these procedures. If, on the other hand, you plan to modify the program or use any of the procedures in programs of your own, take the time to really study the program design parameters that are contained in the documentation book, pages 35 through 46. The individual procedures could, of course, be copied from the source code and turned into separate files with their own file names and extensions (other than .COM or .PAS). They would then have to be integrated into any main program of your own during the compilation procedure, meaning that your main program would have to include the appropriate {$I . . .} directives.

The complete source code for the go-moku game is not shown in the documentation book. If you send it to the printer, you'll be able to see how the main program calls the various procedures while the game is being played, and how these procedures produce the decisions about where you or the computer should place the next piece on the board. All of this is quite complicated, and not something to be mastered overnight. But, if you have the time and inclination, it's fun.

BRIDGE

Playing "Turbo Bridge" is quite an experience. Even if you think you're a really good bridge player, you're likely to find that you will have a rough time beating the computer. Because there are several bridge conventions, it's a good idea to read the information contained in the documentation book, which identifies the convention used by the program as "Simplified Goren with Modifications." The point is that the computer, not being saddled with human emotions, will bid and play in accordance with certain hard and fast rules. If you're unfamiliar with what is meant by certain types of bids, you're likely to lose every time.

You can use this program to improve your bridge game or, if you're unfamiliar with the game, to learn how to play it. The basic rules of the game are given in Appendix C (pages 131 through 134) of the documentation book, and there are, of course, literally hundreds of books on the subject. Appendix D of the documentation lists some of them.

When you first activate the game by typing BRIDGE and ENTER from the DOS prompt, you're confronted by the main menu. It asks which hand you want to play, with South being the default condition. The four hands are identified as North, East, South and West. North and South represent one pair of partners, and East and West the other pair. There seems to be no particular reason to change the default condition unless you've got some kind of an emotional attachment to a direction other than South. The next question asks whether or not you want to see all four hands displayed. The default answer is No, and this, too, should be accepted, except possibly during an early learning period. The final question asks whether you want the computer to cheat by looking at your hand. This seems quite silly and the No default should certainly be accepted.

If you've accepted all default conditions, simply press the space bar and you're ready to play. If you've changed some of the default conditions, press P when you're ready to go. What you'll see is the bridge table more or less in the center of the screen, with the legends North at the top, East at the right, South with the cards that you were dealt at the bottom, and West at the left. In the top right-hand corner is a display of the contract and a progressive display of the number of tricks taken by either side. In the left bottom corner is a constantly updated display of the cards that made up the last four tricks.

At the start of the game you're asked whether or not you want to play your own (and, of course, the dummy's) cards. A Y answer would seem to be indicated, but there are a number of options. You can select autOplay (press O), in which case you just sit there and watch the computer play against itself. In that mode, it is still up to you to bid, but once the bidding is complete, the computer does all of the playing. I used this mode a number of times just to see what would happen and, though I don't claim to be an expert bridge player, I totally and emphatically disagree with the way the computer played the various hands. Another choice available to you when the bidding cycle is complete is Hint. If you press H, the program will display the card that it thinks should be played. If you agree with that choice, press ENTER. If you decide that you want to play a card other than the one suggested, get rid of it by using the backspace and then enter your own selection in the usual manner.

There are times when the program appears to be exasperatingly slow. This is, in fact, quite realistic, because human players would take a certain amount of time to think before deciding which card to play. These pauses are probably the result of the program having to look at enormous numbers of possible choices. Because of the clever way in which the program is written, none of the "players" knows the cards of the others, with the exception of the dummy and whatever information was gleaned from the bidding process. I was using a color monitor, but I assumed that you could also use a monochrome monitor, although the symbols that stand for the four suits (Spades, Hearts, Diamonds and Clubs) would probably be more difficult to recognize. Just to see what would happen, I switched the monitor from color to monochrome and found, to my surprise, that the entire bridge table, along with a lot of other information, simply disappeared. Apparently, a computer equipped with a monochrome card rather than a color graphics card might not be able to handle the game.

If you select several hands that you want to play, you can actually play this game with another person. In this case, the computer will represent only two players, with you and the other person completing the foursome. This would seem to be the only way that two people can play four-handed bridge. It would seem sensible to select, say, South and East or West, rather than South and North, to avoid having one of the human players end up as the dummy. This could, of course, still happen if the computer wins the bidding contract.

CHESS

Before taking a closer look at the chess game, I want to mention once more that, like bridge, the entire chess board disappeared when I switched from color to monochrome. In other words, if yours is a monochrome system, get a demonstration to make certain that the programs work with your system before spending any money.

Chess is a very complicated and difficult game. If you're an experienced player, the Turbo Chess game will present an interesting challenge. If you're a beginner, playing the game over and over will help you become more proficient. By making frequent use of the Hint option (press H), you can let the program teach you what the most logical next move would be. If you don't know how to play chess at all, you'd better study the official rules in Appendix B (pages 123 through 130) in the documentation book before trying to actually work with the program, because knowing what moves are permitted is vitally important. The graphic representation of the individual chess pieces leaves something to be desired, and most would be difficult to identify except for the fact that each is also identified by a letter: K for King, Q for Queen, R for Rook, B for Bishop, N for kNight, and P for Pawn.

The Hint option is, at first, a bit confusing. The command asks that you make a move, and you press H, expecting to see some sort of instruction next to the word MOVE:. That's not the way it works. When you press H and ENTER, be sure to look at the chessboard itself, because the suggested move is made for you to see. A moment later the pieces are returned to their previous positions. If you miss it, type H again. You can do that as often as you like until you're sure that you know what the suggested move is. Not only does the program show you the suggested move, it also shows what the opponent is likely to do as the result of that move. This happens rather quickly, so you really have to pay close attention in order not to miss all of that action. Naturally, you don't have to actually make the suggested move. I played several complete games in order to familiarize myself with Turbo Chess. Some I played using the Hint option for every move, and with others I tried my luck by deciding on the moves myself. Well, either way, I lost every game.

The program also includes an Auto mode that is activated by pressing A. In that mode, the computer plays against itself. It might be useful to play a game or two in this manner, but, again, you really have to keep your eyes glued to the screen because the movements of the individual pieces tend to be extremely quick. There are often long pauses between moves, however, while the computer figures out what the next move should be.

Interestingly, when you look at the source code for the main program, you'll be surprised to find only some 60 lines, at least half of which consist of annotations and explanations. Including all of those comments, it's 1,570 bytes long—not much of a program. The real program is contained in the include files TIMELIB.CH, BOARD.CH, MOVEGEN.CH, DISPLAY.CH, INPUT.CH, SMALL.CH, EVALU.CH, SEARCH.CH, and TALK.CH which, along with all explanations and annotations, add up to 165,689 bytes. Because the compiled version uses only 64,894 bytes, it is assumed that the difference is made up by those explanations.

The documentation book gives a brief explanation of what goes on in all those modules in a section called Program Structure (pages 71 through 87). These comments give you a vague idea of how the program functions, but if you actually look at the source code for those nine include modules, you're confronted by a veritable ocean of hard-to-decipher code. It would take an extremely courageous programmer to try and modify this program in any way. I suggest that you print the source code for some of these modules, just to give you an idea. They are not reproduced in the documentation book and looking at them on the monitor isn't much help, because the portions displayed are just too small.

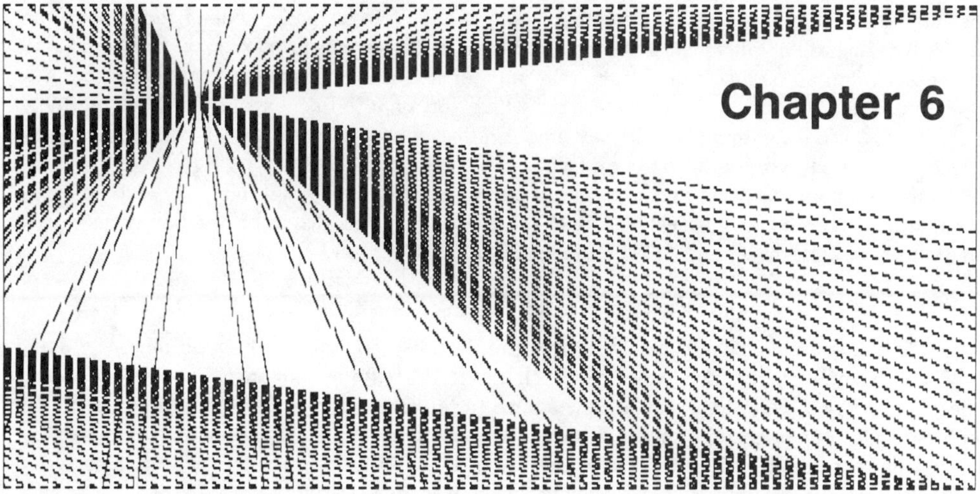

Chapter 6

Sidekick and Turbo Lightning

Sidekick is a RAM-resident program, meaning that you enter it into your computer memory before you start to work on whatever you're planning to do. Then, at any time, you're able to call up any of its functions without exiting the program you're currently working on. Whether you're using a database or spreadsheet program or you're busy writing a program in Pascal, BASIC, or any other language, Sidekick is always lurking underneath, ready to be activated with one or two keystrokes.

Sidekick consists of a note pad that includes a text editor, and that can be used to write notes or comments for temporary storage and subsequent retrieval. It can also be used to write documents or programs. A business calculator that includes a number of special features for programmers and a perpetual calendar to keep a record of appointments are also included. If your system includes a modem, Sidekick will automatically dial telephone numbers stored in a database program, or it will pick up the numbers directly from the screen.

Sidekick makes extensive use of windows, always leaving at least part of what you're currently working on exposed on your screen while it is being used.

Sidekick requires an IBM PC, XT, AT, jr, or true compatible with a minimum of 128K RAM, at least one disk drive and PC DOS or MS DOS 2.0 or better. To use the autodialing function, you'll need an AT&T modem 4000, a Hayes-compatible modem, or an IBM PCjr internal modem.

Like Sidekick, Turbo Lightning is a RAM-resident program that stays in your computer memory while you're busy working on other things. It is an interactive look-up system that gives you immediate access to the complete Random House Concise Dictionary and the Random House Thesaurus, giving you a proofreader and a synonym-finder at your fingertips.

One of the unique features of Turbo Lightning is that it knows when you have misspelled a word as soon as it has been typed, producing a beep. With a keystroke you can call up a list of the likely replacement words, and another keystroke will replace the misspelled word with the correct one. If you find this instant proofreader function an annoyance, you can turn it off and have Turbo Lightning proofread an entire document instead of individual words. Turbo Lightning, though possibly not quite as complete as some other dictionary programs, is more convenient, because it's at your fingertips all the time instead of having to be loaded when needed. Any special words that are not included in the standard dictionary, such as proper names or idioms, may be entered into an auxiliary dictionary that augments Turbo Lightning's vocabulary.

To use the Thesaurus, type the word for which you want to find a synonym. Then, with one keystroke, Turbo Lightning will display an entire list of synonyms. Another keystroke will replace the original word with the one of your choice.

The minimum hardware and software requirements for Turbo Lightning are an IBM PC or compatible computer with at least 128K RAM, two floppy disk drives or one floppy disk drive and one hard disk drive, and PC DOS or MS DOS 2.0 or later.

MAKING A HABIT OF USING SIDEKICK

Sidekick is a nice, convenient little program, because no matter what you might be doing with your computer, if you've loaded Sidekick into RAM before doing anything else, it's always there and ready to be used. You don't even need to return to the system prompt in order to call up one of its convenience programs. Simply type Ctrl and Alt (holding down both keys at the same time), or press both Shift keys at the same time. Either way, Sidekick's main selection menu will pop up, ready for you to select what you want it to do.

The Notepad

For instance, while you're working on something else, the phone rings. It's someone telling you something that you need to make a note of. Just hit those two keys (you can press Ctrl and Alt with your left hand while holding the phone in your right, or vice versa), then press N, and your notepad is ready for use. The notepad is a complete text editor that uses most of the same commands as the Turbo Pascal text editor or, for that matter, the demonstration text editors in the Turbo Editor Toolbox. All of these are largely (though not completely) identical to the traditional WordStar commands (though quite different from those used by WordStar 2000).

There are a number of other conveniences available with the notepad. Pressing ^Q^T (^ means hold down the CTRL key) will print the current date and time, to record when, exactly, the message is being entered. There are also the various editing options. For instance, by pressing the F2 key or using the text-editor command ^K^D, the note you just typed will be saved on the currently logged disk under the default file name NOTES. If you want it saved under another file name, press F3 before saving. You'll be given an opportunity to change the file name to whatever other one you'd like to use, always remembering the limit of an eight character name plus a three character extension.

Another interesting gimmick is the ability to copy a block of text, or whatever, from your current work screen onto the notepad. For instance, you've just typed something fairly complicated, and it occurs to you that you'll be wanting to use this same material in another file. Reading an entire file of many pages and thousands of program lines into another file (using ^K^R), when all you need is a short section, requires that all of the remaining stuff be deleted. This is, at best, a nuisance. Using Sidekick's notepad, you can type F4, and the notepad image will disappear, returning you, momentarily, to your work screen. Mark the block that you want to copy with the block commands—^K^B for the beginning of the block and ^K^K for the end. Type ESC to return to you notepad, or don't mark the end of the block with ^K^K and simply type ESC to mark the end of the block automatically. Then, once again having the notepad in display, move the cursor to where you want the first word of the block to appear. Type ^K^C (for block copy), and the block will appear on your notepad. Save it, and, later on, whenever you need to use this material in another file or program, you can simply read this file into the other. Use ^K^R, followed by the disk drive in which the file you want to copy is located, followed by the file name under which it was saved. Press ENTER, and the copied material will appear in the cursor position in the file on which you're currently working.

The size of the notepad display can be changed by using either the F9 or F10 key. F9 makes it possible to use the arrow keys to expand the size of the display up to a maximum of 23 lines by 78 characters. Pressing F9 again returns the keys to their original function while leaving the notepad display in its new size. F10 does exactly the opposite. It works just like F9 except that the display can be shrunk to as little as three lines by 78 characters, again using the arrow keys.

Another feature that might come in handy is the ability to type foreign characters into the notepad, such as umlauts, characters with accents, and certain limited graphics images. These characters are not normally available with a word processor or text editor. With the notepad text editor, press ^Q^G to activate a limited graphics mode. Then, holding down the Alt key, type the ASCII character code on the NUMERIC KEYPAD with NUMLOCK active. This is a bit tricky—it has to be done quickly because holding the Alt key down too long causes the main selection menu to appear instead. You can find the ASCII character codes by invoking Sidekick and typing A, which displays all the ASCII character codes from 0 through 255, one page at the time. Use the down arrow key to scroll to the next page.

If you want to load a previously saved file into the notepad, use the Read-a-File command, ^K^R, followed by the drive letter and colon (if the material to be copied is not on the logged drive), and then the name of the file to be loaded into the notepad. This comes in handy when you want to look at some notes you made and saved at a different time, and you're not particularly excited about exiting the program on which you're currently working, because that always involves a considerable waste of time.

The Calculator

The calculator is called up by pressing C from the main selection menu, or Alt C if you're already working with one of Sidekick's other facilities. It is capable of displaying up to 18 digits, four of which may be decimal positions. When it is called up, the NUMLOCK is automatically activated. The calculator works in the decimal mode by default, but it can be converted to function in hexadecimal or binary by typing H or B. It also functions in AOS, the algebraic operating system, as opposed to RPN, Reverse Polish Notation. The difference is that, in AOS, you use **X** + **X** = while in RPN you use **X ENTER X** +, with neither equal signs nor parentheses permitted.

The calculator will store values, subtotals, etc. in memory. Data stored in memory can be manipulated, using +, −, *, or /. You can also use AND (A key), OR (O key), or XOR (X key). Data stored in memory are recalled using M R. The E key will clear the display, but won't affect previous entries or subtotals. C clears the display, but leaves data stored in memory untouched. M C will clear the memory. A "Paste" function is also included, meaning that you can assign any currently displayed value to any key or key combination of your choice. Be careful, however, not to select a key that is used for other purposes. For instance, say that the number in display is 654, and you know that you'll have to use it dozens of times in the document that you're currently working on. Press P to activate the Paste mode. If you now press, say, Q, then whenever you subsequently press Q or q, the display will show 654 rather than the letter. This can be a bit disconcerting when you're trying to type a word such as 654uestion. A better idea is to either use a key combination, such as Alt Q, or a symbol that's rarely used.

It says in the documentation book that pressing C in the "programming mode" will clear all keys that were programmed under the paste mode. Well, I never did succeed in doing that, and found that I had to shut the computer down to restore a programmed key to its original function. A number of keys, however, can safely be programmed, because their use is extremely rare. In addition, the function keys (F1 through F10) can be reprogrammed, if necessary. Thus, while data produced by the calculator cannot automatically be saved on disk, they can be saved through the use of reprogrammed keys, though that feature remains active only as long as the computer is not turned off.

The Calendar

If your DOS disk includes a clock, then the calendar, when activated by typing L from the selection menu, will display the correct current date. If not, it will initially display April 1985, which you'll then have to bring up to date. The right and left arrow keys are used to increment or decrement the months, and the up and down arrow keys are used to increment or decrement the years. The calendar is designed to cover the time period from January 1, 1901 through December 31, 2099, which should be ample for most practical purposes. It is most unlikely that any of us would have appointments after 2099, or would want to look at appointments before 1901.

To record appointments, press ENTER if you want to enter something for today's date or, if the appointment is for another date, type in that date and then press ENTER. You'll see a display that covers the time of the day from 8 a.m. to 8:30 p.m. in half-hour increments. The up and down keys are used to move the cursor to a later or earlier time, offering you a chance to enter appointment data for future retrieval. Keep the information short, such as "Lunch with Bob," because there is no wrap-around and anything past the highlighted line is ignored.

In the documentation book, it says that F2 stands for Name and F3 stands for Print, but these two are actually reversed in the program. Press F2, and you're asked for the first and last month for which you want stored appointments to be printed. If you simply press ENTER in reply to each, all data from the first to the last appointment will be printed. Press F3 and the program will ask that you key in a name or initials, using up to eight characters. The program then creates a separate file for each name and, when the name is called up, it displays all appointments for that person and no one else. F4 will cause all appointments to be printed by the printer, and F5 can be used to delete appointments for selected time periods.

The Dialer

The automatic dialer can only be used if your system includes a modem. Mine does not, thus, all I can do here is to tell you what the book says it's supposed to do.

The dialer works in two different ways. It either picks a number to dial off the screen or it selects it from its own directory. It recognizes a telephone number as such because it must be typed onto the screen, or recorded in the directory in compliance with certain style requirements. Valid styles are (505) 555-1234 or 505 555-1234. There are a number of ways to create such a directory. You can use the Notepad facility and store it on disk, or you can use any database program, regardless of the language in which it is written.

Each record in the file may contain up to 78 characters. The suggested format is:

NAME PHONENUMBER COMMENT

NAME can be anything that is distinctive of the person or company, a nickname, initials, or whatever. The first character should always be in column 1, because leading blanks are significant. PHONENUMBER must contain at least one hyphen or one parenthesis in order to be recognized as a telephone number by the dialer. Either of the formats shown above should probably be used consistently. COMMENT can be an address, or anything else that you'd like to remember in connection with the person or company represented by that telephone number.

F2 can be used to give your directory an appropriate file name. It is often desirable to have several such directories, one, say, for personal friends, one for customers, and one for suppliers. F3 asks that you key in the identifier represented by NAME. It then searches for the record that contains the associated telephone number and comments. F4 is used to key in any text that is associated with what you're looking for, and that might be part of the data entered as COMMENTS. The program searches for any match, and displays the record(s) in which such a match is found. F5 stops the search.

The dialer comes pre-installed for a Hayes Smartmodem (300 or 1200 baud) or compatible modem, though other modems may be substituted during the installation procedure.

If the default condition associated with any of Sidekick's programs doesn't appeal to you for some reason, there is an installation program included on the distribution disk that can be used to make any changes that you like. The documentation book explains in detail how the various defaults can be changed.

Sidekick is a rather remarkable achievement. Ever since I learned how to use it, I always, quite automatically, load it before going to work with my word processor (WordStar 2000), writing programs using Turbo Pascal, or activating any other application programs.

THE JOY OF USING TURBO LIGHTNING

Turbo Lightning, despite a name that appears to have nothing to do with the subject of the program, is a dictionary, spelling checker and thesaurus rolled into one. Because it is a RAM-resident program, it's always there, making sure that what you're typing is spelled correctly. In the auto-proof mode, it beeps whenever you type a word that isn't in the dictionary. This can become a major annoyance, especially if you're a hunt-and-peck typist like I am, prone to hitting a wrong key with considerable frequency. To get rid of that beep, type the auto-proof On/Off command key, Alt F5, which is a toggle that can be used as often as you like.

For floppy disk systems, Turbo Lightning is installed by typing LIGHT and ENTER. This should be done before loading Sidekick into RAM, if it is to be used too, and before any applications programs, such as word processors or spreadsheets. If yours is a hard disk system, the documentation book gives detailed instructions. The dictionaries that can be used by systems equipped with a hard disk are more extensive than those available for floppy-disk systems, thus providing greater accuracy, but for average usage the floppy-disk system dictionaries are quite adequate.

As is true of any RAM-resident program, various options are there but not in evidence. Something must be done in order to access them. In the case of Turbo Lightning, pressing SHIFT F8 will cause its main menu to be superimposed over the top area of whatever you're working on at the moment. This menu consists of Environment, Word-Check, Full-Screen-Check, Thesaurus, Setup, and Options, with the first word initially highlighted. Use the arrow keys to select the appropriate subject from this menu, and press ENTER to activate the associated pull-down menu. If you prefer, you can simply type the first letter of any one of the menu items (E, W, F, T, S, O) and the result will be the same. To get rid of the menu without making a selection, press ESC.

The ENVIRONMENT menu lists a collection of word processors and other application programs, each identified by a letter. Move the highlighting to the program that you're using, and press the associated letter to let Turbo Lightning know what you're doing. If your program is not listed, Appendix C in the documentation book explains how to replace one of the listed programs with the one you're interested in.

The WORD-CHECK menu activates the proofreading function in one of two ways. You can either choose to have it check the word currently preceding the cursor, regardless of whether or not it is misspelled, or the last word that actually was misspelled. The choice is displayed as:

A: Check word at cursor
B: Check last bad word

Typing A or B will produce the desired result, with likely replacements for any words that are actually misspelled.

The FULL-SCREEN-CHECK menu also has two choices:

A: Do Full Screen Check

B: Review Last Full Screen Check

Pressing A will cause the program to check all words on the currently active screen, and B will redo the last screen check, once more highlighting any words that are still misspelled (or are not in the dictionary).

The THESAURUS option offers no choices. It simply looks at the word at the cursor and displays as many synonyms as it can find.

The SETUP menu offers four choices:

A: Auxiliary dictionary file name	AUXI
B: Disk dictionary file name	FLP-DISK
C: Thesaurus file name	FLP-THES
D: Save Setup/Options/Environment	

The first three can be used to change file names, if that's what you want to do. The last selection is used to save all changes that you've made in the Environment or in the Options mode on disk, where they'll remain until you'll want to change them again. These changes must be made and saved with a copy of the Turbo Lightning distribution disk in the logged drive. It wouldn't make much sense to record the changes on a disk that's used for entirely different purposes.

When you select OPTIONS, the menu looks like:

A:	Auto proof	OFF
B:	Confirm window	ON
C:	Main menu hot key	ShftF8
D:	Last bad word hot key	AltF10
E:	Check word hot key	AltF9
F:	Screen check hot key	AltF8
G:	Review screen hot key	AltF7
H:	Thesaurus hot key	AltF6
I:	Toggle auto proof hot key	AltF5

It can be used to toggle Auto proof and Confirm window ON/OFF. If there is some reason why such an action is indicated, you can change the "hot" keys to some others. A hot key is a key that lets you address a specific function directly, without first going through the main menu. In other words, if you press Alt and F9 simultaneously, the proofreader will look at the last word you typed and either confirm its spelling, or display some likely replacements.

You must never be lulled into a false sense of security, thinking that if your electronic proofreader didn't find any spelling errors, everything is correct. It doesn't work that way. For instance, you might have meant to type confirm, but you actually typed conform. The spelling program cannot know what you had in mind. It only knows that there's nothing wrong with the spelling of conform, even though it makes absolutely no sense in the context in which it's being used. Using Turbo Lightning, or a comparable program, does not relieve you of the need to proof-read what you've written, to make certain that what's down on paper makes sense.

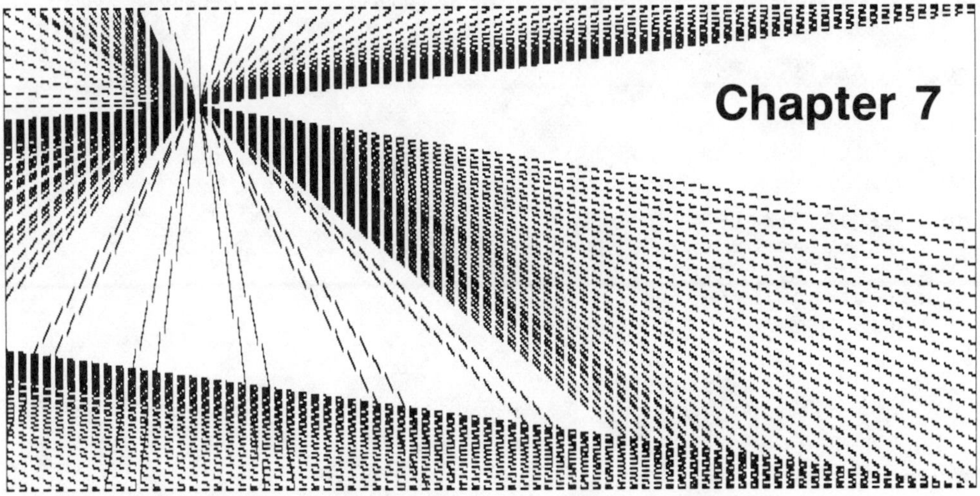

A Grab-Bag of Programs

This chapter contains a collection of different types of programs, most of which use one or another of the toolbox routines.

ASCII CHARACTERS 127 THROUGH 255

In the discussion about the Sidekick program in Chapter 6, I mentioned that one of its subprograms displays the entire range of ASCII characters from 1 through 255. For those who do not have Sidekick, and who might be interested in finding out what's available in addition to the traditional 1-through-126 ASCII character set, I've written a little program called ASCII.Tst (Fig. 7-1). It causes each of those characters to be displayed, along with its decimal number, in the center of the screen, until you press any key to see there next one. How useful these characters might be somewhat doubtful, because they might depend on the printer that you're using.

IT'S A CRAPSHOOT

This program lets you try your luck in a simulated dice game. You can either play against the computer by yourself, or up to 10 players can play against the house. The rules are simple:

7 or 11 on the first throw-- You win
2, 3 or 12 on the first throw------------------------------------- You lose
on subsequent throws:
You make your point--- You win
You throw anything other than a 7--------------------------------- Throw again
You throw a 7--- You lose

The program uses the Turbo Graphix Toolbox routine DefineTextWindow(. . .); to draw the two dice after each throw. A line or two of text explains where each player stands at any given time. The game is fun to play, and it goes on indefinitely until you press Q to quit.

Fig. 7-1. This program causes the characters that are available with the ASCII character codes 127 through 255 to be displayed.

```
program AsciiTest;

var X : integer;

begin

for X := 127 to 255 do begin
    clrscr; gotoxy(35,12);
    writeln(X,'  ',chr(X));
    repeat until KeyPressed;
    end;
end.
```

With 400+ lines, the program (Fig. 7-2), at first, looks a bit forbidding. It's really not that serious, because all those graphics procedures (two through twelve) can simply be copied, one after another, and only the **writeln** lines need to be edited.

GRAPHIC ROUTINES

The program RoutineDemonstration (DEMO.P) (Fig. 7-3) demonstrates some of the graphics routines that were not used in any of the programs discussed in the graphics chapter (Chapter 4) in this book. They are SetLineStyle, DrawCircle, DrawCircleDirect, DrawCross, DrawCross-Diag, DrawDiamond, DrawStar, DrawTextW, and DrawWye. All of these are displayed in a variety of sizes, with a line of text at the bottom, explaining the size being shown. At the start the program asks that you key in three different values that will control the length of short, medium, and long pauses. Typing 50, 500, and 1000 will cause fairly rapid program execution. If specific sizes are to be examined, larger numbers might be called for. At the conclusion of each loop for each of the routines, the program stops and waits for you to press ENTER to continue program execution. Programs like this are worthwhile because they give a fairly clear idea of what happens when one of these routines is included in a program.

It is important to remember the difference between Screen Coordinates and World Coordinates. The various routines in this program begin either with a call to the procedure Start or with the InitGraphic statement. In the first instance, the routines operate in accordance with World Coordinates. Programs using the second statement in the first line operate in accordance with Screen Coordinates, in my case, 640 by 200 (it varies with the graphics cards used by your system). If you inadvertently use World Coordinates with a routine that expects Screen Coordinates, you're likely to get some fairly odd, and probably incomprehensible, results.

A Pulsating Rectangle in Colors

Figure 7-4 is a short graphics program that creates a pulsating rectangle that constantly changes color. The colors are represented by the variable **C := random(14);**. Fourteen is used in this equation, and C+1 in **SetForegroundColor(C + 1)** because it avoids black (0) as one of the random colors. By entering any digit from 0 to 1000 in reply to the opening prompt, the pulsating speed can be varied from quite rapid to exasperatingly slow. Figure 7-5 is a printout of the basic design, produced by using the GRAPHICS.COM program from PC DOS.

A Progressive Abstract Design

PaintDesign (PAINT.P) (Fig. 7-6) produces an abstract design that intermittently changes color and gradually fills the screen with a profusion of random lines, producing some interesting

Fig. 7-2. This program is a dice game (craps) that can be played by up to 10 players. It uses a series of graphic routines to draw the dice for each throw.

```
{CRAPS (DICE) FOR MULTIPLE PLAYERS}
{CRAPS.P  }

program Craps;

{$I TYPEDEF.SYS  }
{$I GRAPHIX.SYS  }
{$I KERNEL.SYS   }
{$I WINDOWS.SYS  }

var     Z, P, TT, T1, T2, W, HP, Q, WW : integer;
        PL                             : array[1..10] of string[10];
        AW                             : array[1..10] of integer;
        CS                             : string[10];
        RET, A                         : char;

procedure lost;
begin
     Z := 1;
     gotoxy(1,20);
     writeln('You threw a ',TT);
     writeln;
     writeln('You lost.  New shooter!');
     writeln;
     write('Press any key to go on     ');
     repeat until KeyPressed;
     LeaveGraphic;
end;


procedure score4;
begin
     if TT = P then begin
     Z := 1;
     gotoxy(1,20);
     writeln('You made your point. You won $',WW,'!');
     end
     else begin
     Z := 2;
     gotoxy(1,20);
     writeln('You threw a ',TT);
     writeln;
     writeln('The point is ',P);
     end;
     writeln;
     write('Press any key to go on     ');
     repeat until KeyPressed;
     LeaveGraphic;
end;


procedure score2;
begin
          case TT of
     2 : score4;
     3 : score4;
```

```
     4 : score4;
     5 : score4;
     6 : score4;
     7 : lost;
     8 : score4;
     9 : score4;
    10 : score4;
    11 : score4;
    12 : score4;
         end;
end;

procedure score3;
begin
     Z := 2;
     gotoxy(1,20);
     writeln('You threw a ',TT);
     writeln('The point is ',P);
     writeln;
     write('Press any key to go on     ');
     repeat until KeyPressed;
     LeaveGraphic;
end;


procedure win;
begin
     Z := 1;
     gotoxy(1,20);
     writeln('You won $',WW,'!');
     writeln;
     write('Press any key to go on     ');
     repeat until KeyPressed;
     LeaveGraphic;
end;

procedure craps;
begin
     Z := 1;
     gotoxy(1,20);
     writeln('Craps!  You lose.');
     writeln;
     write('Press any key to go on     ');
     repeat until KeyPressed;
     LeaveGraphic;
end;

procedure score1;
begin
         case TT of
     2 : craps;
     3 : craps;
     4 : score3;
     5 : score3;
     6 : score3;
     7 : win;
     8 : score3;
     9 : score3;
    10 : score3;
```

```
    11 : win;
    12 : craps;
         end;
end;

procedure score;
begin
         case Z of
     1 : score1;
     2 : score2;
         end;
end;

procedure two;
begin
     initGraphic;
     defineTextWindow(1,40,4,58,12,4);
     defineTextWindow(2,40,14,58,22,4);
     selectWindow(1);
     setForegroundColor(11);
     drawBorder;
     gotoxy(46,8);
     writeln('   o    ');
     selectWindow(2);
     drawBorder;
     gotoxy(46,18);
     writeln('   o    ');
     score;
end;

procedure three;
begin
     initGraphic;
     defineTextWindow(1,40,4,58,12,4);
     defineTextWindow(2,40,14,58,22,4);
     selectWindow(1);
     setForegroundColor(11);
     drawBorder;
     gotoxy(46,8);
     writeln('   o    ');
     selectWindow(2);
     drawBorder;
     gotoxy(46,16);
     writeln('o       ');
     gotoxy(46,20);
     writeln('       o');
     score;
end;

procedure four;
begin
     initGraphic;
     defineTextWindow(1,40,4,58,12,4);
     defineTextWindow(2,40,14,58,22,4);
     selectWindow(1);
     setForegroundColor(11);
     drawBorder;
     gotoxy(46,6);
     writeln('o       ');
```

```
        gotoxy(46,10);
        writeln('        o');
        selectWindow(2);
        drawBorder;
        gotoxy(46,16);
        writeln('o        ');
        gotoxy(46,20);
        writeln('        o');
        score;
end;

procedure five;
begin
        initGraphic;
        defineTextWindow(1,40,4,58,12,4);
        defineTextWindow(2,40,14,58,22,4);
        selectWindow(1);
        setForegroundColor(11);
        drawBorder;
        gotoxy(46,6);
        writeln('o        ');
        gotoxy(46,8);
        writeln('    o    ');
        gotoxy(46,10);
        writeln('        o');
        selectWindow(2);
        drawBorder;
        gotoxy(46,16);
        writeln('o        ');
        gotoxy(46,20);
        writeln('        o');
        score;
end;

procedure six;
begin
        initGraphic;
        defineTextWindow(1,40,4,58,12,4);
        defineTextWindow(2,40,14,58,22,4);
        selectWindow(1);
        setForegroundColor(11);
        drawBorder;
        gotoxy(46,6);
        writeln('o        ');
        gotoxy(46,8);
        writeln('    o    ');
        gotoxy(46,10);
        writeln('        o');
        selectWindow(2);
        drawBorder;
        gotoxy(46,16);
        writeln('o        ');
        gotoxy(46,18);
        writeln('    o    ');
        gotoxy(46,20);
        writeln('        o');
        score;
end;
```

```
procedure seven;
begin
     initGraphic;
     defineTextWindow(1,40,4,58,12,4);
     defineTextWindow(2,40,14,58,22,4);
     selectWindow(1);
     setForegroundColor(11);
     drawBorder;
     gotoxy(46,6);
     writeln('o      o');
     gotoxy(46,8);
     writeln('    o   ');
     gotoxy(46,10);
     writeln('o      o');
     selectWindow(2);
     drawBorder;
     gotoxy(46,16);
     writeln('o       ');
     gotoxy(46,20);
     writeln('       o');
     score;
end;

procedure eight;
begin
     initGraphic;
     defineTextWindow(1,40,4,58,12,4);
     defineTextWindow(2,40,14,58,22,4);
     selectWindow(1);
     setForegroundColor(11);
     drawBorder;
     gotoxy(46,6);
     writeln('o      o');
     gotoxy(46,8);
     writeln('    o   ');
     gotoxy(46,10);
     writeln('o      o');
     selectWindow(2);
     drawBorder;
     gotoxy(46,16);
     writeln('o      ');
     gotoxy(46,18);
     writeln('   o    ');
     gotoxy(46,20);
     writeln('       o');
     score;
end;

procedure nine;
begin
     initGraphic;
     defineTextWindow(1,40,4,58,12,4);
     defineTextWindow(2,40,14,58,22,4);
     selectWindow(1);
     setForegroundColor(11);
     drawBorder;
     gotoxy(46,6);
     writeln('o      o');
```

```
        gotoxy(46,8);
        writeln('    o   ');
        gotoxy(46,10);
        writeln('o       o');
        selectWindow(2);
        drawBorder;
        gotoxy(46,16);
        writeln('o       o');
        gotoxy(46,20);
        writeln('o       o');
        score;
end;
procedure ten;
begin
        initGraphic;
        defineTextWindow(1,40,4,58,12,4);
        defineTextWindow(2,40,14,58,22,4);
        selectWindow(1);
        setForegroundColor(11);
        drawBorder;
        gotoxy(46,6);
        writeln('o       o');
        gotoxy(46,8);
        writeln('    o   ');
        gotoxy(46,10);
        writeln('o       o');
        selectWindow(2);
        drawBorder;
        gotoxy(46,16);
        writeln('o       o');
        gotoxy(46,18);
        writeln('   o    ');
        gotoxy(46,20);
        writeln('o       o');
        score;
end;

procedure eleven;
begin
        initGraphic;
        defineTextWindow(1,40,4,58,12,4);
        defineTextWindow(2,40,14,58,22,4);
        selectWindow(1);
        setForegroundColor(11);
        drawBorder;
        gotoxy(46,6);
        writeln('o       o');
        gotoxy(46,8);
        writeln('    o   ');
        gotoxy(46,10);
        writeln('o       o');
        selectWindow(2);
        drawBorder;
        gotoxy(46,16);
        writeln('o       o');
        gotoxy(46,18);
        writeln('o       o');
        gotoxy(46,20);
        writeln('o       o');
```

```
     score;
end;

procedure twelve;
begin
     initGraphic;
     defineTextWindow(1,40,4,58,12,4);
     defineTextWindow(2,40,14,58,22,4);
     selectWindow(1);
     setForegroundColor(11);
     drawBorder;
     gotoxy(46,6);
     writeln('o      o');
     gotoxy(46,8);
     writeln('o      o');
     gotoxy(46,10);
     writeln('o      o');
     selectWindow(2);
     drawBorder;
     gotoxy(46,16);
     writeln('o      o');
     gotoxy(46,18);
     writeln('o      o');
     gotoxy(46,20);
     writeln('o      o');
     score;
end;

procedure display;
begin
     clrscr;
     TT := T1 + T2;
     if Z = 1 then P := TT;
         case TT of
     2 : two;
     3 : three;
     4 : four;
     5 : five;
     6 : six;
     7 : seven;
     8 : eight;
     9 : nine;
    10 : ten;
    11 : eleven;
    12 : twelve;
         end;
end;

procedure dice;
begin
         repeat
     randomize;
     T1 := random(7);
         until T1 > 0;
         repeat
     randomize;
     T2 := random(7);
         until T2 > 0;
     display;
```

```
end;

procedure shooter;
begin
     clrscr; gotoxy(1,10);
     write('Name or initial of current shooter?   ');
     readln(CS);
     dice;
end;

procedure wagers;
begin
     P := 0;  WW := 0;
     Z := 1;
     clrscr; gotoxy(1,10);
       for W := 1 to HP do begin
     write(PL[W],',  amount of wager?  $');
     readln(AW[W]);
       WW := WW + AW[W];
       end;
     shooter;
end;


procedure players;
begin
     Z := 0;
     clrscr; gotoxy(20,10);
     writeln('Craps (dice) for from 1 to 10 players');
     writeln;
     gotoxy(20,12);
     write('How many players?     ');
     readln(HP);
     writeln;
     gotoxy(20,15);
     writeln('Type the name or initial of each player, please');
     writeln;
       for Q := 1 to HP do begin
     write('                   Player number ',Q,'  ');
     readln(PL[Q]);
       end;
     wagers;
end;


begin
     Z := 1;
     players;
          repeat
          case Z of
     1 : wagers;
     2 : dice;
          end;
     textColor(15);
     gotoxy(1,20);
     write('Press ENTER to go on or type Q to quit     ');
     readln(RET);
          until (RET = 'Q') or (RET = 'q');
 end.
```

Fig. 7-3. This program demonstrates the preprogrammed graphics routines that are contained in the include modules.

```
{This program demonstrates the various graphics routines}
{DEMO.P    }

program RoutineDemonstration;


{$I TYPEDEF.SYS  }
{$I GRAPHIX.SYS  }
{$I KERNEL.SYS   }
{$I WINDOWS.SYS  }
{$I CIRCSEGM.HGH }

const MaxWrldX : real = 1000.0;
      MaxWrldY : real = 1000.0;

var Z, ZZ, ZZZ, ZZZZ, Q, LS : integer;
    CH                      : char;

procedure Start;
begin
     InitGraphic;
     DefineWorld(1,0,MaxWrldY,MaxWrldX,0);
     SelectWorld(1);
     SelectWindow(1);
     DrawBorder;
end;

procedure Demo;
begin
     Start;
     for LS := 0 to 4 do begin
     ClearScreen;
     gotoxy(5,24);
     writeln('DrawLine, Line style: ',LS);
     SetLineStyle(LS);
     DrawLine(0,500,1000,500);
     Delay(ZZ);
     end;
     read(CH);
     LeaveGraphic;

     Start;
     for Z := 1 to 5 do begin
     gotoxy(5,24);
     writeln('DrawCircle, Radius ',Z);
     DrawCircle(500,500,Z);
     Delay(ZZ);
     end;
     read(CH);
     LeaveGraphic;

     Start;
     Z := 0;
     repeat
     Z := Z + 10;
     gotoxy(5,24);
     writeln('DrawCircleDirect, radius: ',Z,' pixels');
```

```
DrawCircleDirect(500,500,Z,true);
Delay(ZZZZ);
until Z = 400;
read(CH);
LeaveGraphic;

InitGraphic;
Z := 0;
repeat
Z := Z + 1;
gotoxy(5,24);
writeln('DrawCross, size: ',Z);
DrawCross(320,100,Z);
Delay(ZZZZ);
until Z = 100;
read(CH);
LeaveGraphic;

InitGraphic;
Z := 0;
repeat
Z := Z + 1;
gotoxy(5,24);
writeln('DrawCrossDiag, size: ',Z);
DrawCrossDiag(320,100,Z);
Delay(ZZZZ);
until Z = 100;
read(CH);
LeaveGraphic;

InitGraphic;
Z := 0;
repeat
Z := Z + 1;
gotoxy(5,24);
writeln('DrawDiamond, size: ',Z);
DrawDiamond(320,100,Z);
Delay(ZZZZ);
until Z = 100;
read(CH);
LeaveGraphic;

InitGraphic;
Z := 0;
repeat
Z := Z + 1;
gotoxy(5,24);
writeln('DrawStar, size: ',Z);
DrawStar(320,100,Z);
Delay(ZZZZ);
until Z = 100;
read(CH);
LeaveGraphic;

Start;
for Z := 1 to 8 do begin
gotoxy(5,24);
writeln('DrawTextW, Size ',Z);
```

```
        DrawTextW(300,500,Z,'H');
        Delay(ZZ);
        end;
        read(CH);
        LeaveGraphic;

        InitGraphic;
        Z := 0;
        repeat
        Z := Z + 1;
        gotoxy(5,24);
        writeln('DrawWye, size: ',Z);
        DrawWye(320,100,Z);
        Delay(ZZZZ);
        until Z = 100;
        read(CH);
        LeaveGraphic;
end;

procedure Pause;
begin
        clrscr;  gotoxy(10,10);
        write('Enter length of short pauses      ');
        readln(ZZZZ);
        gotoxy(10,12);
        write('Enter length of medium pauses     ');
        readln(ZZZ);
        gotoxy(10,14);
        write('Enter length of long pauses       ');
        readln(ZZ);
end;

begin
        Pause;
        if ZZ <> 0 then
        Demo
        else
end.
```

Fig. 7-4. This is one of three just-for-fun programs. This one produces a pulsing three-dimensional effect.

```
{An apparently pulsating 3-D design}
{PULSE.P   }


program Pulse3D;

{$I TYPEDEF.SYS }
{$I GRAPHIX.SYS }
{$I KERNEL.SYS  }

var S, C, X : integer;

procedure Design;
begin

        InitGraphic;
        DefineWorld(1,0,1000,1000,0);
        SelectWorld(1);
```

```
      SelectWindow(1);
      DrawBorder;
           repeat
           C := random(14);
      SetForegroundColor(C+1);
      for X := 1 to 40 do begin
      Delay(S);
      DrawSquare(500 - X * 12.5, 500 - X * 12.5, 500 + X * 12.5,
                                                  500 + X * 12.5, false);
      end;
     { ClearScreen; }
           until KeyPressed;
      LeaveGraphic;
end;

begin
      clrscr; gotoxy(1,10);
      writeln('Enter the desired speed (low digit: fast, high digit: slow) ');
      writeln;
      writeln('To exit program press any key');
      writeln;
      readln(S);
      Design;
end.
```

designs along the way. It's based largely on values selected at random, so the designs that are produced vary from run to run. One of the early stages of the creation of the design is shown in the printout produced by GRAPHICS.COM from PC DOS (Fig. 7-7).

Three Designs in Three Windows

WindowPainting (WIND.P, Fig. 7-8) repeats the two programs described above, and adds the "walking line" program from the distribution disk to demonstrate how several entirely different and independent displays can be placed into different windows on the same screen. Figure 7-9 is a printout of the result.

A PRODUCT INVENTORY FILE

The program entitled ProductInventory (PRD.P, Fig. 7-10) can be used to store records containing the data relative to a particular product. The menu offers 10 choices, one to be use prior to the first data entry (#9), because its purpose is simply to create a file called PROD.DTA if it does not already exist, or to erase previously stored data. When selected, it displays a warning in procedure Start to prevent inadventent erasures. One selection, #0, exits the program to the operating system, while the other seven choices, #2 through #8, offer various parameters for data retrieval. Most include the option to have the displayed record printed (Fig. 7-11).

One of these selections, #6, displays the product for which new quantity-on-hand data are to be entered. It then asks that the new figures be keyed in, and produces a new record with the new quantity-on-hand figure, but with everything else unchanged.

Selection #7 is used to display all stored data alphabetically according to the product names. This selection calls up an external file called STRPROD.COM (Fig. 7-12). In order to use this option, both programs must be compiled using the Option routine from Turbo Pascal (type OCQC). This separate program includes a call to the ($I SORT.BOX) module, which must be present on the logged disk. It will look for the file named PROD.DTA on the currently logged disk, and will then display the stored data in alphabetical order. It will display entire records, requiring

Fig. 7-5. This is a printout of one of the stages of the three-dimensional design.

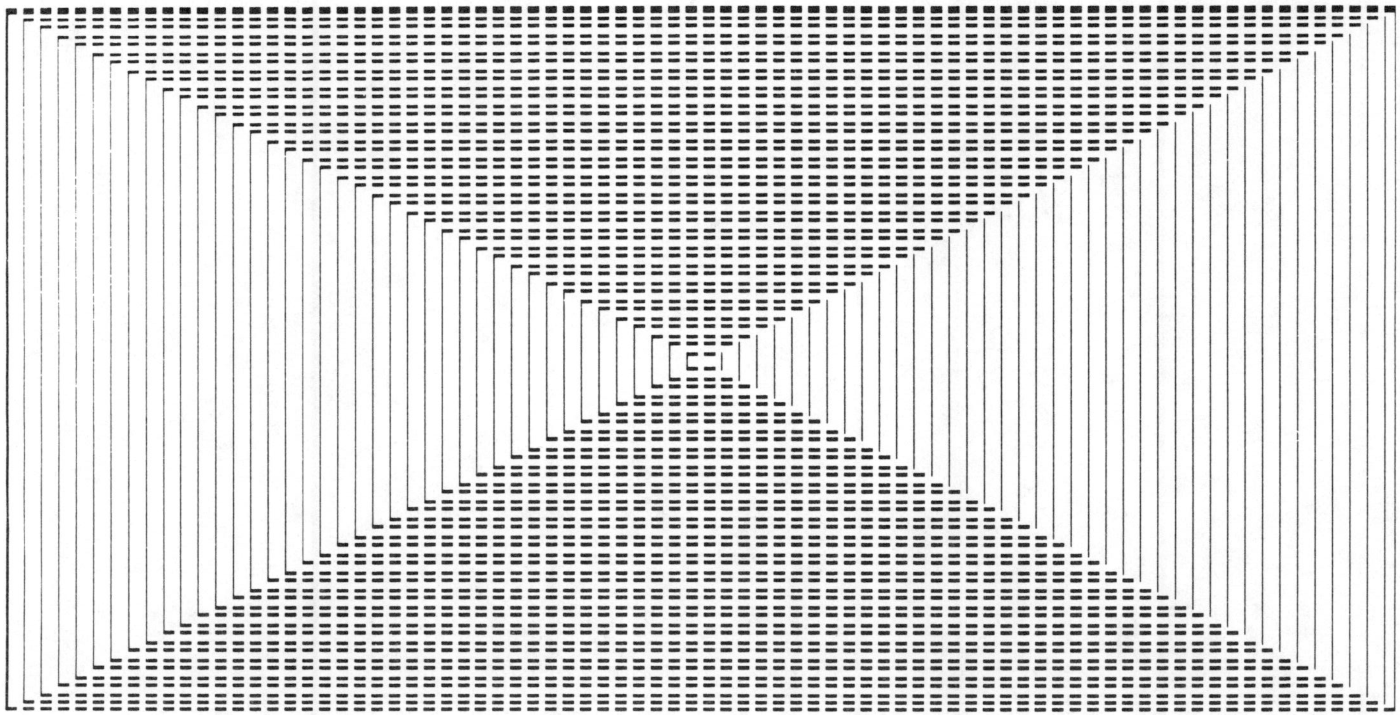

Fig. 7-6. This program creates an ever-changing abstract design.

```
{Painting an abstract design that keeps changing}
{PAINT.P   }

program PaintDesign;

{$I TYPEDEF.SYS }
{$I GRAPHIX.SYS }
{$I KERNEL.SYS  }

var A, B, Z     : real;
    C, X, Y     : integer;
    ENT         : char;

procedure MovingPicture;
begin
     InitGraphic;
     DefineWorld(1,0,30,30,0);
     SelectWorld(1);
     SelectWindow(1);
     DrawBorder;
     Y := 14;
        repeat
     SetForegroundColor(Y);
     Z := 0.0;
     A := random(30);
     B := random(30);
        repeat
     Z := Z + 1;
     for X := 0 to 30 do begin
     DrawLine(X * 5 + Z,0,A,B);
     DrawLine(A,B,30 - X - Z,30);
     DrawLine(30,Y + X,A,B);
     DrawLine(A,B,0,30 - X - Y);
     DrawLine(0,A,0,B);
     DrawLine(A+B,Y,X,B - A);
     end;
        until Z > 1.0;
DELAY(10000);
 Y := Y - 1;
     if Y = 1 then Y := Y + 1;
        until KeyPressed;
end;

begin
     clrscr;  gotoxy(1,10);
     writeln('To exit the program, press any key');
     writeln;
     write('Press ENTER to start       ');
     readln(ENT);
     MovingPicture;
end.
```

that ENTER be pressed after each, otherwise they'd scroll by too fast to be read. The program can, of course, be modified fairly easily to be used to store other types of data.

BLACKJACK

The program called Blackjack (BJ.P, the main program, plus the include files CHCKCARD.BJ,

Fig. 7-7. This is a printout of one stage of the abstract design produced when the program is run.

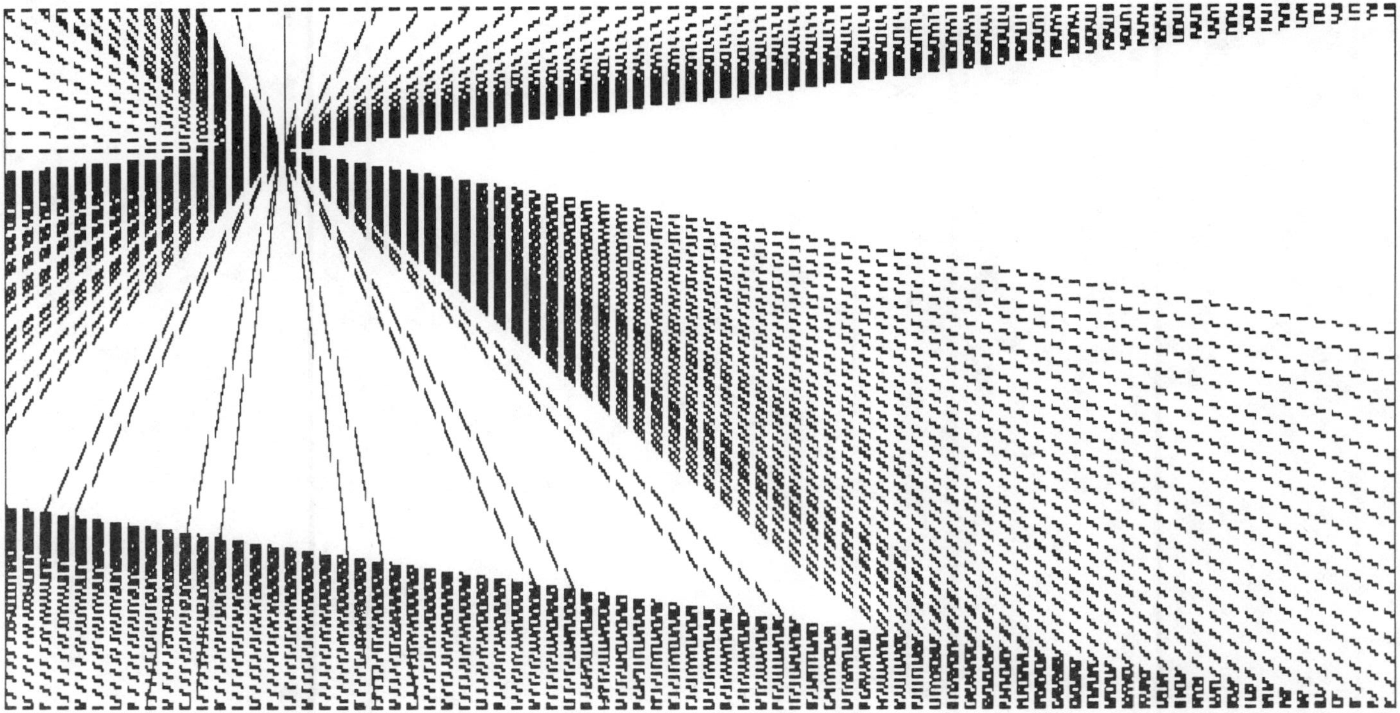

Fig. 7-8. This program places three different designs into three windows.

```
{Window Painting}
{WIND.P    }

program WindowPainting;

{$I TYPEDEF.SYS }
{$I GRAPHIX.SYS }
{$I KERNEL.SYS  }
{$I WINDOWS.SYS }

var ENT : char;

procedure Rectang;

var S, C, X : integer;

begin
     SetForegroundColor(11);
     for X := 1 to 40 do begin
     DrawSquare(500 - X * 12.5, 500 - X * 12.5, 500 + X * 12.5,
                                              500 + X * 12.5, false);
     end;
end;

procedure Paint;

var A, B, Z     : real;
    C, X, Y     : integer;

begin
     SetForegroundColor(12);
     Z := 0.0;
     A := random(30);
     B := random(30);
        repeat
     Z := Z + 1;
     for X := 0 to 30 do begin
     DrawLine(X * 5 + Z,0,A,B);
     DrawLine(A,B,30 - X - Z,30);
     DrawLine(30,Y + X,A,B);
     DrawLine(A,B,0,30 - X - Y);
     DrawLine(0,A,0,B);
     DrawLine(A+B,Y,X,B - A);
     end;
        until Z > 1.0;
end;

procedure Lines;

var I : integer;

begin
     SetForegroundColor(13);
     for I := 1 to 20 do DrawLine(I * 50,0,1000 - I * 50,I * 50);
end;

procedure Display;
```

```
begin
     InitGraphic;
     DrawBorder;
     DefineWindow(1,trunc(XMaxGlb/10),trunc(YMaxGlb/10),
                    trunc(XMaxGlb/2),trunc(YMaxGlb/2));
     DefineHeader(1,'THIS IS THE PULSATING PICTURE');
     DefineWorld(1,0,1000,1000,0);
     DefineWindow(2,trunc(XMaxGlb/3),trunc(YMaxGlb/3),
                    trunc((XMaxGlb*2)/3),trunc((YMaxGlb*2)/3));
     DefineHeader(2,'THIS IS THE ABTRACT PAINTING');
     DefineWorld(2,0,30,30,0);
     DefineWindow(3,trunc(XMaxGlb/2),trunc(YMaxGlb/2),
                    trunc((XMaxGlb*9)/10),trunc((YMaxGlb*9)/10))
     DefineHeader(3,'TIS IS THE WALKING LINE');
     DefineWorld(3,0,1000,1000,0);

     SelectWorld(1);
     SelectWindow(1);
     SetHeaderOn;
     SetBackground(0);
     DrawBorder;
     Rectang;
     SelectWorld(2);
     SelectWindow(2);
     SetHeaderOn;
     SetBackground(0);
     DrawBorder;
     Paint;
     SelectWorld(3);
     SelectWindow(3);
     SetHeaderOn;
     SetBackground(0);
     DrawBorder;
     Lines;
repeat until KeyPressed;
LeaveGraphic;
end;

begin
     clrscr; gotoxy(1,10);
     writeln('To exit the program press any key');
     writeln;
     write('Press ENTER to start     ');
     readln(ENT);
     Display;
 end.
```

DEALCARD.BJ, LOOKCARD.BJ and PLAYCARD.BJ) is shown in Figs. 7-13 through 7-17. It is on electronic version of a very popular gambling game, adhering to the rules by which it is played in Las Vegas and Atlantic City.

The rules are as follows: The dealer deals a card, face down, to the player and another, also face down, to him- or herself. The player then receives a second card, face down, and the dealer a second card, face up. After that, the player may ask for as many additional cards as desired. The values of the cards are 10 for all face cards, 1 or 11 for aces, and the face value for cards 2 through 10. The object of the game is to come as close as possible to 21, but not to go over. If the player ends up with more points than the dealer, but with 21 or less, the player wins the amount of the wager. Otherwise the dealer wins, taking the player's wager. If the player makes

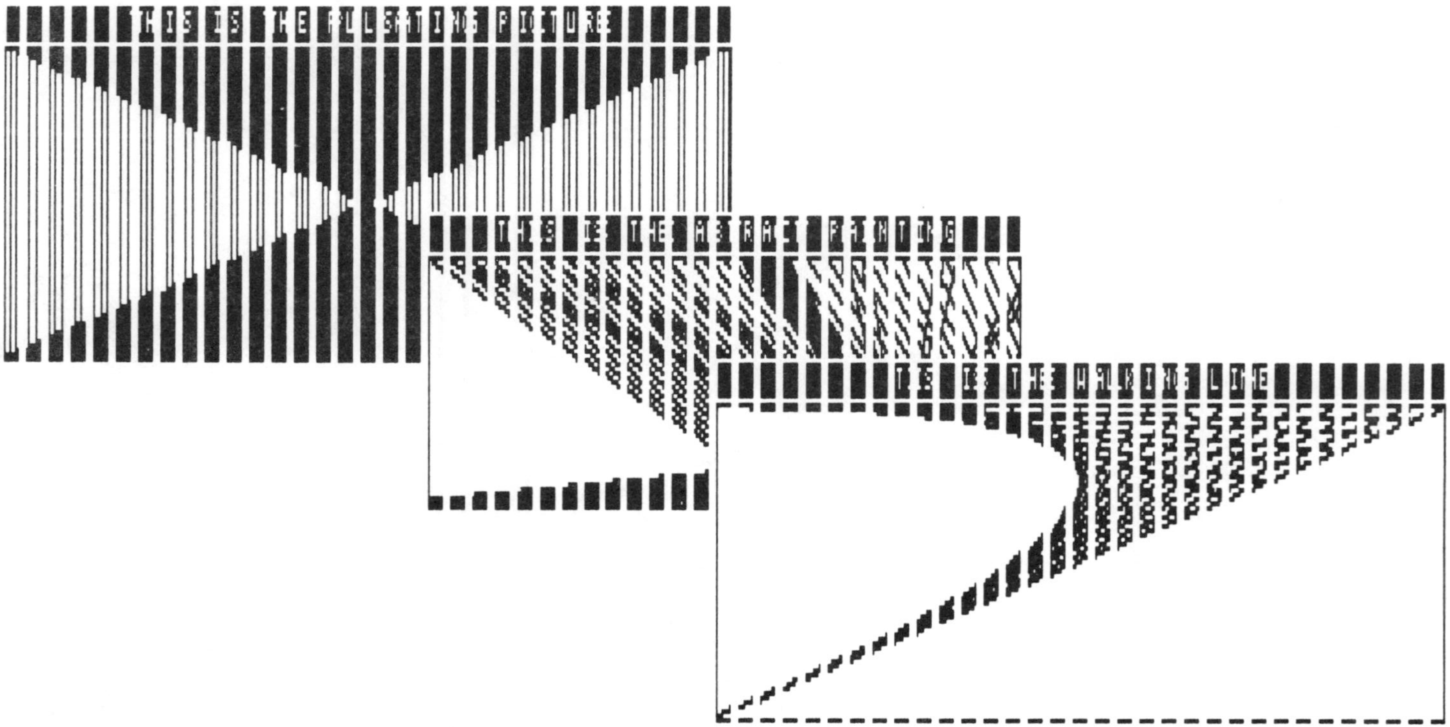

Fig. 7-9. This is a printout of three windows at one stage of program execution.

Fig. 7-10. This is a simple inventory file program.

```
{Product Inventory File Program}
{PRD.P    }

program ProductInventory;

var PRODUCT : file of string[50];
    EXTRN   : file;
    DESCR, REORDER, ONHAND, COST, PRICE, SUPPLIER, COMMENT, ID : string[50];
    NME, REOR, HI, LO, CHI, CLO, NUM                          : string[50];
    WHICH   : integer;
    Y       : char;

procedure Print;
begin
     writeln(Lst,'Product name/description.............',DESCR);
     writeln(Lst,'Product ID number...................',ID);
     writeln(Lst,'Product reorder number...............',REORDER);
     writeln(Lst,'Quantity on hand.....................',ONHAND);
     writeln(Lst,'Purchase price.......................',COST);
     writeln(Lst,'Resale price.........................',PRICE);
     writeln(Lst,'Supplier.............................',SUPPLIER);
     writeln(Lst,'Comments.............................',COMMENT);
     writeln(Lst,'  ');
end;

procedure Display;
begin
     clrscr;  gotoxy(1,5);
     writeln('Product name/description.............',DESCR);
     writeln('Product ID number...................',ID);
     writeln('Product reorder number...............',REORDER);
     writeln('Quantity on hand.....................',ONHAND);
     writeln('Purchase price.......................',COST);
     writeln('Resale price.........................',PRICE);
     writeln('Supplier.............................',SUPPLIER);
     writeln('Comments.............................',COMMENT);
     writeln;
     write('Printout?   (Y/N)    ');
     readln(Y);
         if UpCase(Y) = 'Y' then
     Print;
     writeln;
     write('Press ENTER to go on      ');
     readln(Y);
end;

procedure Enter;
begin
     clrscr; gotoxy(1,10);
     repeat
     assign(Product,'PROD.DTA');
     reset(Product);
     Seek(Product,FileSize(Product));
     write('Enter Product name or description      ');
     readln(DESCR);
     write('Enter Product ID number                ');
     readln(ID);
```

```
      write('Enter Product Reorder number           ');
      readln(REORDER);
      write('Enter quantity on hand                 ');
      readln(ONHAND);
      write('Enter Product Purchase Price          $');
      readln(COST);
      write('Enter Product Resale Price            $');
      readln(PRICE);
      write('Enter Supplier                         ');
      readln(SUPPLIER);
      write('Enter comments                         ');
      readln(COMMENT);
      write(Product,DESCR);
      write(Product,ID);
      write(Product,REORDER);
      write(Product,ONHAND);
      write(Product,COST);
      write(Product,PRICE);
      write(Product,SUPPLIER);
      write(Product,COMMENT);
      close(Product);
      writeln;
      write('Another entry?  (Y/N)   ');
      readln(Y);
           until UpCase(y) = 'N';
end;

procedure Description;
begin
     clrscr; gotoxy(1,10);
     write('Enter Product name or description    ');
     readln(NME);
     assign(Product,'PROD.DTA');
     reset(Product);
          repeat
     read(Product,DESCR);
     read(Product,ID);
     read(Product,REORDER);
     read(Product,ONHAND);
     read(Product,COST);
     read(Product,PRICE);
     read(Product,SUPPLIER);
     read(Product,COMMENT);
         if NME = DESCR then
         Display;
         until eof(Product);
     close(Product);
end;

Procedure ReorderNumber;
begin
     clrscr; gotoxy(1,10);
     write('Enter Product Reorder number    ');
     readln(REOR);
     assign(Product,'PROD.DTA');
     reset(Product);
          repeat
     read(Product,DESCR);
     read(Product,ID);
```

```
     read(Product,REORDER);
     read(Product,ONHAND);
     read(Product,COST);
     read(Product,PRICE);
     read(Product,SUPPLIER);
     read(Product,COMMENT);
         if REOR >= ONHAND then
         Display;
         until eof(Product);
     close(Product);
end;

procedure ComparePrice;
begin
     clrscr; gotoxy(1,10);
     write('Enter upper price limit     ');
     readln(HI);
     write('Enter lower price limit     ');
     readln(LO);
     assign(Product,'PROD.DTA');
     reset(Product);
          repeat
     read(Product,DESCR);
     read(Product,ID);
     read(Product,REORDER);
     read(Product,ONHAND);
     read(Product,COST);
     read(Product,PRICE);
     read(Product,SUPPLIER);
     read(Product,COMMENT);
         if (PRICE < HI) and (PRICE > LO) then
         Display;
         until eof(Product);
     close(Product);
end;

procedure CompareCost;
begin
     clrscr; gotoxy(1,10);
     write('Enter upper cost limit     ');
     readln(CHI);
     write('Enter lower cost limit     ');
     readln(CLO);
     assign(Product,'PROD.DTA');
     reset(Product);
          repeat
     read(Product,DESCR);
     read(Product,ID);
     read(Product,REORDER);
     read(Product,ONHAND);
     read(Product,COST);
     read(Product,PRICE);
     read(Product,SUPPLIER);
     read(Product,COMMENT);
         if (COST < CHI) and (COST > CLO) then
         Display;
         until eof(Product);
     close(Product);
end;
```

```
procedure QuantityOnHand;
begin
     clrscr; gotoxy(1,10);
     write('Enter Product name or description    ');
     readln(NME);
     write('Enter lower cost limit    ');
     readln(CLO);
     assign(Product,'PROD.DTA');
     reset(Product);
          repeat
     read(Product,DESCR);
     read(Product,ID);
     read(Product,REORDER);
     read(Product,ONHAND);
     read(Product,COST);
     read(Product,PRICE);
     read(Product,SUPPLIER);
     read(Product,COMMENT);
         if NME = DESCR then
         Display;
         until eof(Product);
     close(Product);
end;

procedure Alpha;
begin
     assign(Extrn,'SRTPROD.COM');
     execute(Extrn);
end;

procedure ByNumber;
begin
     clrscr; gotoxy(1,10);
     write('Enter product ID number    ');
     readln(NUM);
     assign(Product,'PROD.DTA');
     reset(Product);
          repeat
     read(Product,DESCR);
     read(Product,ID);
     read(Product,REORDER);
     read(Product,ONHAND);
     read(Product,COST);
     read(Product,PRICE);
     read(Product,SUPPLIER);
     read(Product,COMMENT);
         if NUM = ID then
         Display;
         until eof(Product);
     close(Product);
end;

procedure Start;
begin
     clrscr;  gotoxy(1,10);
     TextColor(12);
     writeln('                                        WARNING!');
     writeln('                                        ========');
     writeln;
```

```
     writeln('                           All previous entries will be erased!');
     writeln('                           ------------------------------------');
     writeln;
     TextColor(14);
     write('                             Go ahead?                   (Y/N)    ');
     readln(Y);
               if UpCase(Y) = 'Y' then begin
           assign(Product,'PROD.DTA');
           rewrite(Product);
           close(Product);
               end
               else
end;

procedure Menu;
begin
     clrscr; gotoxy(1,8);
     TextColor(11);
     writeln('                           PRODUCT INVENTORY');
     writeln('                           =================');
     Delay(2000);
     gotoxy(1,12);
     TextColor(10);
     writeln('                                  MENU');
     writeln('                                  ----');
     TextColor(12);
     write('        1    ');
     TextColor(13);
     writeln('Add new product to inventory');
     writeln('            ================================================');
     TextColor(12);
     write('        2    ');
     TextColor(13);
     writeln('Retrieve data for one product');
     writeln('            ------------------------------------------------');
     TextColor(12);
     write('        3    ');
     TextColor(13);
     writeln('Retrieve all products below reorder level');
     writeln('            ------------------------------------------------');
     TextColor(12);
     write('        4    ');
     TextColor(13);
     writeln('Retrieve all products between price levels');
     writeln('            ------------------------------------------------');
     TextColor(12);
     write('        5    ');
     TextColor(13);
     writeln('Retrieve all products between cost levels');
     writeln('            ================================================');
     TextColor(12);
     write('        6    ');
     TextColor(13);
     writeln('Enter new quantity on hand for one product');
     writeln('            ------------------------------------------------');
     TextColor(12);
     TextColor(12);
     write('        7    ');
     TextColor(13);
```

```
      writeln('Retrieve all products alphabetically');
      writeln('       ------------------------------------------------');
      TextColor(12);
      write('        8    ');
      TextColor(13);
      writeln('Retrieve all products by ID number');
      writeln('       ================================================');
      TextColor(12);
      write('        9    ');
      TextColor(13);
      writeln('Erase.  Start from scratch');
      writeln('       ================================================');
      TextColor(12);
      write('        0    ');
      TextColor(13);
      writeln('Exit program');
      writeln('       ------------------------------------------------');
      TextColor(14);
      write('        Which?          ');
      readln(WHICH);
         case WHICH of
      1 : Enter;
      2 : Description;
      3 : ReorderNumber;
      4 : ComparePrice;
      5 : CompareCost;
      6 : QuantityOnHand;
      7 : Alpha;
      8 : ByNumber;
      9 : Start;
      0 : end;
end;

begin
         repeat
      Menu;
         until WHICH = 0;
end.
```

Fig. 7-11. This printout was produced by the inventory file program.

```
Product name/description.............GADGET
Product ID number....................102
Product reorder number...............50
Quantity on hand.....................40
Purchase price.......................15
Resale price.........................28.95
Supplier.............................XYZ CO.
Comments.............................NONE
```

Fig. 7-12. A companion to Product Inventory, this program sorts products alphabetically by product name or description.

```
{External companion file to Product Inventory,
                              to sort by product name alphabetically}
{SRTPROD.P    }


{$C-}
```

```
program SortAFileAlphabetically;

type
  NameString = string[50];
  ProdRec = record
              Number    : integer;
              DESCR     : NameString;
              ID        : string[50];
              REORDER   : string[50];
              ONHAND    : string[50];
              COST      : string[50];
              PRICE     : string[50];
              SUPPLIER  : string[50];
              COMMENT   : string[50];
            end;

  ProdFileType = file of ProdRec;

var
  ProdFile : ProdFileType;
  Product  : ProdRec;
  Results  : integer;
  CHOICE   : char;
  LIST     : file;

{$I SORT.BOX }

procedure OpenFile(var f : ProdFileType; Name : NameString);

begin
       clrscr;
  {$I-}
  reset(f);
  {$I+}
  if IOresult <> 0 then
  begin
    writeln(^G, '  -- Cannot find ', Name);
    halt;
  end;
end;

procedure Inp;

var
  rec : integer;
begin
  rec := 0;
  writeln;
  writeln('Input routine -- sending ', FileSize(ProdFile),
          ' records to sort:');
  repeat
    rec := rec + 1;
    write(#13, rec:6);
    read(ProdFile,Product);
    SortRelease(Product);
  until eof(ProdFile);
  writeln;
  writeln;
  writeln('Done with input -- sorting ',
```

```
            FileSize(ProdFile), ' records . . .');
end;

function Less;

var
  FirstProd:  ProdRec absolute X;
  SecondProd: ProdRec absolute Y;
begin
  Less := FirstProd.DESCR < SecondProd.DESCR;
end;

procedure OutP;

var
  i      : integer;
  GO, Y : char;


begin

  repeat
      clrscr;
    SortReturn(Product);
      with Product do begin
     clrscr;  gotoxy(1,5);
     writeln('Product name/description.............',DESCR);
     writeln('Product ID number....................',ID);
     writeln('Product reorder number...............',REORDER);
     writeln('Quantity on hand.....................',ONHAND);
     writeln('Purchase price.......................',COST);
     writeln('Resale price.........................',PRICE);
     writeln('Supplier.............................',SUPPLIER);
     writeln('Comments.............................',COMMENT);
     writeln;
     end;
     writeln;
     write('Press ENTER to go on       ');
     readln(GO);

          until SortEOS;
  end;

procedure DisplayResults(results : integer);
begin
  writeln;
  writeln;
  case Results of
     0 : writeln('Done with sort and display.');
     3 : writeln('Error:  not enough memory to sort');
     8 : writeln('Error:  illegal item length.');
     9 : writeln('Error:  can only sort ', MaxInt, ' records.');
    10 : writeln('Error:  disk full or disk write error.');
    11 : writeln('Error:  disk error during read.');
    12 : writeln('Error:  directory full or invalid path name');
  end;
end;

begin
```

```
    OpenFile(ProdFile,'PROD.DTA');
    Results := TurboSort(SizeOf(ProdRec));
    DisplayResults(Results);
end.
```

Fig. 7-13. With this program, you can play blackjack against the computer. Be prepared to lose your shirt.

```
{Blackjack (21) according to Las Vegas rules}
{BJ.P   }

program blackjack;

var   W                  : real;
      X, Z, WL           : integer;
      A, AA              : array[1..10] of integer;
      AC                 : array[1..10] of boolean;
      CARD, CARD1        : string[9];
      AP, AD, SC         : integer;
      YN, Y              : char;

{$I CHCKCARD.BJ   }
{$I DEALCARD.BJ   }
{$I LOOKCARD.BJ   }
{$I PLAYCARD.BJ   }

procedure Wager;
begin
      gotoxy(10,20);
      write('Enter the amount of your wager (0 to quit)  $');
      readln(W);
      X := 0; WL := 5;
      if W <> 0 then
      Play1
      else
end;

begin
          repeat
      TextColor(15);
      clrscr; gotoxy(1,10);
      writeln('                                 BLACKJACK (21)');
      writeln('                                 ==============');
      Wager;
          until W = 0;
end.
```

Fig. 7-14. The first of four include files used by the blackjack program, CHCKCARD.BJ is used to determine wins and losses.

```
{Procedures WinLose, Result, Push}
{CHCKCARD.BJ   }

procedure WinLose;
begin
          case WL of
      0 : begin
          clrscr; gotoxy(10,10);
          TextColor(12);
          write('Player loses ');
          TextColor(11);
```

```
        writeln('$',W:2:2);
        TextColor(15);
        gotoxy(50,24);
        writeln('Press any key to continue');
        repeat until KeyPressed;
        end;
    1 : begin
        clrscr; gotoxy(10,10);
        TextColor(12);
        write('Player wins ');
        TextColor(11);
        writeln('$',W:2:2);
        TextColor(15);
        gotoxy(50,24);
        writeln('Press any key to continue');
        repeat until KeyPressed;
        end;
    end;
end;

procedure Result;
begin
    if AD > AP then WL := 0
    else WL := 1;
end;

procedure Push;
begin
    clrscr;
    gotoxy(10,10);
    TextColor(12);
    write('Player has ');
    TextColor(11);
    writeln(AP);
    gotoxy(10,14);
    TextColor(10);
    write('Dealer has ');
    TextColor(14);
    writeln(AD);
    gotoxy(20,16);
    TextColor(15);
    writeln('PUSH!   Nobody wins or loses!');
    TextColor(15);
    gotoxy(50,24);
    writeln('Press any key to continue');
    repeat until KeyPressed;
    WL := 5;
end;
```

Fig. 7-15. DEALCARD.BJ assigns card denominations to the string variable CARD.

```
{Procedures Ace, DealACard}
{DEALCARD.BJ  }

procedure Ace;
begin
    if A[X] = 0 then AC[X] := true;
end;
```

```
procedure DealACard;
begin
     X := X + 1;
     randomize;
     A[X] := random(14);
     if A[X] = 11 then CARD := ' a Jack';
     if A[X] = 12 then CARD := ' a Queen';
     if A[X] = 13 then CARD := ' a King';
     if A[X] > 10 then AA[X] := 10;
     if A[X] = 0  then CARD := ' an Ace';
     if A[X] = 1  then CARD := ' a Two';
     if A[X] = 2  then CARD := ' a Three';
     if A[X] = 3  then CARD := ' a Four';
     if A[X] = 4  then CARD := ' a Five';
     if A[X] = 5  then CARD := ' a Six';
     if A[X] = 6  then CARD := ' a Seven';
     if A[X] = 7  then CARD := ' an Eight';
     if A[X] = 8  then CARD := ' a Nine';
     if A[X] = 9  then CARD := ' a Ten';
     if A[X] = 0  then AA[X] := 11;
     if (A[X] > 0) and (A[X] < 10) then AA[X] := A[X]+1;
     Ace;
end;
```

Fig. 7-16. LOOKCARD.BJ is used if the player has blackjack, and to show the cards of the dealer.

```
{Procedures Bjack, Stand, Adjust}
{LOOKCARD.BJ   }

procedure Bjack;
begin
     clrscr;
     DealACard;
     AD := AD + AA[X];
     if AD = 21 then Push else
     gotoxy(10,10);
     TextColor(12);
     write('Player has blackjack!  Player wins');
     TextColor(11);
     writeln(' $',W * 1.5:2:2);
     TextColor(15);
     gotoxy(50,24);
     writeln('Press any key to continue');
     repeat until KeyPressed;
end;

procedure Stand;
begin
     clrscr;
     gotoxy(20,10);
     TextColor(12);
     write('Player has ');
     TextColor(11);
     writeln(AP);
     gotoxy(20,14);
     TextColor(10);
     write('Dealer''s down card is ');
     TextColor(14);
```

```
      write(CARD1);
      TextColor(10);
      write('. Dealer has ');
      TextColor(14);
      writeln(AD);
      TextColor(15);
      gotoxy(50,24);
      writeln('Press any key to continue');
      repeat until KeyPressed;
      if AD = AP then Push
      else begin
      gotoxy(14,16);
      TextColor(9);
      writeln('Dealer must draw on 16 or less, stand on 17 or more');
      end;
      TextColor(15);
      gotoxy(50,24);
      writeln('Press any key to continue');
      repeat until KeyPressed;
      if AD > 16 then Result
      else
      begin
          repeat
      TextColor(10);
      DealACard;
      gotoxy(20,18);
      write('Dealer has drawn');
      TextColor(14);
      write(CARD);
      AD := AD + AA[X];
      TextColor(10);
      write('. Dealer now has ');
      TextColor(14);
      writeln(AD,'       ');
      TextColor(15);
      gotoxy(50,24);
      writeln('Press any key to continue');
      repeat until KeyPressed;
         until AD >= 17;
      if (AD > AP) and (AD < 22) then
      WL := 0 else WL := 1;
      WinLose;
      end;
end;

procedure Adjust;
begin
      for Z := 1 to X do begin
      if AC[Z] = true then AP := AP - 10
      else
      WinLose;
      end;
end;
```

Fig. 7-17. PLAYCARD.BJ asks whether the player wants the dealer to deal another card.

```
{Procedures Play3, Decide, DealPlay2, Play2, DealPlay1, Play1}
{PLAYCARD.BJ  }
```

```
procedure Play3;
begin
        repeat
     DealACard;
     gotoxy(10,10);
     TextColor(12);
     write('Player''s next card is');
     TextColor(11);
     writeln(CARD,'                ');
     AP := AP + AA[X];
     gotoxy(10,12);
     TextColor(12);
     write('Player now has ');
     TextColor(11);
     write(AP);
     if AP > 21 then begin
     TextColor(15);
     gotoxy(50,24);
     writeln('Press any key to continue');
     repeat until KeyPressed;
     Adjust;
     end
     else
     TextColor(10);
     write(' and Dealer has ');
     TextColor(14);
     write(SC);
     TextColor(10);
     writeln(' showing.');
     gotoxy(20,16);
     writeln('                                                   ');
     gotoxy(20,18);
     TextColor(12);
     write('Another card for the Player?  (Y/N)    ');
     readln(Y);
        until UpCase(Y) <> 'Y';
     Stand;
end;

procedure Decide;
begin
     TextColor(12);
     gotoxy(20,16);
     write('Player has ');
     TextColor(11);
     write(AP);
     TextColor(10);
     write(' and Dealer has ');
     TextColor(14);
     write(AA[X]);
     TextColor(10);
     writeln(' showing.');
     gotoxy(20,18);
     TextColor(12);
     write('Another card for the Player?  (Y/N)    ');
     readln(YN);
          case YN of
     'Y','y' : Play3;
     'N','n' : Stand;
```

```
            end;
end;

procedure DealPlay2;
begin
     DealACard;
     TextColor(10);
     gotoxy(10,10);
     write('Dealer''s second card is');
     TextColor(14);
     writeln(CARD,'         ');
     SC := AA[X];
     AD := AD + AA[X];
     if AD = 22 then AD := 12;
     TextColor(15);
     gotoxy(50,24);
     writeln('Press any key to continue');
     repeat until KeyPressed;
     Decide;
end;

procedure Play2;
begin
     DealACard;
     gotoxy(10,10);
     TextColor(12);
     write('Player''s second card is');
     TextColor(11);
     writeln(CARD,'           ');
     AP := AP + AA[X];
     gotoxy(10,12);
     TextColor(12);
     write('Player now has ');
     TextColor(11);
     writeln(AP);
     repeat until KeyPressed;
     if AP = 21 then Bjack else
     if AP = 22 then Adjust else
     DealPlay2;
end;

procedure DealPlay1;
begin
     DealACard;
     TextColor(10);
     gotoxy(10,10);
     write('Dealer''s first card is face down');
     CARD1 := CARD;
     AD := AA[X];
     TextColor(15);
     gotoxy(50,24);
     writeln('Press any key to continue');
     repeat until KeyPressed;
     Play2;
end;

procedure Play1;
begin
     clrscr;
```

```
        gotoxy(20,22);
        TextColor(15);
        writeln('DEALING...');
        Delay(500);
        DealACard;
        gotoxy(10,10);
        TextColor(12);
        write('Player''s first card is');
        TextColor(11);
        writeln(CARD);
        AP := AA[X];
        TextColor(15);
        gotoxy(50,24);
        writeln('Press any key to continue');
        repeat until KeyPressed;
        DealPlay1;
end;
```

21 in two cards (Ace plus 10, Jack, Queen, or King), the player has BLACKJACK, and (unless the dealer also has 21 in two cards) the winnings are 1.5 times the wager. If the dealer also has 21 in two cards, it is called "push," and no money changes hands. The same is true if player and dealer end up with the same number of points. If the player ends up with more than 21 points, the wager is lost, and if the dealer goes over 21 while the player remains under 21, the player wins regardless of the point counts. While the player may elect to stand on any number of points, the dealer, according to the rules, must draw another card if the point count is 16 or less, and may not draw another card if the point count is 17 or more.

As written, the program assumes a color monitor. If yours is a monochrome system, you can simply ignore or eliminate all of the **TextColor(. . .) ;** statements that add color to the game.

A CREDIT CARD REGISTER

The CreditCards (CREDIT.CRD) program, can be used to store credit card numbers. Its print option is useful if you have to submit an entire list of all of your credit cards to, for example, a credit-card protection organization that insure you against charges made on lost or stolen cards.

The program consists of four separate units. The main program declares the variables, presents the main menu, and, prior to the first run of the program, creates a data file called CREDIT.DTA in the procedure Start (Fig. 7-18). The other three are include files. INDATA.CC is used to enter and store data (Fig. 7-19), OUTDATA.CC is used to retrieve and display previously stored data (Fig. 7-20), and HARDCOPY.CC is used to produce the optional printout (Fig. 7-21)

This program, too, was written for a color monitor. If used with a monochrome display, the **TextColor(. . .);** lines can either be ignored or eliminated.

PROGRAMS FOR HOBBYISTS

The program ModelRailroad (MRR.P) (Fig. 7-22) is a collection of 13 subprograms. Six of them are strictly related to model railroading, while the others can be used in a variety of general applications.

The subprograms dealing specifically with model railroading (Figs. 7-23 through 7-27) are contained in the include files LINEAR.MRR, SPEED.MRR, TIME.MRR, SPDDIST.MRR, and DISTSPD.MRR. All of these first call GAUGE.MRR (Fig. 7-28) in order to determine in which of the seven popular scales the conversions are to be conducted. LINEAR.MRR converts linear measures to scale measures or vice versa. SPEED.MRR converts prototype miles per hour to feet per minute in the selected scale. TIME.MRR converts actual time either to time based on

Fig. 7-18. This program keeps a record of credit card numbers. It uses three include files during execution.

```
{Keeping a record of credit card numbers}
{CREDIT.CRD  }

program CreditCards;

var  WHICH                : integer;
     AMEX, VISA, MC, DC : string[20];
     EXX, TEX, MOB, SLL : string[20];
     GLF, CNO, P66      : string[20];
     CB, SR, X1, X2, X3 : string[20];
     OLX1, OLX2, OLX3   : string[20];
     OX1, OX2, OX3, RX1 : string[20];
     RX2, RX3, HX1, HX2 : string[20];
     HX3, HH, SH, HI    : string[20];
     SFA, NMS, BWY, BLD : string[20];
     RS, MW, JCP        : string[20];
     CREDIT             : file of string[20];
     Y                  : char;

{$I INDATA.CC   }
{$I HARDCOPY.CC }
{$I OUTDATA.CC  }

procedure Start;
begin
     clrscr;  gotoxy(1,10);
     TextColor(11);
     writeln('          WARNING!  All previous entries will be erased!');
     writeln;
     write('                         Go ahead? (Y/N) ');
     readln(Y);
            if UpCase(Y) = 'Y' then begin
            assign(Credit,'CREDIT.DTA');
            rewrite(Credit);
            close(credit);
            end
            else
end;

procedure Menu;
begin
     clrscr; gotoxy(1,7);
     TextColor(11);
     writeln('              CREDIT CARD REGISTER');
     writeln('              ********************');
     writeln;
     TextColor(10);
     writeln('                        MENU');
     writeln('                        ----');
     writeln;
     TextColor(12);
     write('        1');
     TextColor(14);
     writeln('      Enter new credit card data');
     writeln;
     TextColor(12);
     write('        2');
```

```
    TextColor(14);
    writeln('     Retrieve credit card data');
    TextColor(11);
    writeln('--------------------------------------------------');
    TextColor(12);
    write('        0');
    TextColor(14);
    writeln('      Exit program');
    TextColor(11);
    writeln('--------------------------------------------------');
    TextColor(12);
    write('        3');
    TextColor(14);
    writeln('      Erase;  start from scratch');
    TextColor(11);
    writeln('--------------------------------------------------');
    TextColor(15);
    write('         Which?            ');
    readln(WHICH);
      case WHICH of
    1 : Enter;
    2 : Retrieve;
    3 : Start;
    0 : end;
end;

begin
    repeat
    menu;
    until WHICH = 0;
end.
```

Fig. 7-19. The first include file, INDATA.CC, is used to enter

```
{Include file used to enter and store data}
{INDATA.CC  }

procedure GeneralPurpose;
begin
    clrscr; gotoxy(1,10);
    TextColor(10);
    writeln('      Enter card numbers for:');
    TextColor(11);
    writeln('------------------------------------------------------');
    TextColor(14);
    write('     American Express?       ');
    readln(AMEX);
    write('     Visa                    ');
    readln(VISA);
    write('     MasterCard              ');
    readln(MC);
    write('     Diner''s Club            ');
    readln(DC);
    write('     Carte Blanche           ');
    readln(CB);
    write('     Discover                ');
    readln(SR);
```

```
    write('     Extra 1                    ');
    readln(X1);
    write('     Extra 2                    ');
    readln(X2);
    write('     Extra 3                    ');
    readln(X3);
          write(Credit,AMEX);
          write(Credit,VISA);
          write(Credit,MC);
          write(Credit,DC);
          write(Credit,CB);
          write(Credit,SR);
          write(Credit,X1);
          write(Credit,X2);
          write(Credit,X3);
    TextColor(11);
    writeln('--------------------------------------------------');
          close(Credit);
end;

procedure Oil;
begin
    clrscr; gotoxy(1,10);
    TextColor(10);
    writeln('     Enter card numbers for:');
    TextColor(11);
    writeln('--------------------------------------------------');
    TextColor(14);
    write('     Exxon                      ');
    readln(EXX);
    write('     Texaco                     ');
    readln(TEX);
    write('     Mobil                      ');
    readln(MOB);
    write('     Shell                      ');
    readln(SLL);
    write('     Gulf                       ');
    readln(GLF);
    write('     Conoco                     ');
    readln(CNO);
    write('     Phillips 66                ');
    readln(P66);
    write('     Extra 1                    ');
    readln(OLX1);
    write('     Extra 2                    ');
    readln(OLX2);
    write('     Extra 3                    ');
    readln(OLX3);
          write(Credit,EXX);
          write(Credit,TEX);
          write(Credit,MOB);
          write(Credit,SLL);
          write(Credit,GLF);
          write(Credit,CNO);
          write(Credit,P66);
          write(Credit,OLX1);
          write(Credit,OLX2);
          write(Credit,OLX3);
     TextColor(11);
```

```
     writeln('--------------------------------------------------------------');
            close(Credit);
end;

procedure Retail;
begin
     TextColor(10);
     writeln('      Enter card numbers for:');
     TextColor(11);
     writeln('--------------------------------------------------------------');
     TextColor(14);
     write('      Saks Fifth Avenue        ');
     readln(SFA);
     write('      Neiman Marcus            ');
     readln(NMS);
     write('      Broadway                 ');
     readln(BWY);
     write('      Bloomingdale''s           ');
     readln(BLD);
     write('      Sears Roebuck            ');
     readln(RS);
     write('      Montgomery Ward          ');
     readln(MW);
     write('      J C Penney               ');
     readln(JCP);
     write('      Extra 1                  ');
     readln(RX1);
     write('      Extra 2                  ');
     readln(RX2);
     write('      Extra 3                  ');
     readln(RX3);
            write(Credit,SFA);
            write(Credit,NMS);
            write(Credit,BWY);
            write(Credit,BLD);
            write(Credit,RX1);
            write(Credit,RX2);
            write(Credit,RX3);
            write(Credit,RS);
            write(Credit,MW);
            write(Credit,JCP);
     TextColor(11);
     writeln('--------------------------------------------------------------');
            close(Credit);
end;

procedure Hotel;
begin
     clrscr; gotoxy(1,10);
     TextColor(10);
     writeln('      Enter card numbers for:');
     TextColor(11);
     writeln('--------------------------------------------------------------');
     TextColor(14);
     write('     Hilton                    ');
     readln(HH);
     write('     Sheraton                  ');
     readln(SH);
     write('     Holiday Inn               ');
```

```
     readln(HI);
     write('     Extra 1                  ');
     readln(HX1);
     write('     Extra 2                  ');
     readln(HX2);
     write('     Extra 3                  ');
     readln(HX3);
          write(Credit,HH);
          write(Credit,SH);
          write(Credit,HI);
          write(Credit,HX1);
          write(Credit,HX2);
          write(Credit,HX3);
          close(Credit);
end;

procedure Other;
begin
     clrscr; gotoxy(1,10);
     TextColor(10);
     writeln('     Enter card numbers for:');
     TextColor(11);
     writeln('----------------------------------------------------------------');
     TextColor(14);
     write('     Other 1                  ');
     readln(OX1);
     write('     Other 2                  ');
     readln(OX2);
     write('     Other 3                  ');
     readln(OX3);
          write(Credit,OX1);
          write(Credit,OX2);
          write(Credit,OX3);
          close(Credit);
end;

procedure Enter;
begin
            assign(Credit,'CREDIT.DTA');
            reset(Credit);
            seek(Credit,FileSize(Credit));
     clrscr; gotoxy(1,7);
     TextColor(10);
     writeln('Enter card numbers for:');
     TextColor(11);
     writeln('-------------------------------');
     TextColor(12);
     write('     1');
     TextColor(14);
     writeln('     General credit cards');
     TextColor(12);
     write('     2');
     TextColor(14);
     writeln('     Oil Company cards');
     TextColor(12);
     write('     3');
     TextColor(14);
     writeln('     Department and retail stores');
     TextColor(12);
```

```
     write('       4');
     TextColor(14);
     writeln('     Restaurants, Hotels, Motels');
     TextColor(12);
     write('       5');
     TextColor(14);
     writeln('     Other');
     TextColor(11);
     writeln('-------------------------------------------------');
     TextColor(15);
     write('     Which?      ');
     readln(WHICH);
        case WHICH of
     1 : GeneralPurpose;
     2 : Oil;
     3 : Retail;
     4 : Hotel;
     5 : Other;
        end;
end;
```

Fig. 7-20. OUTDATA.CC retrieves and displays stored data.

```
{Include file used to retrieve stored data}
{OUTDATA.CC  }

procedure RetAllCardData;
begin
            read(Credit,AMEX);
            read(Credit,VISA);
            read(Credit,MC);
            read(Credit,DC);
            read(Credit,CB);
            read(Credit,SR);
            read(Credit,X1);
            read(Credit,X2);
            read(Credit,X3);
     clrscr; gotoxy(1,10);
     TextColor(10);
     writeln('     Card numbers for:');
     TextColor(11);
     writeln('----------------------------------------------------------');
     TextColor(14);
     writeln('     American Express:          ',AMEX);
     writeln('     Visa                       ',VISA);
     writeln('     MasterCard                 ',MC);
     writeln('     Diner''s Club               ',DC);
     writeln('     Carte Blanche              ',CB);
     writeln('     Discover                   ',SR);
     writeln('     Extra 1                    ',X1);
     writeln('     Extra 2                    ',X2);
     writeln('     Extra 3                    ',X3);
     TextColor(11);
     writeln('----------------------------------------------------------');
     repeat until KeyPressed;
            read(Credit,EXX);
            read(Credit,TEX);
            read(Credit,MOB);
```

```
       read(Credit,SLL);
       read(Credit,GLF);
       read(Credit,CNO);
       read(Credit,P66);
       read(Credit,OLX1);
       read(Credit,OLX2);
       read(Credit,OLX3);
clrscr; gotoxy(1,10);
TextColor(10);
writeln('     Card numbers for:');
TextColor(11);
writeln('-------------------------------------------------------');
TextColor(14);
writeln('     Exxon                    ',EXX);
writeln('     Texaco                   ',TEX);
writeln('     Mobil                    ',MOB);
writeln('     Shell                    ',SLL);
writeln('     Gulf                     ',GLF);
writeln('     Conoco                   ',CNO);
writeln('     Phillips 66              ',P66);
writeln('     Extra 1                  ',OLX1);
writeln('     Extra 2                  ',OLX2);
writeln('     Extra 3                  ',OLX3);
TextColor(11);
writeln('-------------------------------------------------------');
repeat until KeyPressed;
clrscr; gotoxy(1,10);
       read(Credit,SFA);
       read(Credit,NMS);
       read(Credit,BWY);
       read(Credit,BLD);
       read(Credit,RX1);
       read(Credit,RX2);
       read(Credit,RX3);
       read(Credit,RS);
       read(Credit,MW);
       read(Credit,JCP);
TextColor(10);
writeln('      Card numbers for:');
TextColor(11);
writeln('-------------------------------------------------------');
TextColor(14);
writeln('      Saks Fifth Avenue       ',SFA);
writeln('      Neiman Marcus           ',NMS);
writeln('      Broadway                ',BWY);
writeln('      Bloomingdale''s          ',BLD);
writeln('      Sears Roebuck           ',RS);
writeln('      Montgomery Ward         ',MW);
writeln('      J C Penney              ',JCP);
writeln('      Extra 1                 ',RX1);
writeln('      Extra 2                 ',RX2);
writeln('      Extra 3                 ',RX3);
TextColor(11);
writeln('-------------------------------------------------------');
repeat until KeyPressed;
     read(Credit,HH);
     read(Credit,SH);
     read(Credit,HI);
     read(Credit,HX1);
```

```
          read(Credit,HX2);
          read(Credit,HX3);
     clrscr; gotoxy(1,10);
     TextColor(10);
     writeln('     Card numbers for:');
     TextColor(11);
     writeln('-------------------------------------------------------');
     TextColor(14);
     writeln('     Hilton                     ',HH);
     writeln('     Sheraton                   ',SH);
     writeln('     Holiday Inn                ',HI);
     writeln('     Extra 1                    ',HX1);
     writeln('     Extra 2                    ',HX2);
     writeln('     Extra 3                    ',HX3);
     repeat until KeyPressed;
          read(Credit,OX1);
          read(Credit,OX2);
          read(Credit,OX3);
     clrscr; gotoxy(1,10);
     TextColor(10);
     writeln('     Retrieve card numbers for:');
     TextColor(11);
     writeln('-------------------------------------------------------');
     TextColor(14);
     writeln('     Other 1                    ',OX1);
     writeln('     Other 2                    ',OX2);
     writeln('     Other 3                    ',OX3);
     repeat until KeyPressed;
          close(Credit);
end;

procedure Retrieve;
begin
            assign(Credit,'CREDIT.DTA');
            reset(Credit);
     clrscr; gotoxy(1,7);
     TextColor(10);
     writeln('Retrieve all card numbers ');
     TextColor(11);
     writeln('-----------------------------');
     TextColor(12);
     write('     1');
     TextColor(14);
     writeln('     Display all');
     TextColor(12);
     write('     2');
     TextColor(14);
     writeln('     Print all');
     TextColor(11);
     writeln('--------------------------------------------');
     TextColor(15);
     write('     Which?      ');
     readln(WHICH);
        case WHICH of
     1 : RetAllCardData;
     2 : RetPrint;
        end;
end;
```

Fig. 7-21. HARDCOPY.CC produces a hard copy of the stored data.

```
{This include file retrieves and prints all data}
{HARDCOPY.CC  }

procedure RetPrint;
begin
          read(Credit,AMEX);
          read(Credit,VISA);
          read(Credit,MC);
          read(Credit,DC);
          read(Credit,CB);
          read(Credit,SR);
          read(Credit,X1);
          read(Credit,X2);
          read(Credit,X3);
    writeln(Lst,'     American Express:         ',AMEX);
    writeln(Lst,'     Visa                      ',VISA);
    writeln(Lst,'     MasterCard                ',MC);
    writeln(Lst,'     Diner''s Club              ',DC);
    writeln(Lst,'     Carte Blanche             ',CB);
    writeln(Lst,'     Discover                  ',SR);
    writeln(Lst,'     Extra 1                   ',X1);
    writeln(Lst,'     Extra 2                   ',X2);
    writeln(Lst,'     Extra 3                   ',X3);
    writeln(Lst,'---------------------------------------------------');
          read(Credit,EXX);
          read(Credit,TEX);
          read(Credit,MOB);
          read(Credit,SLL);
          read(Credit,GLF);
          read(Credit,CNO);
          read(Credit,P66);
          read(Credit,OLX1);
          read(Credit,OLX2);
          read(Credit,OLX3);
    writeln(Lst,'     Exxon                     ',EXX);
    writeln(Lst,'     Texaco                    ',TEX);
    writeln(Lst,'     Mobil                     ',MOB);
    writeln(Lst,'     Shell                     ',SLL);
    writeln(Lst,'     Gulf                      ',GLF);
    writeln(Lst,'     Conoco                    ',CNO);
    writeln(Lst,'     Phillips 66               ',P66);
    writeln(Lst,'     Extra 1                   ',OLX1);
    writeln(Lst,'     Extra 2                   ',OLX2);
    writeln(Lst,'     Extra 3                   ',OLX3);
    writeln(Lst,'---------------------------------------------------');
          read(Credit,SFA);
          read(Credit,NMS);
          read(Credit,BWY);
          read(Credit,BLD);
          read(Credit,RX1);
          read(Credit,RX2);
          read(Credit,RX3);
          read(Credit,RS);
          read(Credit,MW);
          read(Credit,JCP);
    writeln(Lst,'     Saks Fifth Avenue         ',SFA);
    writeln(Lst,'     Neiman Marcus             ',NMS);
```

```
    writeln(Lst,'     Broadway                         ',BWY);
    writeln(Lst,'     Bloomingdale''s                   ',BLD);
    writeln(Lst,'     Sears Roebuck                    ',RS);
    writeln(Lst,'     Montgomery Ward                  ',MW);
    writeln(Lst,'     J C Penney                       ',JCP);
    writeln(Lst,'     Extra 1                          ',RX1);
    writeln(Lst,'     Extra 2                          ',RX2);
    writeln(Lst,'     Extra 3                          ',RX3);
    writeln(Lst,'-------------------------------------------------------');
         read(Credit,HH);
         read(Credit,SH);
         read(Credit,HI);
         read(Credit,HX1);
         read(Credit,HX2);
         read(Credit,HX3);
    writeln(Lst,'     Hilton                           ',HH);
    writeln(Lst,'     Sheraton                         ',SH);
    writeln(Lst,'     Holiday Inn                      ',HI);
    writeln(Lst,'     Extra 1                          ',HX1);
    writeln(Lst,'     Extra 2                          ',HX2);
    writeln(Lst,'     Extra 3                          ',HX3);
         read(Credit,OX1);
         read(Credit,OX2);
         read(Credit,OX3);
    writeln(Lst,'     Other 1                          ',OX1);
    writeln(Lst,'     Other 2                          ',OX2);
    writeln(Lst,'     Other 3                          ',OX3);
         close(Credit);
end;
```

Fig. 7-22. This program is actually a collection of 12 programs primarily for use by hobbyists.

```
{A selection of programs for model railroad hobbyists}
{MRR.P  }

program ModelRailroad;

var WHICH          : integer;
    RET            : char;
    G              : real;

{$I GAUGE.MRR     }
{$I LINEAR.MRR    }
{$I SPEED.MRR     }
{$I TIME.MRR      }
{$I CLOCK.MRR     }
{$I SPDDIST.MRR   }
{$I DISTSPD.MRR   }
{$I ELEV.MRR      }
{$I BEND.MRR      }
{$I OHMS.MRR      }
{$I RESIST.MRR    }
{$I FRACT.MRR     }
{$I GEARSPD.MRR   }

procedure LinearMeasures;
begin
    Scale;
```

```
     PrototypeMeasures;
end;

procedure MphFpm;
begin
     Scale;
     SpeedConversion;
end;

procedure RealTime;
begin
     Scale;
     TimeConversion;
end;

procedure DigitalClock;
begin
     StartDigital;
end;

procedure PrototypeSpeed;
begin
     Scale;
     DetermineSpeed;
end;

procedure DistanceCovered;
begin
     Scale;
     DetermineDistance;
end;

procedure Grade;
begin
     DetermineGradeData;
end;

procedure Curve;
begin
     DetermineCurveLength;
end;

procedure OhmsLaw;
begin
     Electricity;
end;

procedure Wire;
begin
     FindResistance;
end;

procedure FractionDecimal;
begin
     ConversionTable;
end;


procedure Gears;
```

```
begin
     ConvertGearSpeeds;
end;

procedure Menu;
begin
     clrscr;  gotoxy(1,3);
     TextColor(10);
     writeln('                    SELECTION OF PROGRAMS FOR MODEL RAILROADING');
     writeln('                    ~~~~~~~~~~~~~~~~~~~~~~~~~~~~~~~~~~~~~~~~~~~');
     writeln;
     TextColor(12);
     write('          1');
     TextColor(13);
     writeln('     Convert linear measures');
     TextColor(12);
     write('          2');
     TextColor(13);
     writeln('     Convert miles per hour to feet per minute');
     TextColor(12);
     write('          3');
     TextColor(13);
     writeln('     Convert real time to scale time');
     TextColor(12);
     write('          4');
     TextColor(13);
     writeln('     Activate the digital scale-time clock');
     TextColor(12);
     write('          5');
     TextColor(13);
     writeln('     Determine prototype speed by distance covered');
     TextColor(12);
     write('          6');
     TextColor(13);
     writeln('     Determine distance covered by prototype speed');
     TextColor(12);
     write('          7');
     TextColor(13);
     writeln('     Determine grade versus distance');
     TextColor(12);
     write('          8');
     TextColor(13);
     writeln('     Determine length of curve by radius');
     TextColor(12);
     write('          9');
     TextColor(13);
     writeln('     Ohm''s Law (Volt/Ampere/Ohm)');
     TextColor(12);
     write('         10');
     TextColor(13);
     writeln('     Determine resistance of electrical wire');
     TextColor(12);
     write('         11');
     TextColor(13);
     writeln('     Display fraction-to-decimal conversion chart');
     TextColor(12);
     write('         12');
     TextColor(13);
     writeln('     Determine gear speeds');
```

```
     TextColor(11);
     writeln('       ==========================================================');
     TextColor(12);
     write('         0');
     TextColor(13);
     writeln('     Exit program');
     TextColor(11);
     writeln('       ==========================================================');
     TextColor(14);
     write('          Which?      ');
     readln(WHICH);
           case WHICH of
     1 : LinearMeasures;
     2 : MphFpm;
     3 : RealTime;
     4 : DigitalClock;
     5 : PrototypeSpeed;
     6 : DistanceCovered;
     7 : Grade;
     8 : Curve;
     9 : OhmsLaw;
    10 : Wire;
    11 : FractionDecimal;
    12 : Gears;
     0 : end;
end;

begin
     repeat
     Menu;
     until WHICH = 0;
end.
```

Fig. 7-23. This subprogram, LINEAR.MRR, converts linear measures.

```
{Include file for MRR program: Linear measures}
{LINEAR.MRR}

procedure PrototypeMeasures;

var LINEAR       : integer;
    FEET, SCALE : real;

procedure Prototype;
begin
     clrscr;  gotoxy(1,10);
     TextColor(11);
     write('Prototype measure to be converted?    ');
     readln(FEET);
     FEET := FEET / G;
     writeln;
     TextColor(12);
     writeln('Scale measure:                                    ',FEET:5:1);
     TextColor(10);
     gotoxy(60,24);
     writeln('Press any key');
     repeat until KeyPressed;
end;
```

```
procedure Measures;
begin
     clrscr;  gotoxy(1,10);
     TextColor(11);
     write('Scale measure to be converted?        ');
     readln(SCALE);
     SCALE :=SCALE * G;
     writeln;
     TextColor(12);
     writeln('Prototype measure:                      ',SCALE:5:1);
     TextColor(10);
     gotoxy(60,24);
     writeln('Press any key');
     repeat until KeyPressed;
end;

begin
     clrscr;  gotoxy(1,8);
     TextColor(10);
     writeln('          Do you want to convert');
     writeln('          ----------------------');
     TextColor(12);
     write('      1');
     TextColor(13);
     writeln('  Prototype Measures to Scale Measures');
     writeln;
     TextColor(12);
     write('      2');
     TextColor(13);
     writeln('  Scale Measures to Prototype Measures');
     TextColor(11);
     writeln('      ---------------------------------------------');
     TextColor(14);
     write('      Which?     ');
     readln(LINEAR);
          case LINEAR of
     1 : Prototype;
     2 : Measures;
          end;
end;
```

Fig. 7-24. This subprogram converts prototype and scale speeds.

```
{Include file for MRR: Speed conversions}
{SPEED.MRR}

procedure SpeedConversion;

var MPH, FPM : real;

begin
     clrscr;  gotoxy(1,10);
     TextColor(10);
     write(' Enter prototype miles per hour      ');
     readln(MPH);
     writeln;
     FPM := MPH * 5280 / G / 60;
     TextColor(12);
```

```
     write(MPH:3:0,' miles per hour represent ',FPM:5:2,' feet per minute');
     writeln(' in your gauge.');
     TextColor(14);
     gotoxy(60,24);
     writeln('Press any key');
     repeat until KeyPressed;
end;
```

Fig. 7-25. This subprogram converts time.

```
{Include file for MRR: Time conversion}
{TIME.MRR}

procedure TimeConversion;

var TIME, TIME1, TIME2, TIME3, HOURS, MINUTES, PER : real;
    CHOICE                                         : integer;

procedure YourGauge;
begin
     clrscr;  gotoxy(1,8);
     TextColor(10);
     write('Time to be converted (hours.minutes)    ');
     readln(TIME);
     TextColor(12);
     writeln;
     TIME1   := trunc(TIME);
     TIME2   := TIME - TIME1;
     TIME3   := TIME2 / 0.6;
     TIME    := TIME1 + TIME3;
     TIME    := TIME / G;
     HOURS   := trunc(TIME);
     MINUTES := (TIME - HOURS) * 0.6 * 100;
     write('Scale time in your gauge is ',HOURS:2:0,' hours and ');
     writeln(MINUTES:2:0,' minutes');
     TextColor(14);
     gotoxy(60,24);
     writeln('Press any key');
     repeat until KeyPressed;
end;

procedure Percentage;
begin
     clrscr;  gotoxy(1,8);
     TextColor(10);
     write('Time to be converted (hours.minutes)    ');
     readln(TIME);
     writeln;
     write('Enter conversion percentage             ');
     readln(PER);
     TextColor(12);
     writeln;
     TIME1   := trunc(TIME);
     TIME2   := TIME - TIME1;
     TIME3   := TIME2 / 0.6;
     TIME    := TIME1 + TIME3;
     TIME    := TIME * (PER / 100);
     HOURS   := trunc(TIME);
```

```
     MINUTES := (TIME - HOURS) * 0.6 * 100;
     write('Converted time at ',PER:2:0,'% is ',HOURS:2:0,' hours and ');
     writeln(MINUTES:2:0,' minutes');
     TextColor(14);
     gotoxy(60,24);
     writeln('Press any key');
     repeat until KeyPressed;
end;

begin
     clrscr;  gotoxy(1,8);
     TextColor(10);
     writeln('Do you want to convert time according to:');
     writeln('-----------------------------------------');
     writeln;
     TextColor(12);
     write('   1');
     TextColor(13);
     writeln('   your gauge?');
     writeln;
     TextColor(12);
     write('   2');
     TextColor(13);
     writeln('   percentage?');
     TextColor(11);
     writeln('-----------------------------------------');
     TextColor(14);
     write('   Which?      ');
     readln(CHOICE);
         case CHOICE of
     1 : YourGauge;
     2 : Percentage;
         end;
end;
```

Fig. 7-26. SPDDIST.MRR is one of two speed-versus-distance subprograms.

```
{Include file for MRR: determine prototype speed}
{SPDDIST.MRR }

procedure DetermineSpeed;

var FEET, TIME, TIME1, TIME2, SPEED : real;

begin
     clrscr;  gotoxy(1,10);
     TextColor(10);
     write('    Enter distance covered on your pike in feet     ');
     readln(FEET);
     writeln;
     write('    Enter time for that distance in minutes.seconds ');
     readln(TIME);
     TIME1 := trunc(TIME);
     TIME2 := (TIME - TIME1) / 0.6;
     TIME  := TIME1 + TIME2;
     FEET  := FEET * G;
     FEET  := FEET / 5280;
     TIME  := TIME / 60;
```

```
     SPEED := FEET / TIME;
     SPEED := trunc(SPEED + 0.5);
     gotoxy(1,15);
     TextColor(12);
     writeln('    Prototype speed is ',SPEED:3:0,' miles per hour');
     gotoxy(60,24);
     TextColor(11);
     writeln('Press any key');
     repeat until KeyPressed;
end;
```

Fig. 7-27. DISTSPD.MRR is the other speed-versus-distance subprogram.

```
{Include file for MRR: Determine scale distance by prototype speed}
{DISTSPD.MRR }

procedure DetermineDistance;

var SPEED, TIME, TIME1, TIME2, FEET : real;

begin
     clrscr;  gotoxy(1,10);
     TextColor(10);
     write('     Enter prototype speed in miles per hour    ');
     readln(SPEED);
     writeln;
     write('     Enter the time frame in minutes.seconds    ');
     readln(TIME);
     TIME1 := trunc(TIME);
     TIME2 := (TIME - TIME1) / 0.6;
     TIME  := TIME1 + TIME2;
     FEET  := SPEED * 5280 / 60 * TIME / G;
     gotoxy(1,15);
     TextColor(12);
     writeln('     The distance covered on your pike is ',FEET:3:1,' feet');
     gotoxy(60,24);
     TextColor(14);
     writeln('Press any key');
     repeat until KeyPressed;
end;
```

Fig. 7-28. This subprogram is used by model railroaders to determine the gauge to be used in conversion calculations.

```
{Include file for MRR: determines gauge selection}
{GAUGE.MRR }

procedure Scale;

var GAGE : char;

begin
     clrscr;  gotoxy(1,6);
     TextColor(10);
     writeln('This program can be used with any of the seven popular');
     writeln;
     writeln('gauges.          Please select the one you want to use.');
     writeln('______________________________________________________');
     writeln;
```

```
        TextColor(12);
        write('           1');
        TextColor(13);
        writeln('    "O"  gauge');
        TextColor(12);
        write('           2');
        TextColor(13);
        writeln('    "S"  gauge');
        TextColor(12);
        write('           3');
        TextColor(13);
        writeln('    "OO" gauge');
        TextColor(12);
        write('           4');
        TextColor(13);
        writeln('    "HO" gauge');
        TextColor(12);
        write('           5');
        TextColor(13);
        writeln('    "TT" gauge');
        TextColor(12);
        write('           6');
        TextColor(13);
        writeln('    "N"  gauge');
        TextColor(12);
        write('           7');
        TextColor(13);
        writeln('    "Z"  gauge');
        TextColor(11);
        writeln('        ------------------------------------------');
        TextColor(14);
        write('        Which?      ');
        readln(GAGE);
            case GAGE of
        '1' : G := 48;
        '2' : G := 64;
        '3' : G := 76.2;
        '4' : G := 87.1;
        '5' : G := 120;
        '6' : G := 160;
        '7' : G := 220;
            end;
end;
```

the scale being used, or to any percentage of actual time. SPDDIST.MRR and DISTSPD.MRR convert the distances covered by prototype trains in terms of miles per hour, to the distance covered by model trains on the layout, or vice versa.

The other seven subprograms (Figs. 7-29 through 7-35) perform more general functions. CLOCK.MRR converts the computer into a digital timer, operating either in actual time or in any faster or slower time selected by the user. ELEV.MRR performs various computations about grades, such as the distance needed to achieve a given change in elevation at a specified percent grade. BEND.MRR determines the length of a curve based on the radius of that curve and the portion of a full circle represented by it. OHMS.MRR deals with Ohm's Law, determining values for volts, amperes and ohms. RESIST.MRR determines the resistance of electrical wires, based on the length of such wires and wire diameter. FRACT.MRR displays a table in which all fractions from 1/2 to 63/64 are converted to their decimal equivalents. Finally, GEARSPD.MRR determines the difference in revolutions per minute between two shafts driven by gears of different

Fig. 7-29. This subprogram converts your computer into a digital clock.

```
{Include fuile for MRR: digital clock}
{CLOCK.MRR}

procedure StartDigital;

var LIMIT, LIMIT1, LIMIT2, A, B, C, PER : real;
    BBB, CCC, SSS, HHH                  : string[8];
    SPEED, X                            : integer;
    ENT                                 : char;

begin
     A := 0;  B := 0;  C := 0;
     clrscr; gotoxy(1,10);
     TextColor(10);
     writeln('This program converts your screen into a digital clock');
     writeln('-------------------------------------------------------');
     writeln('You may use actual time or you may speed up the time ');
     writeln('to suit your gauge and operating requirements.');
     writeln('-------------------------------------------------------');
     writeln;
     TextColor(13);
     write('Timing Speed? (actual time: approx. 1000)     ');
     readln(SPEED);
     PER := (SPEED / 1000) * 100;
     writeln;
     write('Time limit in scale hours.minutes?            ');
     readln(LIMIT);
     LIMIT1 := trunc(LIMIT);
     LIMIT2 := (LIMIT - LIMIT1) * 100;
     clrscr;  gotoxy(1,10);
     TextColor(12);
     write('         To start the clock, press any key');
     repeat until KeyPressed;
     clrscr; gotoxy(15,2);
     writeln('Selected timing speed is ',PER:3:0,' percent of real time');
     gotoxy(15,4);
     if LIMIT1 = 1 then HHH := 'hour' else HHH := 'hours';
     write('The selected time limit is ',LIMIT1:2:0,' ',HHH,' and ');
     writeln(LIMIT2:2:0,' minutes');
     TextColor(14);
     gotoxy(20,7);
     writeln('_________________________________________');
     for X := 1 to 10 do begin
     gotoxy(20,8 + X);
     write(chr(179));
     gotoxy(60,8 + X);
     writeln(chr(179));
     end;
     gotoxy(1,18);
     writeln('                  _________________________________________');
     repeat
     Delay(SPEED);
     A := A + 1;
     if A = 60 then begin
     A := 0;
     B := B + 1;
     end;
```

```
        if B = 60 then begin
        B := 0;
        C := C + 1;
        end;
        if A = 1 then SSS := 'second' else SSS := 'seconds';
        if B = 1 then BBB := 'minute' else BBB := 'minutes';
        if C = 1 then CCC := 'hour'   else CCC := 'hours';
        TextColor(12);
        gotoxy(35,11);
        writeln(C:2:0,' ',CCC);
        gotoxy(35,13);
        writeln(B:2:0,' ',BBB);
        gotoxy(35,15);
        writeln(A:2:0,' ',SSS);
        until C + (B / 100)= LIMIT;
        TextColor(10);
        gotoxy(60,24);
        writeln('Press any key');
        repeat until KeyPressed;
end;
```

Fig. 7-30. This subprogram deals with elevation and grades.

```
{Include file for MRR: determine grade data}
{ELEV.MRR }

procedure FirstOption;

var PER, DISTANCE, ELEVATION : real;

begin
     clrscr;  gotoxy(1,10);
     TextColor(10);
     write('  Enter the desired percent grade              ');
     readln(PER);
     writeln;
     write('  Enter amount of climb/descent in inches      ');
     readln(ELEVATION);
     DISTANCE := 100 / PER * ELEVATION;
     gotoxy(1,20);
     TextColor(12);
     writeln('  The needed distance is ',DISTANCE:3:1,' inches');
     gotoxy(60,24);
     TextColor(14);
     writeln('Press any key');
     repeat until KeyPressed;
end;

Procedure SecondOption;

var DISTANCE, INCH, PER  : real;

begin
     clrscr;  gotoxy(1,10);
     TextColor(10);
     write('  Enter the available distance in inches             ');
     readln(DISTANCE);
     writeln;
```

```
     write('  Enter the number of inches to climb or descend     ');
     readln(INCH);
     PER := INCH / DISTANCE * 100;
     gotoxy(1,20);
     TextColor(12);
     writeln('  The resulting percent grade is ',PER:2:1,'%');
     gotoxy(60,24);
     TextColor(14);
     writeln('Press any key');
     repeat until KeyPressed;
end;

procedure ThirdOption;

var  DISTANCE, PER, ELEVATION  : real;

begin
     clrscr;  gotoxy(1,10);
     TextColor(10);
     write('  Enter the available distance in inches              ');
     readln(DISTANCE);
     writeln;
     write('  Enter the desired percent grade                      ');
     readln(PER);
     ELEVATION := PER / 100 * DISTANCE;
     gotoxy(1,20);
     TextColor(12);
     write('  The resulting change in elevation is ');
     writeln(ELEVATION:2:1,' inches');
     gotoxy(60,24);
     TextColor(14);
     writeln('Press any key');
     repeat until KeyPressed;
end;

procedure DetermineGradeData;

var GRADE   : integer;

begin
     clrscr; gotoxy(1,10);
     TextColor(12);
     write('   1');
     TextColor(13);
     writeln('   Determine distance by grade percent and elevation change');
     writeln;
     TextColor(12);
     write('   2');
     TextColor(13);
     writeln('   Determine percent grade by distance and elevation change');
     writeln;
     write('  The resulting change in elevation is ');
     writeln(ELEVATION:2:1,' inches');
     gotoxy(60,24);
     TextColor(14);
     writeln('Press any key');
     repeat until KeyPressed;
end;
```

```
procedure DetermineGradeData;

var GRADE   : integer;

begin
     clrscr; gotoxy(1,10);
     TextColor(12);
     write('   1');
     TextColor(13);
     writeln('   Determine distance by grade percent and elevation change');
     writeln;
     TextColor(12);
     write('   2');
     TextColor(13);
     writeln('   Determine percent grade by distance and elevation change');
     writeln;
     TextColor(12);
     write('   3');
     TextColor(13);
     writeln('   Determine elevation change by grade percent and distance');
     TextColor(14);
     write('   -------------------------------------');
     writeln('----------------------------');
     TextColor(10);
     write('   Which?       ');
     readln(GRADE);
         case GRADE of
     1 : FirstOption;
     2 : SecondOption;
     3 : ThirdOption;
         end;
end;
```

Fig. 7-31. This subprogram measures the linear length of a curve.

```
{Include file for MRR: Determine the length of a given curve}
{BEND.MRR }

procedure DetermineCurveLength;

var  RADIUS, CIRCLE, INCH  : real;

begin
     clrscr;  gotoxy(1,10);
     TextColor(10);
     write('  Enter the average radius of the curve in inches  ');
     readln(RADIUS);
     writeln;
     write('  The curve is what percent of a circle?           ');
     readln(CIRCLE);
     CIRCLE := CIRCLE / 100;
     INCH := RADIUS * (2 * 3.14159) * CIRCLE;
     gotoxy(1,16);
     TextColor(12);
     writeln('  The length of that curve is ',INCH:3:1,' inches');
     gotoxy(60,24);
     TextColor(14);
     writeln('Press any key');
     repeat until KeyPressed;
end;
```

Fig. 7-32. This subprogram performs the calculations known as Ohm's Law.

```
{Include file for MRR: Ohm's Law}
{OHMS.MRR }


procedure FindOhms;

var OHM, AMP, VOLT : real;

begin
     clrscr; gotoxy(1,10);
     TextColor(10);
     write('    Enter number of volts      ');
     readln(VOLT);
     writeln;
     write('    Enter number of amperes    ');
     readln(AMP);
     OHM := VOLT / AMP;
     gotoxy(1,16);
     TextColor(12);
     writeln('    The number of Ohms is ',OHM:3:1);
     gotoxy(60,24);
     TextColor(14);
     writeln('Press any key');
     repeat until KeyPressed;
end;

procedure FindAmps;

var OHM, VOLT, AMP  : real;

begin
     clrscr; gotoxy(1,10);
     TextColor(10);
     write('    Enter number of volts      ');
     readln(VOLT);
     writeln;
     write('    Enter number of ohms      ');
     readln(OHM);
     AMP := VOLT / OHM;
     gotoxy(1,16);
     TextColor(12);
     writeln('    The number of Amperes is ',AMP:3:1);
     gotoxy(60,24);
     TextColor(14);
     writeln('Press any key');
     repeat until KeyPressed;
end;

procedure FindVolts;

var OHM, VOLT, AMP : real;

begin
     clrscr; gotoxy(1,10);
     TextColor(10);
     write('    Enter number of ohms        ');
     readln(OHM);
```

```
     writeln;
     write('    Enter number of amperes    ');
     readln(AMP);
     VOLT := AMP * OHM;
     gotoxy(1,16);
     TextColor(12);
     writeln('     The number of Volts is ',VOLT:3:1);
     gotoxy(60,24);
     TextColor(14);
     writeln('Press any key');
     repeat until KeyPressed;
end;

procedure Electricity;

var CHOICE : integer;

begin
     clrscr;  gotoxy(1,10);
     TextColor(12);
     write('   1');
     TextColor(13);
     writeln('         Find Ohms');
     writeln;
     TextColor(12);
     write('   2');
     TextColor(13);
     writeln('         Find Amperes');
     writeln;
     TextColor(12);
     write('   3');
     TextColor(13);
     writeln('         Find Volts');
     TextColor(11);
     writeln('   ------------------------------------------');
     TextColor(10);
     write('   Which?      ');
     readln(CHOICE);
        case CHOICE of
     1 : FindOhms;
     2 : FindAmps;
     3 : FindVolts;
        end;
end;
```

Fig. 7-33. This subprogram calculates the resistance of electrical wire.

```
{Include file for MRR: Wire resistance}
{RESIST.MRR }

procedure FindResistance;

var  WIRE, MILS, OHM : real;

begin
     clrscr; gotoxy(1,10);
     TextColor(10);
     write('   Enter length of wire in inches         ');
```

```
     readln(WIRE);
     writeln;
     write('   Enter diameter of wire in mils        ');
     readln(MILS);
     OHM := 10.4 * WIRE / MILS;
     gotoxy(1,16);
     TextColor(12);
     writeln('   Resistance of that wire is ',OHM:3:1,' ohms');
     gotoxy(60,24);
     TextColor(14);
     writeln('Press any key');
     repeat until KeyPressed;
end;
```

Fig. 7-34. This subprogram displays the decimal equivalents for all fractions from 1/2 to 63/64.

```
{Include file for MRR:  fractions versus decimals}
{FRACT.MRR }

procedure ConversionTable;

var X                  : char;
    A, B, C, D, E, F   :  real;
begin
     A := 1 / 2;
     B := 1 / 4;
     C := 1 / 8;
     D := 1 / 16;
     E := 1 / 32;
     F := 1 / 64;
     clrscr; gotoxy(1,5);
     TextColor(11);
     writeln(' 1/2  = ',A:1:1);
     TextColor(12);
     write('----------------------------------------');
     writeln('------------------------------');
     TextColor(11);
     writeln(' 1/4  = ',B:1:2,'        3/4  = ',B * 3:1:2);
     TextColor(12);
     write('----------------------------------------');
     writeln('------------------------------');
     TextColor(11);
     write(' 1/8  = ',C:1:3,'       3/8  = ',C * 3:1:3);
     writeln('       5/8  = ',C * 5:1:3,'       7/8  = ',C * 7:1:3);
     TextColor(12);
     write('----------------------------------------');
     writeln('------------------------------');
     TextColor(11);
     write(' 1/16 = ',D:1:4,'      3/16 = ',D * 3:1:4);
     write('       5/16 = ',D * 5:1:4,'       7/16 = ',D * 7:1:4);
     write('             9/16 = ',D * 9:1:4,'     11/16 = ',D * 11:1:4);
     writeln('      13/16 = ',D * 13:1:4,'      15/16 = ',D * 15:1:4);
     TextColor(12);
     write('----------------------------------------');
     writeln('------------------------------');
     TextColor(11);
     write(' 1/32 = ',E:1:4,'      3/32 = ',E * 3:1:4);
     writeln('      5/32 = ',E * 5:1:4,'       7/32 = ',E * 7:1:4);
```

```
     write(' 9/32 = ',E *  9:1:4,'       11/32 = ',E * 11:1:4);
     writeln('      13/32 = ',E * 13:1:4,'       15/32 = ',E * 15:1:4);
     write('17/32 = ',E * 17:1:4,'       19/32 = ',E * 19:1:4);
     writeln('      21/32 = ',E * 21:1:4,'       23/32 = ',E * 23:1:4);
     write('25/32 = ',E * 25:1:4,'       27/32 = ',E * 27:1:4);
     writeln('      29/32 = ',E * 29:1:4,'       31/32 = ',E * 31:1:4);
     TextColor(12);
     write('----------------------------------------');
     writeln('------------------------------');
     TextColor(11);
     write(' 1/64 = ',F:1:4,'       3/64 = ',F * 3:1:4);
     writeln('       5/64 = ',F * 5:1:4,'        7/64 = ',F * 7:1:4);
     write(' 9/64 = ',F *  9:1:4,'       11/64 = ',F * 11:1:4);
     writeln('      13/64 = ',F * 13:1:4,'       15/64 = ',F * 15:1:4);
     write('17/64 = ',F * 17:1:4,'       19/64 = ',F * 19:1:4);
     writeln('      21/64 = ',F * 21:1:4,'       23/64 = ',F * 23:1:4);
     write('25/64 = ',F * 25:1:4,'       27/64 = ',F * 27:1:4);
     writeln('      29/64 = ',F * 29:1:4,'       31/64 = ',F * 31:1:4);
     write('33/64 = ',F * 33:1:4,'       35/64 = ',F * 35:1:4);
     writeln('      37/64 = ',F * 37:1:4,'       39/64 = ',F * 39:1:4);
     write('41/64 = ',F * 41:1:4,'       43/64 = ',F * 43:1:4);
     writeln('      45/64 = ',F * 45:1:4,'       47/64 = ',F * 47:1:4);
     write('49/64 = ',F * 49:1:4,'       51/64 = ',F * 51:1:4);
     writeln('      53/64 = ',F * 53:1:4,'       55/64 = ',F * 55:1:4);
     write('57/64 = ',F * 57:1:4,'       59/64 = ',F * 59:1:4);
     writeln('      61/64 = ',F * 61:1:4,'       63/64 = ',F * 63:1:4);
     TextColor(12);
     write('----------------------------------------');
     writeln('------------------------------');
     TextColor(11);
     gotoxy(63,24);
     TextColor(14);
     write('Press any key');
     repeat until KeyPressed;
end;
```

Fig. 7-35. This subprogram calculates the shaft speeds for two shafts driven by gears.

```
{Include file for MRR:  converting gear speeds}
{GEARSPD.MRR }

procedure SmallGear;

var LARGE, SMALL, RPM, LRPM, DIFF : real;

begin
     clrscr;  gotoxy(1,10);
     TextColor(10);
     write('     Enter number of teeth of the larger gear       ');
     readln(LARGE);
     writeln;
     write('     Enter number of teeth on the smaller gear      ');
     readln(SMALL);
     writeln;
     write('     Enter known rpm figure or 100 for large gear  ');
     readln(LRPM);
     DIFF := SMALL / LARGE;
     RPM  := LRPM / DIFF;
```

```
     writeln;
     TextColor(12);
     writeln('     The small gear turns at ',RPM:5:0,' rpm.');
     gotoxy(60,24);
     TextColor(14);
     writeln('Press any key');
     Repeat until KeyPressed;
end;

procedure LargeGear;

var LARGE, SMALL, RPM, SRPM, DIFF : real;

begin
     clrscr;  gotoxy(1,10);
     TextColor(10);
     write('     Enter number of teeth of the larger gear      ');
     readln(LARGE);
     writeln;
     write('     Enter number of teeth on the smaller gear     ');
     readln(SMALL);
     writeln;
     write('     Enter known rpm figure or 100 for small gear  ');
     readln(SRPM);
     DIFF := SMALL / LARGE;
     RPM  := SRPM * DIFF;
     writeln;
     TextColor(12);
     writeln('     The large gear turns at ',RPM:5:0,' rpm.');
     gotoxy(60,24);
     TextColor(14);
     writeln('Press any key');
     Repeat until KeyPressed;
end;

procedure ConvertGearSpeeds;

var Z              : char;

begin
     clrscr;  gotoxy(1,10);
     TextColor(10);
     writeln(' This program determines the difference in rpm between');
     writeln;
     writeln(' shafts driven by gears of different sizes.');
     writeln('-------------------------------------------------------');
     TextColor(10);
     writeln(' If neither rpm is known, enter 100 for either gear');
     writeln;
     write(' Which rpm figure do you want?  L)arger or S)maller ');
     readln(Z);
        case Z of
     'L','l' : LargeGear;
     'S','s' : SmallGear;
        end
end;
```

sizes with different numbers of teeth.

If you have use for some of these programs but not all, it would be a simple matter to write a different main program that asks only for the include files that are applicable to your specific needs.

A VALUE COMPARISON PROGRAM

The program ValueComparison (SPREAD.P, Figs. 7-36 and 7-37) is designed to permit the user to enter known data about up to eight different products, after which the program determines certain results based on these data.

The required inputs are the product name, the cost of the product to the dealer, the resale price, the number sold during any given period, and the commission percentage paid to the salesperson. Based on these data, the program computes the markup percentage, the gross amount received, the total cost, the total paid in commissions, and the profit or loss for each individual product, plus the total number of all products sold, the total gross received, the total commissions paid, the total cost of acquisition, and the total profit or loss.

The resultant display consists of nine vertical and ten horizontal columns, with the headings for the vertical columns reading:

PRODUCT NAME COST PRCE Mup% SOLD GRSS COMM COST PROF

PRCE means price, Mup% stands for the markup percentage, GRSS is gross receipts, COMM holds commissions paid, the second COST represents the total acquisition cost, and PROF indicates profit or loss. The bottom line, the 9th horizontal row, displays the aggregate totals. The program includes an option to have the resultant screen display printed (Fig. 7-38).

Fig. 7-36. This might be called a "poor man's spreadsheet" program. It compares different products based on input.

```
{This program can be used to compare various conditions}
{SPREAD.P    }

program ValueComparison;

{$I TYPEDEF.SYS   }
{$I GRAPHIX.SYS   }
{$I KERNEL.SYS    }

var WHICH, NUM, X : integer;
    Y             : char;
    DtaFile       : file of real;
    NAM           : array[1..8] of string[12];
    SOLD          : array[1..8] of integer;
    COST, PRICE   : array[1..8] of real;
    GRSS, COMM    : array[1..8] of real;
    TCST, PROF    : array[1..8] of real;
    MKUP, PERC    : array[1..8] of real;
    PRC1          : array[1..8] of real;
    TSLD          : integer;
    TGRS, TEXP    : real;
    TPFL, TPRC    : real;

procedure Display;

{$I LAYOUT.SPD   }

begin
     LayoutPage;
```

```
end;

procedure Enter;
begin
     TSLD := 0;
     TPRC := 0;
     TGRS := 0;
     TEXP := 0;
     TPFL := 0;
     clrscr;  gotoxy(1,10);
     TextColor(10);
     write('Enter number of products for which you wish to enter data  ');
     readln(NUM);
     clrscr;
     for X := 1 to NUM do begin
     clrscr;  gotoxy(1,10);
     write('Name of product #',X,' (to 12 characters)      ');
     readln(NAM[X]);
     write('Cost of ',NAM[X],'                 $');
     readln(COST[X]);
     write('Resale price of ',NAM[X],'        $');
     readln(PRICE[X]);
     write('Number of ',NAM[X],' sold?          ');
     readln(SOLD[X]);
     write('Commission percentage?             %');
     readln(COMM[X]);

     MKUP[X] := (PRICE[X] - COST[X]) / COST[X] * 100;
     GRSS[X] := PRICE[X] * SOLD[X];
     PRC1[X] := PRICE[X] * (COMM[X] / 100);
     TCST[X] := (COST[X] + PRC1[X]) * SOLD[X];
     PERC[X] := TCST[X] * (COMM[X] /100);

     PROF[X] := GRSS[X] - TCST[X];
     end;

     writeln('---------------------------------------------------');
     write('Will you want to the results printed?  (Y/N)    ');
     readln(Y);

     for X := 1 to NUM do begin
     TSLD := TSLD + SOLD[X];
     TGRS := TGRS + GRSS[X];
     TEXP := TEXP + TCST[X];
     TPFL := TPFL + PROF[X];
     TPRC := TPRC + PERC[X];
     end;

     Display;
end;

procedure Menu;
begin
     clrscr; gotoxy(1,10);
     TextColor(10);
     writeln('                         MENU');
     TextColor(11);
     writeln('                         ****');
     writeln;
```

```
     TextColor(12);
     write('        1');
     TextColor(14);
     writeln('        Enter data for examination');
     writeln;
     TextColor(11);
     writeln('--------------------------------------------------------------');
     TextColor(12);
     write('        0');
     TextColor(14);
     writeln('        Exit Program');
     TextColor(11);
     writeln('--------------------------------------------------------------');
     writeln;
     TextColor(15);
     write('        Which?      ');
     readln(WHICH);
                    case WHICH of
                    1 : Enter;
                    0 : end;
end;

begin
     repeat
     Menu;
     until WHICH = 0;
end.
```

Fig. 7-37. This is the include file that draws the layout for the spreadsheet on the screen.

```
{Include file to create the page layout}
{LAYOUT.SPD  }

procedure DrawLines;
begin
     DrawLine(20,100,980,100);
     DrawLine(20,105,980,105);
     DrawLine(20,200,980,200);
     DrawLine(20,300,980,300);
     DrawLine(20,400,980,400);
     DrawLine(20,500,980,500);
     DrawLine(20,600,980,600);
     DrawLine(20,700,980,700);
     DrawLine(20,800,980,800);
     DrawLine(20,900,980,900);
     DrawLine(200,20,200,980);
     DrawLine(205,20,205,980);
     DrawLine(300,20,300,980);
     DrawLine(400,20,400,980);
     DrawLine(500,20,500,980);
     DrawLine(600,20,600,980);
     DrawLine(700,20,700,980);
     DrawLine(800,20,800,980);
     DrawLine(900,20,900,980);
     gotoxy(3,2); writeln('PRODUCT NAME');
     gotoxy(19,2); writeln('COST');
     gotoxy(27,2); writeln('PRCE');
     gotoxy(35,2); writeln('Mup%');
```

```
gotoxy(43,2); writeln('SOLD');
gotoxy(51,2); writeln('GRSS');
gotoxy(59,2); writeln('COMM');
gotoxy(67,2); writeln('COST');
gotoxy(75,2); writeln('PROF');

gotoxy(18,4); writeln('$');
gotoxy(26,4); writeln('$');
gotoxy(39,4); writeln('%');
gotoxy(50,4); writeln('$');
gotoxy(58,4); writeln('$');
gotoxy(66,4); writeln('$');
gotoxy(74,4); writeln('$');

gotoxy(3,4);  writeln(NAM[1]);
gotoxy(19,4); writeln(COST[1]:2:2);
gotoxy(27,4); writeln(PRICE[1]:2:2);
gotoxy(35,4); writeln(MKUP[1]:2:1);
gotoxy(43,4); writeln(SOLD[1]);
gotoxy(51,4); writeln(GRSS[1]:2:2);
gotoxy(59,4); writeln(PERC[1]:2:2);
gotoxy(67,4); writeln(TCST[1]:2:2);
gotoxy(75,4); writeln(PROF[1]:2:2);

gotoxy(18,7); writeln('$');
gotoxy(26,7); writeln('$');
gotoxy(39,7); writeln('%');
gotoxy(50,7); writeln('$');
gotoxy(58,7); writeln('$');
gotoxy(66,7); writeln('$');
gotoxy(74,7); writeln('$');

gotoxy(3,7);  writeln(NAM[2]);
gotoxy(19,7); writeln(COST[2]:2:2);
gotoxy(27,7); writeln(PRICE[2]:2:2);
gotoxy(35,7); writeln(MKUP[2]:2:1);
gotoxy(43,7); writeln(SOLD[2]);
gotoxy(51,7); writeln(GRSS[2]:2:2);
gotoxy(59,7); writeln(PERC[2]:2:2);
gotoxy(67,7); writeln(TCST[2]:2:2);
gotoxy(75,7); writeln(PROF[2]:2:2);

gotoxy(18,9); writeln('$');
gotoxy(26,9); writeln('$');
gotoxy(39,9); writeln('%');
gotoxy(50,9); writeln('$');
gotoxy(58,9); writeln('$');
gotoxy(66,9); writeln('$');
gotoxy(74,9); writeln('$');

gotoxy(3,9);  writeln(NAM[3]);
gotoxy(19,9); writeln(COST[3]:2:2);
gotoxy(27,9); writeln(PRICE[3]:2:2);
gotoxy(35,9); writeln(MKUP[3]:2:1);
gotoxy(43,9); writeln(SOLD[3]);
gotoxy(51,9); writeln(GRSS[3]:2:2);
gotoxy(59,9); writeln(PERC[3]:2:2);
gotoxy(67,9); writeln(TCST[3]:2:2);
gotoxy(75,9); writeln(PROF[3]:2:2);
```

```
gotoxy(18,12); writeln('$');
gotoxy(26,12); writeln('$');
gotoxy(39,12); writeln('%');
gotoxy(50,12); writeln('$');
gotoxy(58,12); writeln('$');
gotoxy(66,12); writeln('$');
gotoxy(74,12); writeln('$');

gotoxy(3,12);  writeln(NAM[4]);
gotoxy(19,12); writeln(COST[4]:2:2);
gotoxy(27,12); writeln(PRICE[4]:2:2);
gotoxy(35,12); writeln(MKUP[4]:2:1);
gotoxy(43,12); writeln(SOLD[4]);
gotoxy(51,12); writeln(GRSS[4]:2:2);
gotoxy(59,12); writeln(PERC[4]:2:2);
gotoxy(67,12); writeln(TCST[4]:2:2);
gotoxy(75,12); writeln(PROF[4]:2:2);

gotoxy(18,14); writeln('$');
gotoxy(26,14); writeln('$');
gotoxy(39,14); writeln('%');
gotoxy(50,14); writeln('$');
gotoxy(58,14); writeln('$');
gotoxy(66,14); writeln('$');
gotoxy(74,14); writeln('$');

gotoxy(3,14);  writeln(NAM[5]);
gotoxy(19,14); writeln(COST[5]:2:2);
gotoxy(27,14); writeln(PRICE[5]:2:2);
gotoxy(35,14); writeln(MKUP[5]:2:1);
gotoxy(43,14); writeln(SOLD[5]);
gotoxy(51,14); writeln(GRSS[5]:2:2);
gotoxy(59,14); writeln(PERC[5]:2:2);
gotoxy(67,14); writeln(TCST[5]:2:2);
gotoxy(75,14); writeln(PROF[5]:2:2);

gotoxy(18,17); writeln('$');
gotoxy(26,17); writeln('$');
gotoxy(39,17); writeln('%');
gotoxy(50,17); writeln('$');
gotoxy(58,17); writeln('$');
gotoxy(66,17); writeln('$');
gotoxy(74,17); writeln('$');

gotoxy(3,17);  writeln(NAM[6]);
gotoxy(19,17); writeln(COST[6]:2:2);
gotoxy(27,17); writeln(PRICE[6]:2:2);
gotoxy(35,17); writeln(MKUP[6]:2:1);
gotoxy(43,17); writeln(SOLD[6]);
gotoxy(51,17); writeln(GRSS[6]:2:2);
gotoxy(59,17); writeln(PERC[6]:2:2);
gotoxy(67,17); writeln(TCST[6]:2:2);
gotoxy(75,17); writeln(PROF[6]:2:2);

gotoxy(18,19); writeln('$');
gotoxy(26,19); writeln('$');
gotoxy(39,19); writeln('%');
gotoxy(50,19); writeln('$');
gotoxy(58,19); writeln('$');
```

```
     gotoxy(66,19); writeln('$');
     gotoxy(74,19); writeln('$'):

     gotoxy(3,19);  writeln(NAM[7]);
     gotoxy(19,19); writeln(COST[7]:2:2);
     gotoxy(27,19); writeln(PRICE[7]:2:2);
     gotoxy(35,19); writeln(MKUP[7]:2:1);
     gotoxy(43,19); writeln(SOLD[7]);
     gotoxy(51,19); writeln(GRSS[7]:2:2);
     gotoxy(59,19); writeln(PERC[7]:2:2);
     gotoxy(67,19); writeln(TCST[7]:2:2);
     gotoxy(75,19); writeln(PROF[7]:2:2);

     gotoxy(18,22); writeln('$');
     gotoxy(26,22); writeln('$');
     gotoxy(39,22); writeln('%');
     gotoxy(50,22); writeln('$');
     gotoxy(58,22); writeln('$');
     gotoxy(66,22); writeln('$');
     gotoxy(74,22); writeln('$');

     gotoxy(3,22);  writeln(NAM[8]);
     gotoxy(19,22); writeln(COST[8]:2:2);
     gotoxy(27,22); writeln(PRICE[8]:2:2);
     gotoxy(35,22); writeln(MKUP[8]:2:1);
     gotoxy(43,22); writeln(SOLD[8]);
     gotoxy(51,22); writeln(GRSS[8]:2:2);
     gotoxy(59,22); writeln(PERC[8]:2:2);
     gotoxy(67,22); writeln(TCST[8]:2:2);
     gotoxy(75,22); writeln(PROF[8]:2:2);

     gotoxy(50,24); writeln('$');
     gotoxy(58,24); writeln('$');
     gotoxy(66,24); writeln('$');
     gotoxy(74,24); writeln('$');

     gotoxy(43,24); writeln(TSLD);
     gotoxy(51,24); writeln(TGRS:2:2);
     gotoxy(59,24); writeln(TPRC:2:2);
     gotoxy(67,24); writeln(TEXP:2:2);
     gotoxy(75,24); writeln(TPFL:2:2);

     repeat until KeyPressed;

     if UpCase(Y) = 'Y' then HardCopy(false,1)
     else
end;

procedure LayoutPage;

const MaxWorldX : real = 1000.0;
      MaxWorldY : real = 1000.0;

begin
     InitGraphic;
     DefineWorld(1,0,MaxWorldY,MaxWorldX,0);
     SetForegroundColor(11);
     SelectWorld(1);
     SelectWindow(1);
```

```
        DrawBorder;
        DrawLines;
        LeaveGraphic;
end;
```

ROULETTE

Roulette (R.P), shown in Figs. 7-39 and 7-40, permits you to try your luck in roulette against the house. It starts by offering you a number of choices. You may bet on one, two, three, or four numbers, on one of three rows of numbers, or on black or red or odd or even. These last two happen to be the same, because all odd numbers are red and all even numbers are black. Once you've made your selection, the program continues by drawing a representation of the roulette table layout, asking the amount you wish to wager and the manner in which you want to place your bet (Fig. 7-41). After that's been done, it displays the winning number. Then, when any key is pressed, it displays the amount of your winnings or losses.

The rules are as follows:

You may choose to place your bet on a single number. If that number comes up, your winnings are 35 to 1. If you place your bet on two adjoining numbers, and either number comes up, your winnings are 17 to one. If you place your bet on the bottom edge of any number in the bottom row, you're actually betting on three numbers. For instance, if you place your bet on the edge of 10, you're betting on 10, 11 and 12. If any of those numbers come up, you're paid

Fig. 7-38. This is a sample spreadsheet printout with arbitrary figures.

PRODUCT NAME	COST	PRCE	Mup%	SOLD	GRSS	COMM	COST	PROF
NUTS	$0.03	$0.05	66.7%	66	$3.30	$0.23	$2.31	$0.99
BOLTS	$0.06	$0.10	66.7%	49	$4.90	$0.34	$3.43	$1.47
WIDGETS	$1.05	$1.95	85.7%	27	$52.65	$3.36	$33.61	$19.04
GADGETS	$0.67	$1.29	92.5%	37	$47.73	$2.96	$29.56	$18.17
GIMMICKS	$0.95	$1.69	77.9%	28	$47.32	$3.13	$31.33	$15.99
GASKETS	$0.08	$0.15	87.5%	51	$7.65	$0.48	$4.84	$2.81
NAILS	$0.05	$0.09	80.0%	95	$8.55	$0.56	$5.60	$2.95
SCREWS	$0.03	$0.05	66.7%	71	$3.55	$0.25	$2.48	$1.07
				424	$175.65	$11.32	$113.18	$62.47

Fig. 7-39. Here is a second gambling program—a roulette game.

```
{Roulette}
{R.P    }

program Roulette;

{$I TYPEDEF.SYS  }
{$I GRAPHIX.SYS  }
{$I KERNEL.SYS   }
{$I WINDOWS.SYS  }

{$I BOARD.R      }

var WHICH, X                                   : integer;
    BET1, BET21, BET22, BET31, BET32, BET33 : string[2];
    BET41, BET42, BET43, BET44, BET5, BET6   : string[2];
    WAGER                                      : real;
    NUMBER                                     : array[0..37] of string[2];
    ENT                                        : char;

procedure WinLose;

label NEXT;

begin
        case WHICH of
     1 : begin
        if BET1 = NUMBER[X] then begin
        gotoxy(30,12);
        TextColor(12);
        writeln('YOU''VE WON $',WAGER * 35:4:2);
        gotoxy(60,24);
        TextColor(14);
        write('Press ENTER    ');
        readln(ENT);
        end
        else
        gotoxy(30,12);
        TextColor(10);
        writeln('YOU LOST $',WAGER:4:2);
        gotoxy(60,24);
        TextColor(14);
        write('Press ENTER     ');
        readln(ENT);
        end;
     2 : begin
        if (BET21 = NUMBER[X]) or (BET22 = NUMBER[X]) then begin
        gotoxy(30,12);
        TextColor(12);
        writeln('YOU''VE WON $',WAGER * 17:4:2);
        gotoxy(60,24);
        TextColor(14);
        write('Press ENTER    ');
        readln(ENT);
        end
        else
        gotoxy(30,12);
        TextColor(10);
```

```
        writeln('YOU LOST $',WAGER:4:2);
        gotoxy(60,24);
        TextColor(14);
        write('Press ENTER       ');
        readln(ENT);
        end;
    3 : begin
        if (BET31 = NUMBER[X]) or (BET32 = NUMBER[X])
                                 or (BET33 = NUMBER[X]) then begin
        gotoxy(30,12);
        TextColor(12);
        writeln('YOU''VE WON $',WAGER * 11:4:2);
        gotoxy(60,24);
        TextColor(14);
        write('Press ENTER      ');
        readln(ENT);
        end
        else
        gotoxy(30,12);
        TextColor(10);
        writeln('YOU LOST $',WAGER:4:2);
        gotoxy(60,24);
        TextColor(14);
        write('Press ENTER       ');
        readln(ENT);
        end;
    4 : begin
        if (BET41 = NUMBER[X]) or (BET42 = NUMBER[X])
        or (BET43 = NUMBER[X]) or (BET44 = NUMBER[X]) then begin
        gotoxy(30,12);
        TextColor(12);
        writeln('YOU''VE WON $',WAGER * 8:4:2);
        gotoxy(60,24);
        TextColor(14);
        write('Press ENTER      ');
        readln(ENT);
        end
        else
        gotoxy(30,12);
        TextColor(10);
        writeln('YOU LOST $',WAGER:4:2);
        gotoxy(60,24);
        TextColor(14);
        write('Press ENTER       ');
        readln(ENT);
        end;
    5 : begin
        if (BET5 = '34')  then X := 1;
        if (BET5 = '35')  then X := 2;
        if (BET5 = '36')  then X := 3;
               case X of
           1 : begin
                          if (NUMBER[X] = '1')
                          or (NUMBER[X] = '4')
                          or (NUMBER[X] = '7')
                          or (NUMBER[X] = '10')
                          or (NUMBER[X] = '13')
                          or (NUMBER[X] = '16')
                          or (NUMBER[X] = '19')
```

```
                       or (NUMBER[X] = '22')
                       or (NUMBER[X] = '25')
                       or (NUMBER[X] = '28')
                       or (NUMBER[X] = '31')
                       or (NUMBER[X] = '34') then begin
gotoxy(30,12);
TextColor(12);
writeln('YOU''VE WON $',WAGER * 2:4:2);
gotoxy(60,24);
TextColor(14);
write('Press ENTER    ');
readln(ENT);
goto NEXT;
end
else
gotoxy(30,12);
TextColor(10);
writeln('YOU LOST $',WAGER:4:2);
gotoxy(60,24);
TextColor(14);
write('Press ENTER     ');
readln(ENT);
end;
  2 : begin            if (NUMBER[X] = '2')
                       or (NUMBER[X] = '5')
                       or (NUMBER[X] = '8')
                       or (NUMBER[X] = '11')
                       or (NUMBER[X] = '14')
                       or (NUMBER[X] = '17')
                       or (NUMBER[X] = '20')
                       or (NUMBER[X] = '23')
                       or (NUMBER[X] = '26')
                       or (NUMBER[X] = '29')
                       or (NUMBER[X] = '32')
                       or (NUMBER[X] = '35') then begin
gotoxy(30,12);
TextColor(12);
writeln('YOU''VE WON $',WAGER * 2:4:2);
gotoxy(60,24);
TextColor(14);
write('Press ENTER    ');
readln(ENT);
goto NEXT;
end
else
gotoxy(30,12);
TextColor(10);
writeln('YOU LOST $',WAGER:4:2);
gotoxy(60,24);
TextColor(14);
write('Press ENTER     ');
readln(ENT);
end;
  3 : begin            if (NUMBER[X] = '3')
                       or (NUMBER[X] = '6')
                       or (NUMBER[X] = '9')
                       or (NUMBER[X] = '12')
                       or (NUMBER[X] = '15')
                       or (NUMBER[X] = '18')
```

```
                                    or (NUMBER[X] = '21')
                                    or (NUMBER[X] = '24')
                                    or (NUMBER[X] = '27')
                                    or (NUMBER[X] = '30')
                                    or (NUMBER[X] = '33')
                                    or (NUMBER[X] = '36') then begin
                 gotoxy(30,12);
                 TextColor(12);
                 writeln('YOU''VE WON $',WAGER * 2:4:2);
                 gotoxy(60,24);
                 TextColor(14);
                 write('Press ENTER     ');
                 readln(ENT);
                 goto NEXT;
                 end
                 else
                 gotoxy(30,12);
                 TextColor(10);
                 writeln('YOU LOST $',WAGER:4:2);
                 gotoxy(60,24);
                 TextColor(14);
                 write('Press ENTER      ');
                 readln(ENT);
                 end;
                 end;
        NEXT:
        end;
             6 : begin
                    case BET6 of
                 'R','r','O','o' : begin if
                                       (NUMBER[X] = '1')
                                    or (NUMBER[X] = '3')
                                    or (NUMBER[X] = '5')
                                    or (NUMBER[X] = '7')
                                    or (NUMBER[X] = '9')
                                    or (NUMBER[X] = '11')
                                    or (NUMBER[X] = '13')
                                    or (NUMBER[X] = '15')
                                    or (NUMBER[X] = '17')
                                    or (NUMBER[X] = '19')
                                    or (NUMBER[X] = '21')
                                    or (NUMBER[X] = '23')
                                    or (NUMBER[X] = '25')
                                    or (NUMBER[X] = '27')
                                    or (NUMBER[X] = '29')
                                    or (NUMBER[X] = '31')
                                    or (NUMBER[X] = '33')
                                    or (NUMBER[X] = '35') then begin
                 gotoxy(30,12);
                 TextColor(12);
                 writeln('YOU''VE WON $',WAGER:4:2);
                 gotoxy(60,24);
                 TextColor(14);
                 write('Press ENTER     ');
                 readln(ENT);
                 goto NEXT;
                 end
                 else
                 gotoxy(30,12);
```

```
        TextColor(10);
        writeln('YOU LOST $',WAGER:4:2);
        gotoxy(60,24);
        TextColor(14);
        write('Press ENTER     ');
        readln(ENT);
        end;
        'B','b','E','e' : begin if
                                      (NUMBER[X] = '2')
                                   or (NUMBER[X] = '4')
                                   or (NUMBER[X] = '6')
                                   or (NUMBER[X] = '8')
                                   or (NUMBER[X] = '10')
                                   or (NUMBER[X] = '12')
                                   or (NUMBER[X] = '14')
                                   or (NUMBER[X] = '16')
                                   or (NUMBER[X] = '18')
                                   or (NUMBER[X] = '20')
                                   or (NUMBER[X] = '22')
                                   or (NUMBER[X] = '24')
                                   or (NUMBER[X] = '26')
                                   or (NUMBER[X] = '28')
                                   or (NUMBER[X] = '30')
                                   or (NUMBER[X] = '32')
                                   or (NUMBER[X] = '34')
                                   or (NUMBER[X] = '36') then begin
        gotoxy(30,12);
        TextColor(12);
        writeln('YOU''VE WON $',WAGER:4:2);
        gotoxy(60,24);
        TextColor(14);
        write('Press ENTER    ');
        readln(ENT);
        goto NEXT;
        end
        else
        gotoxy(30,12);
        TextColor(10);
        writeln('YOU LOST $',WAGER:4:2);
        gotoxy(60,24);
        TextColor(14);
        write('Press ENTER     ');
        readln(ENT);
        end;
      end;
    end;
  end;
end;

procedure Identify;
begin
     NUMBER[0] := '0';
     NUMBER[1] := '1';
     NUMBER[2] := '2';
     NUMBER[3] := '3';
     NUMBER[4] := '4';
     NUMBER[5] := '5';
     NUMBER[6] := '6';
     NUMBER[7] := '7';
```

```
     NUMBER[8] := '8';
     NUMBER[9] := '9';
     NUMBER[10] := '10';
     NUMBER[11] := '11';
     NUMBER[12] := '12';
     NUMBER[13] := '13';
     NUMBER[14] := '14';
     NUMBER[15] := '15';
     NUMBER[16] := '16';
     NUMBER[17] := '17';
     NUMBER[18] := '18';
     NUMBER[19] := '19';
     NUMBER[20] := '20';
     NUMBER[21] := '21';
     NUMBER[22] := '22';
     NUMBER[23] := '23';
     NUMBER[24] := '24';
     NUMBER[25] := '25';
     NUMBER[26] := '26';
     NUMBER[27] := '27';
     NUMBER[28] := '28';
     NUMBER[29] := '29';
     NUMBER[30] := '30';
     NUMBER[31] := '31';
     NUMBER[32] := '32';
     NUMBER[33] := '33';
     NUMBER[34] := '34';
     NUMBER[35] := '35';
     NUMBER[36] := '36';
     NUMBER[37] := '00';
end;


procedure Decision;
begin
     randomize;
     X := random(38);
     Identify;
     Delay(1000);
     gotoxy(40,22);
     writeln('The winning number is: ',NUMBER[X]);
     gotoxy(60,24);
     writeln('Press any key');
     repeat until KeyPressed;
     LeaveGraphic;
     WinLose;
end;

procedure AmountOfWager;
begin
     gotoxy(5,16);
     write('How much do you wish to wager?    $');
     readln(WAGER);
end;

procedure OneNumber;
begin
     Table;
     AmountOfWager;
```

```
     gotoxy(5,20);
     write('Place your bet (any one number)    ');
     readln(BET1);
     Decision;
end;

procedure TwoNumbers;
begin
     Table;
     AmountOfWager;
     gotoxy(5,18);
     writeln('Bet on any two adjoining numbers');
     gotoxy(5,20);
     write('First number?  ');
     read(BET21);
     write('  Second number?  ');
     readln(BET22);
     Decision;
end;

procedure ThreeNumbers;
begin
     Table;
     AmountOfWager;
     gotoxy(5,18);
     writeln('Place bet on any number, bottom row');
     gotoxy(5,20);
     write('Number in bottom row?  ');
     readln(BET31);
     if BET31 = '1' then begin BET32 := '2'; BET33 := '3'; end;
     if BET31 = '4' then begin BET32 := '5'; BET33 := '6'; end;
     if BET31 = '7' then begin BET32 := '8'; BET33 := '9'; end;
     if BET31 = '10' then begin BET32 := '11'; BET33 := '12'; end;
     if BET31 = '13' then begin BET32 := '14'; BET33 := '15'; end;
     if BET31 = '16' then begin BET32 := '17'; BET33 := '18'; end;
     if BET31 = '19' then begin BET32 := '20'; BET33 := '21'; end;
     if BET31 = '22' then begin BET32 := '17'; BET33 := '24'; end;
     if BET31 = '25' then begin BET32 := '26'; BET33 := '27'; end;
     if BET31 = '28' then begin BET32 := '29'; BET33 := '30'; end;
     if BET31 = '31' then begin BET32 := '32'; BET33 := '33'; end;
     if BET31 = '34' then begin BET32 := '35'; BET33 := '36'; end;
     Decision;
end;

procedure FourNumbers;
begin
     Table;
     AmountOfWager;
     gotoxy(5,18);
     writeln('Bet on any four adjoining numbers');
     gotoxy(5,20);
     write('1st number? ');
     read(BET41);
     write('  2nd number? ');
     read(BET42);
     write('  3rd number? ');
     read(BET43);
     write('  4th number? ');
     readln(BET44);
```

```
     Decision;
end;

procedure RedBlack;
begin
     Table;
     AmountOfWager;
     gotoxy(5,20);
     write('Bet on R)ed or B)lack or O)dd or E)ven?    ');
     readln(BET6);
     Decision;
end;

procedure OneRow;
begin
     Table;
     AmountOfWager;
     gotoxy(5,20);
     write('Place your bet on 34, 35 or 36 for the row    ');
     readln(BET5);
     Decision;
end;

procedure Play;
begin
         repeat
     clrscr;  gotoxy(1,10);
     TextColor(9);
     writeln('                You have the following choices:');
     writeln('                -------------------------------');
     TextColor(12);
     write('        1');
     TextColor(9);
     writeln('        Play one number              (Odds: 35:1)');
     TextColor(12);
     write('        2');
     TextColor(9);
     writeln('        Play two numbers             (Odds: 17:1)');
     TextColor(12);
     write('        3');
     TextColor(9);
     writeln('        Play three numbers           (Odds: 11:1)');
     TextColor(12);
     write('        4');
     TextColor(9);
     writeln('        Play four numbers            (Odds:  7:1)');
     TextColor(12);
     write('        5');
     TextColor(9);
     writeln('        One row, 12 numbers          (Odds:  2:1)');
     TextColor(12);
     write('        6');
     TextColor(9);
     writeln('        Play red/black or odd/even  (Odds:  1:1)');
     TextColor(11);
     write('       -----------------------------');
     writeln('-------------------------------------');
     TextColor(12);
     write('        0');
```

```
     TextColor(9);
     writeln('       Quit the game');
     TextColor(11);
     write('       -----------------------------');
     writeln('----------------------------------');
     TextColor(14);
     write('        Which?              ');
     readln(WHICH);
           case WHICH of
       1 : OneNumber;
       2 : TwoNumbers;
       3 : ThreeNumbers;
       4 : FourNumbers;
       5 : OneRow;
       6 : RedBlack;
       0 : end;
           until WHICH = 0;
end;

procedure Menu;
begin
     clrscr;  gotoxy(1,10);
     TextColor(12);
     writeln('                                ROULETTE');
     writeln('                                ++++++++');
     writeln;
     write('            1');
     TextColor(10);
     writeln('            Start the game');
     writeln;
     TextColor(12);
     write('            0');
     TextColor(10);
     writeln('            Exit the program');
     writeln;
     TextColor(12);
     writeln('           -------------------------------------------------');
     TextColor(14);
     write('           Which?         ');
     readln(WHICH);
           case WHICH of
       1 : Play;
       0 : end;
end;


begin
     repeat
     Menu;
     until WHICH = 0;
end.
```

Fig. 7-40. The include file BOARD.R produces the roulette table display.

```
{Roulette Table Layout}
{BOARD.R   }

procedure DrawLines;
```

```
begin
     DrawLine(50,190,970,190);
     DrawLine(50,130,970,130);
     DrawLine(50,70,970,70);
     DrawLine(50,10,970,10);
     DrawLine(50,190,50,10);
     DrawLine(970,190,970,10);
     DrawLine(10,160,50,160);
     DrawLine(10,100,50,100);
     DrawLine(10,40,50,40);
     DrawLine(10,160,10,40);
     DrawLine(100,10,100,190);
     DrawLine(150,10,150,190);
     DrawLine(200,10,200,190);
     DrawLine(250,10,250,190);
     DrawLine(300,10,300,190);
     DrawLine(350,10,350,190);
     DrawLine(400,10,400,190);
     DrawLine(450,10,450,190);
     DrawLine(500,10,500,190);
     DrawLine(550,10,550,190);
     DrawLine(600,10,600,190);

     DrawTextW(61,170,1,'RED');
     DrawTextW(61,150,1,' 3 ');
     DrawTextW(110,170,1,'BLACK');
     DrawTextW(110,150,1,'  6  ');
     DrawTextW(161,170,1,'RED');
     DrawTextW(161,150,1,' 9 ');
     DrawTextW(210,170,1,'BLACK');
     DrawTextW(210,150,1,' 12  ');
     DrawTextW(261,170,1,'RED');
     DrawTextW(261,150,1,' 15');
     DrawTextW(310,170,1,'BLACK');
     DrawTextW(310,150,1,' 18 ');
     DrawTextW(361,170,1,'RED');
     DrawTextW(361,150,1,' 21');
     DrawTextW(410,170,1,'BLACK');
     DrawTextW(410,150,1,' 24');
     DrawTextW(461,170,1,'RED');
     DrawTextW(461,150,1,' 27');
     DrawTextW(510,170,1,'BLACK');
     DrawTextW(510,150,1,' 30');
     DrawTextW(561,170,1,'RED');
     DrawTextW(561,150,1,' 33');
     DrawTextW(610,170,1,'BLACK');
     DrawTextW(610,150,1,' 36');

     DrawTextW(20,140,1,' 0');
     DrawTextW(20,70,1,'0 0');

     DrawTextW(60,110,1,'BLACK');
     DrawTextW(60,90,1,'  2  ');
     DrawTextW(111,110,1,'RED');
     DrawTextW(111,90,1,' 5 ');
     DrawTextW(160,110,1,'BLACK');
     DrawTextW(160,90,1,'  8  ');
     DrawTextW(211,110,1,'RED');
     DrawTextW(211,90,1,' 11');
```

```
     DrawTextW(260,110,1,'BLACK');
     DrawTextW(260,90,1,' 14 ');
     DrawTextW(311,110,1,'RED');
     DrawTextW(311,90,1,' 17');
     DrawTextW(360,110,1,'BLACK');
     DrawTextW(360,90,1,' 20');
     DrawTextW(411,110,1,'RED');
     DrawTextW(411,90,1,' 23');
     DrawTextW(460,110,1,'BLACK');
     DrawTextW(460,90,1,' 26');
     DrawTextW(511,110,1,'RED');
     DrawTextW(511,90,1,' 29');
     DrawTextW(560,110,1,'BLACK');
     DrawTextW(560,90,1,' 32');
     DrawTextW(611,110,1,'RED');
     DrawTextW(611,90,1,' 35');

     DrawTextW(60,50,1,'RED');
     DrawTextW(60,30,1,' 1  ');
     DrawTextW(111,50,1,'BLACK');
     DrawTextW(111,30,1,' 4 ');
     DrawTextW(160,50,1,'RED');
     DrawTextW(160,30,1,' 7  ');
     DrawTextW(211,50,1,'BLACK');
     DrawTextW(211,30,1,' 10');
     DrawTextW(260,50,1,'RED');
     DrawTextW(260,30,1,' 13 ');
     DrawTextW(311,50,1,'BLACK');
     DrawTextW(311,30,1,' 16');
     DrawTextW(360,50,1,'RED');
     DrawTextW(360,30,1,' 19');
     DrawTextW(411,50,1,'BLACK');
     DrawTextW(411,30,1,' 22');
     DrawTextW(460,50,1,'RED');
     DrawTextW(460,30,1,' 25');
     DrawTextW(511,50,1,'BLACK');
     DrawTextW(511,30,1,' 28');
     DrawTextW(560,50,1,'RED');
     DrawTextW(560,30,1,' 31');
     DrawTextW(611,50,1,'BLACK');
     DrawTextW(611,30,1,' 34');

end;

procedure Table;

begin

     InitGraphic;
     SetForegroundColor(11);
     DrawBorder;
     DefineWindow(1,2,20,XMaxGlb-2,YMaxGlb - 100);
     DefineHeader(1,'ROULETTE TABLE');
     SetHeaderOn;
     SelectWindow(1);
     SelectWorld(1);
     DefineWorld(1,0,1000,1000,0);
     DrawBorder;
     DrawLines;
end;
```

Fig. 7-41. A sample printout of the roulette table layout shows some of the prompts displayed by the program.

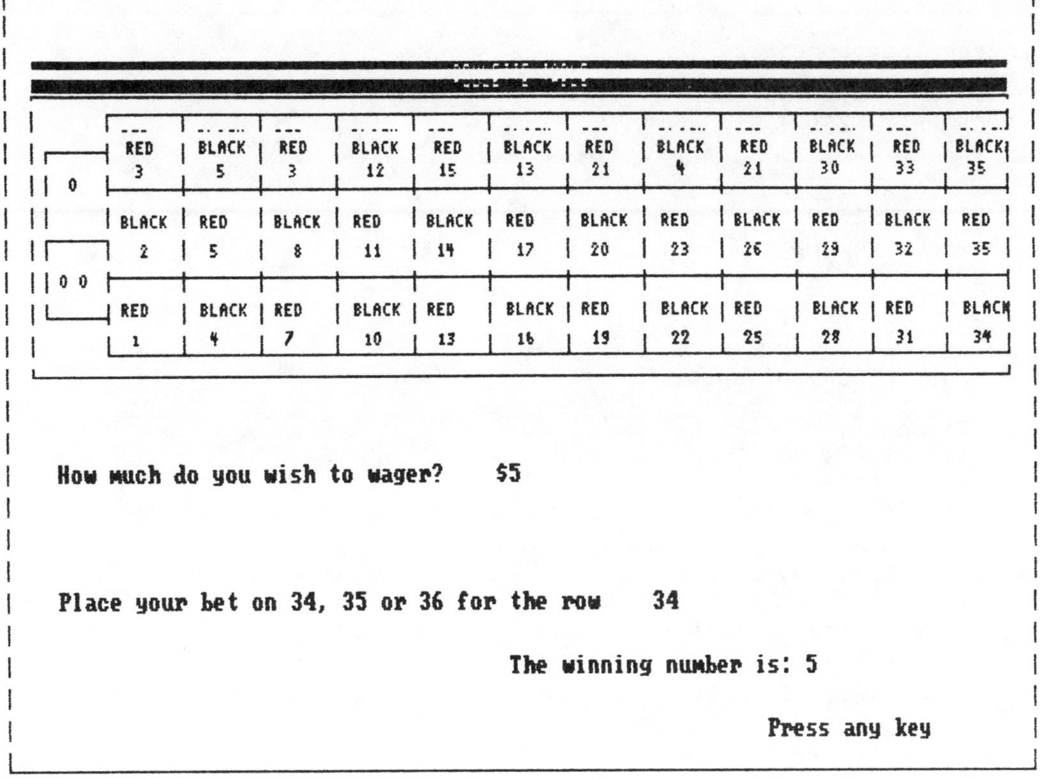

at 11 to 1. If you elect to play four adjoining numbers, the odds are 8 to 1. The odds are reduced to 2 to 1 if you select an entire row of 12 numbers by placing your bet on 34, 35 or 36. And red/black or odd/even simply pay even money. It's a lot of fun, but be prepared to lose your shirt.

FUN WITH TRIGONOMETRY

The Trigonometry program (TRIG.P, Figs 7-42 and 7-43) deals with the lengths of sides and degrees of angles of right triangles. It offers a variety of choices, the first six of which ask that you key in certain values for different variables, automatically producing the correct result. It also displays a right triangle with the sides identified as X (horizontal), Y (vertical) and H (hypotenuse), and the angles identified as A, B and C, where C is the right angle.

The seventh choice also asks that you key in certain values. It then displays the approximate shape of the triangle resulting from those keyed-in values. In addition, you're asked to key in the values of other parameters, and the program checks whether or not your entries are correct. When using this selection, you can repeat each section of it as often as you might like, to produce and examine different triangle shapes resulting from the keyed-in values.

AN ADDRESS PRINTER

The program AdressPrinting, or ADDR.P (Fig. 7-44), prints addresses in four different

Fig. 7-42. This trigonometry program deals with the relationships between the sides and angles of right triangles.

```
{Playing with trigonometric functions}
{TRIG.P    }

program Trigonometry;

{$I TYPEDEF.SYS  }
{$I GRAPHIX.SYS  }
{$I KERNEL.SYS   }

var X, Y, H : real;
    A, B, C : real;
    ENT     : char;
    WHICH   : integer;

{$I TRIGPIC.PG   }

procedure FindHypotenuse;
begin
     Triangle;
     gotoxy(22,14);
     writeln('X');
     gotoxy(42,8);
     writeln('Y');
     gotoxy(22,6);
     writeln('H');
     gotoxy(10,18);
     write('Enter length of side X           ');
     readln(X);
     gotoxy(10,20);
     write('Enter length of side Y           ');
     readln(Y);
     gotoxy(10,22);
     H := SQRT(SQR(X) + SQR(Y));
     writeln('The length of side H : ',H:4:2,' measures.');
     gotoxy(60,24);
     writeln('Press any key');
     repeat until KeyPressed;
     LeaveGraphic;
end;

procedure FindX;
begin
     Triangle;
     gotoxy(22,14);
     writeln('X');
     gotoxy(42,8);
     writeln('Y');
     gotoxy(22,6);
     writeln('H');
     gotoxy(10,18);
     write('Enter length of side H           ');
     readln(H);
     gotoxy(10,20);
     write('Enter length of side Y           ');
     readln(Y);
     gotoxy(10,22);
     X := SQRT(SQR(H) - SQR(Y));
```

```
        writeln('The length of side X : ',X:4:2,' measures.');
        gotoxy(60,24);
        writeln('Press any key');
        repeat until KeyPressed;
        LeaveGraphic;
end;

procedure FindY;
begin
        Triangle;
        gotoxy(22,14);
        writeln('X');
        gotoxy(42,8);
        writeln('Y');
        gotoxy(22,6);
        writeln('H');
        gotoxy(10,18);
        write('Enter length of side H          ');
        readln(H);
        gotoxy(10,20);
        write('Enter length of side X          ');
        readln(X);
        gotoxy(10,22);
        Y := SQRT(SQR(H) - SQR(X));
        writeln('The length of side Y : ',Y:4:2,' measures.');
        gotoxy(60,24);
        writeln('Press any key');
        repeat until KeyPressed;
        LeaveGraphic;
end;

procedure FindAngles;
begin
        Triangle;
        gotoxy(40,2);
        writeln('A');
        gotoxy(40,14);
        writeln('C');
        gotoxy(4,13);
        writeln('B');
        gotoxy(10,18);
        write('Enter degrees of angle A          ');
        readln(A);
        gotoxy(10,20);
        B := 90 - A;
        writeln('The degrees of angle B : ',B:2:2);
        gotoxy(60,24);
        writeln('Press any key');
        repeat until KeyPressed;
        LeaveGraphic;
        Triangle;
        gotoxy(40,2);
        writeln('A');
        gotoxy(40,14);
        writeln('C');
        gotoxy(4,13);
        writeln('B');
        gotoxy(10,18);
```

```
     write('Enter degrees of angle B          ');
     readln(A);
     gotoxy(10,20);
     A := 90 - B;
     writeln('The degrees of angle A : ',A:2:2);
     gotoxy(60,24);
     writeln('Press any key');
     repeat until KeyPressed;
     LeaveGraphic;
end;

procedure FindSides;
begin
     Triangle;
     gotoxy(40,2);
     writeln('A');
     gotoxy(40,14);
     writeln('C');
     gotoxy(4,13);
     writeln('B');
     gotoxy(22,14);
     writeln('X');
     gotoxy(42,8);
     writeln('Y');
     gotoxy(22,6);
     writeln('H');
     gotoxy(10,18);
     write('Enter degrees of angle A          ');
     readln(A);
     gotoxy(10,20);
     write('Enter length of side H            ');
     readln(H);
     gotoxy(10,22);
     Y := H * SIN(A); X := H * COS(A); B := 90 - A;
     writeln('Side X: ',X:4:2,'  side Y: ',Y:4:2);
     gotoxy(10,23);
     writeln('The degrees of angle B: ',B:2:2);
     gotoxy(60,24);
     writeln('Press any key');
     repeat until KeyPressed;
     LeaveGraphic;
end;

procedure FindHypotenuseAndAngles;

const PI = 3.14159;

begin
     Triangle;
     gotoxy(40,2);
     writeln('A');
     gotoxy(40,14);
     writeln('C');
     gotoxy(4,13);
     writeln('B');
     gotoxy(22,14);
     writeln('X');
     gotoxy(42,8);
     writeln('Y');
```

```
     gotoxy(22,6);
     writeln('H');
     gotoxy(10,18);
     write('Enter length of side X          ');
     readln(X);
     gotoxy(10,20);
     write('Enter length of side Y            ');
     readln(Y);
     gotoxy(10,22);
     H := SQRT(SQR(X) + SQR(Y));
     B := ArcTan(X/Y); B := B * (180 / PI);
     A := 90 - B;
     writeln('Side H: ',H:4:2);
     gotoxy(10,23);
     writeln('The degrees of angle A: ',A:2:2,' and angle B: ',B:2:2);
     gotoxy(60,24);
     writeln('Press any key');
     repeat until KeyPressed;
     LeaveGraphic;
end;

procedure Exercise5;

const PI = 3.14159;

var HH, HA, HB : real;

begin
          repeat
     clrscr; gotoxy(1,10);
     TextColor(10);
     write('Enter a length for side X (horizontal)     ');
     readln(X);
     write('Enter a length for side Y (vertical)       ');
     readln(Y);
     H := SQRT(SQR(X) + SQR(Y));
     B := ArcTan(X/Y); B := B * (180 / PI);
     A := 90 - B;
     PrintResult;
     gotoxy(50,10);
     write('Length of side H?  ');
     readln(HH);
     gotoxy(50,12);
     write('Degrees, angle A?  ');
     readln(HA);
     gotoxy(50,14);
     write('Degrees, angle B?  ');
     readln(HB);
     gotoxy(50,16);
     if (HH = trunc(H + 0.5))
     and
     (HA = trunc(A + 0.5))
     and (HB = trunc(B + 0.5))  then writeln('That''s right!')
     else writeln('Sorry, no.');
     gotoxy(50,18);
     writeln('Side H is   ',trunc(H + 0.5):4);
     gotoxy(50,20);
     writeln('Angle A is  ',trunc(A + 0.5):2);
     gotoxy(50,22);
```

```
     writeln('Angle B is  ',trunc(B + 0.5):2);
     gotoxy(60,24);
     writeln('Press any key');
     repeat until KeyPressed;
     LeaveGraphic;
     clrscr; gotoxy(50,22);
     write('Press Q)uit, R)epeat  ');
     readln(ENT);
     until UpCase(ENT) <> 'R';
end;

procedure Exercise4;

var HX, HY, HB  : real;

begin
          repeat
     clrscr; gotoxy(1,10);
     TextColor(10);
     write('Enter a length for side H (hypotenuse)     ');
     readln(H);
     write('Enter degrees of angle A                   ');
     readln(A);
     Y := H * SIN(A);
     X := H * COS(A);
     B := 90 - A;
     PrintResult;
     gotoxy(50,10);
     write('Length of side Y?  ');
     readln(HY);
     gotoxy(50,12);
     write('Length of side X?  ');
     readln(HX);
     gotoxy(50,14);
     write('Degrees, angle B?  ');
     readln(HB);
     gotoxy(50,16);
     if (HY = trunc(Y + 0.5))
     and
     (HX = trunc(X + 0.5))
     and (HB = B)  then writeln('That''s right!')
     else writeln('Sorry, no.');
     gotoxy(50,18);
     writeln('Side Y is  ',trunc(Y + 0.5):4);
     gotoxy(50,20);
     writeln('Side X is  ',trunc(X + 0.5):4);
     gotoxy(50,22);
     writeln('Angle B is ',B:2:0);
     gotoxy(60,24);
     writeln('Press any key');
     repeat until KeyPressed;
     LeaveGraphic;
     clrscr; gotoxy(50,22);
     write('Press Q)uit, R)epeat, C)ontinue  ');
     readln(ENT);
     until UpCase(ENT) <> 'R';
     if UpCase(ENT) = 'C' then Exercise5
     else
end;
```

```
procedure Exercise3;

var HH : real;
begin
        repeat
     clrscr; gotoxy(1,10);
     TextColor(10);
     write('Enter a length for side H (hypotenuse)    ');
     readln(H);
     write('Enter a length for side X (horizontal)    ');
     readln(X);
     Y := SQRT(SQR(H) - SQR(X));
     PrintResult;
     gotoxy(50,10);
     write('Length of side Y?  ');
     readln(HH);
     gotoxy(50,12);
     if HH = trunc(Y + 0.5) then writeln('That''s right!')
     else writeln('Sorry, no. It''s ',trunc(Y + 0.5):4);
     gotoxy(60,24);
     writeln('Press any key');
     repeat until KeyPressed;
     LeaveGraphic;
     clrscr; gotoxy(50,22);
     write('Press Q)uit, R)epeat, C)ontinue  ');
     readln(ENT);
     until UpCase(ENT) <> 'R';
     if UpCase(ENT) = 'C' then Exercise4
     else
end;

procedure Exercise2;

var HH : real;
begin
        repeat
     clrscr; gotoxy(1,10);
     TextColor(10);
     write('Enter a length for side H (hypotenuse)    ');
     readln(H);
     write('Enter a length for side Y (vertical)      ');
     readln(Y);
     X := SQRT(SQR(H) - SQR(Y));
     PrintResult;
     gotoxy(50,10);
     write('Length of side X?  ');
     readln(HH);
     gotoxy(50,12);
     if HH = trunc(X + 0.5) then writeln('That''s right!')
     else writeln('Sorry, no. It''s ',trunc(X + 0.5):4);
     gotoxy(60,24);
     writeln('Press any key');
     repeat until KeyPressed;
     LeaveGraphic;
     clrscr; gotoxy(50,22);
     write('Press Q)uit, R)epeat, C)ontinue  ');
     readln(ENT);
     until UpCase(ENT) <> 'R';
     if UpCase(ENT) = 'C' then Exercise3
```

```
     else
end;

procedure Exercise;

var HH : real;

begin
     repeat
     clrscr; gotoxy(1,10);
     TextColor(10);
     write('Enter a length for side X (horizontal)    ');
     readln(X);
     write('Enter a length for side Y (vertical)      ');
     readln(Y);
     H := SQRT(SQR(X) + SQR(Y));
     PrintResult;
     gotoxy(50,10);
     write('Length of hypotenuse? ');
     readln(HH);
     gotoxy(50,12);
     if HH = trunc(H + 0.5) then writeln('That''s right!')
     else writeln('Sorry, no. It''s ',trunc(H + 0.5):4);
     gotoxy(60,24);
     writeln('Press any key');
     repeat until KeyPressed;
     LeaveGraphic;
     clrscr; gotoxy(50,22);
     write('Press Q)uit, R)epeat, C)ontinue  ');
     readln(ENT);
     until UpCase(ENT) <> 'R';
     if UpCase(ENT) = 'C' then Exercise2
     else
end;

procedure Menu;
begin
     clrscr;  gotoxy(1,3);
     TextColor(10);
     writeln('                    A BIT OF FUN WITH TRIGONOMETRY');
     writeln('                    ~~~~~~~~~~~~~~~~~~~~~~~~~~~~~~');
     writeln;
     TextColor(12);
     writeln('               Find the lengths of the sides of a right triangle');
     writeln('               -------------------------------------------------');
     write('               1');
     TextColor(13);
     writeln('      Find the hypotenuse');
     TextColor(12);
     write('               2');
     TextColor(13);
     writeln('      Find the horizontal length');
     TextColor(12);
     write('               3');
     TextColor(13);
     writeln('      Find the hypotenuse');
     TextColor(12);
     write('               2');
```

```
     TextColor(13);
     writeln('      Find the horizontal length');
     TextColor(12);
     write('             3');
     TextColor(13);
     writeln('      Find the vertical length');
     writeln;
     TextColor(12);
     writeln('                 Find the angles of a right triangle');
     writeln('                 -----------------------------------');
     write('             4');
     TextColor(13);
     writeln('      Find the degrees of the unknown angles');
     TextColor(12);
     writeln;
     writeln('               Find four unknowns based on two knowns');
     writeln('               --------------------------------------');
     write('             5');
     TextColor(13);
     writeln('      Find sides based on hypotenuse and one angle');
     TextColor(12);
     write('             6');
     TextColor(13);
     writeln('      Find hypotenuse and two angles by two sides');
     TextColor(12);
     write('           =========================');
     writeln('==============================');
     write('             7');
     TextColor(13);
     writeln('      Do some exercises');
     TextColor(12);
     write('           =========================');
     writeln('==============================');
     write('             0');
     TextColor(13);
     writeln('      Exit program');
     write('           =========================');
     writeln('==============================');
     TextColor(14);
     write('             Which?         ');
     readln(WHICH);
        case WHICH of
     1 : FindHypotenuse;
     2 : FindX;
     3 : FindY;
     4 : FindAngles;
     5 : FindSides;
     6 : FindHypotenuseAndAngles;
     7 : Exercise;
     0 : end;

end;

begin
     repeat
     Menu;
     until WHICH = 0;
end.
```

Fig. 7-43. The include file for the trigonometry program displays the right triangle.

```
{Include file for trigonometry program, drawing the geometric shape}
{TRIGPIC.PG  }

procedure SetUp;

begin
     InitGraphic;
     DefineWorld(1,0,1000,333,0);
     SetForegroundColor(11);
     DrawBorder;
     SelectWorld(1);
     SelectWindow(1);
end;

procedure Triangle;
begin
     SetUp;
     DrawLine(500,30,500,200);
     DrawLine(100,200,500,200);
     DrawLine(100,200,500,30);
end;

procedure PrintResult;
begin
     SetUp;
     DrawLine(500,30,500,Y * 20);
     DrawLine(500 - (X * 20),Y * 20,500,Y * 20);
     DrawLine(500 - (X * 20),Y * 20,500,30);
end;
```

Fig. 7-44. This program prints address labels in five different styles.

```
{Address Printing Program}
{ADDR.P  }

program AddressPrinting;

{$I NUM10.ADR      }
{$I LRG1.ADR       }
{$I UNPAR.ADR      }
{$I SENDER.ADR     }
{$I PRNTSNDR.ADR   }

var WHICH : integer;

procedure Menu;
begin
     clrscr;  gotoxy(1,10);
     TextColor(10);
     writeln('                          MENU');
     writeln('                          ~~~~');
     writeln;
     TextColor(12);
     write('     1');
     TextColor(13);
     writeln('   Number 10 envelopes (no return address)');
     TextColor(12);
```

```
        write('     2');
        TextColor(13);
        writeln('   Large manila envelope, First Class');
        TextColor(12);
        write('     3');
        TextColor(13);
        writeln('   UPS label');
        TextColor(11);
        writeln('    ----------------------------------------------------');
        TextColor(12);
        write('     4');
        TextColor(13);
        writeln('   Enter or change return address');
        TextColor(11);
        writeln('    ----------------------------------------------------');
        TextColor(12);
        write('     0');
        TextColor(13);
        writeln('   Exit program');
        TextColor(11);
        writeln('    ----------------------------------------------------');
        TextColor(14);
        write('    Which?      ');
        readln(WHICH);
            case WHICH of
        1 : Number10;
        2 : begin
                PrintReturnAddress;
                LargeFirst;
            end;
        3 : begin
                PrintReturnAddress;
                UPS;
            end;
        4 : ReturnAddr;
        0 : end;
end;

begin
        repeat
        Menu;
        until WHICH = 0;

end.
```

formats. Each format is contained in a separate include file which would make it possible for the user to eliminate a format that might not be of use. Conversely, some users might want to add some different formats that could easily be contained in additional include files, requiring only the appropriate **{$I FILERNAME.EXT}** lines in the main program. In addition to writing addresses, the program stores the return address in a separate data file. It is printed automatically for all format selections except the one used with Number 10 envelopes, which are assumed to have the return address preprinted.

The first include file, SENDER.ADR (Fig. 7-45), is used to enter and store the return address. It first displays a warning if a previously stored return address will be erased. If that's fine, the program accepts the return-address data and creates a data file called SNDR.RET to store that return address for future use. If you want to include a company name, simply add the appropriate line and the necessary additional string variable.

PRNTSNDR.ADR (Fig. 7-46) is the include file that prints the return address. If you've added a line to include a company name in the previous include file, be sure to do the same thing here. Also, add that extra string variable.

NUM10.ADR (Fig. 7-47) is the include file that prints addresses on Number 10 envelopes, which include a preprinted return address.

LRG1.ADR (Fig. 7-48) is used to print First Class Mail addresses, including the return address on large manila envelopes. If your large envelopes have a preprinted return address, eliminate the PrintReturnAddress portion in the second selection of the **case WHICH of** portion of the main program.

Finally, UNPAR.ADR (Fig. 7-49) is the include file that prints labels for shipments via United Parcel Service. What was said about preprinted return addresses above, holds true here too.

Fig. 7-45. This include file stores the return address.

```
{Include file to store or change return address}
{SENDER.ADR }

procedure ReturnAddr;

var  Address                : file of string[25];
     NME, ADR, CTY, ST, ZIP : string[25];
     Y                      : char;

begin
     clrscr; gotoxy(1,10);
     TextColor(11);
     writeln('                                          WARNING!');
     writeln('                                          ********');
     writeln;
     writeln('                    The stored return address will be erased!');
     writeln('                    -----------------------------------------');
     writeln;
     TextColor(10);
     write('                  Go ahead?   (Y/N)        ');
     readln(Y);
          if UpCase(Y) = 'Y' then begin
     clrscr;  gotoxy(1,10);
     TextColor(10);
     writeln('Each entry may be up to 25 characters in length');
     writeln;
     TextColor(14);
          repeat
     write('Enter name of sender                         ');
     readln(NME);
     write('Enter street address or P.O.Box              ');
     readln(ADR);
     write('Enter city                                   ');
     readln(CTY);
     write('Enter state name or ID                       ');
     readln(ST);
     write('Enter zip code                               ');
     readln(ZIP);
     writeln('-----------------------------------------------');
     write('Entries correct?  (Y/N)                      ');
     readln(Y);
          until UpCase(Y) = 'Y';
```

```
     assign(Address,'SNDR.RET');
     rewrite(Address);
     write(Address,NME);
     write(Address,ADR);
     write(Address,CTY);
     write(Address,ST);
     write(Address,ZIP);
     close(Address);
     end
     else
end;
```

Fig. 7-46. This include file prints the return address.

```
{Include file that prints the stored return address}
{PRNTSNDR.ADR }

procedure PrintReturnAddress;

var  Address                  : file of string[25];
     NME, ADR, CTY, ST, ZIP : string[25];
     Y                        : char;
     X                        : integer;

begin
     assign(Address,'SNDR.RET');
     reset(Address);
     read(Address,NME);
     read(Address,ADR);
     read(Address,CTY);
     read(Address,ST);
     read(Address,ZIP);
     close(Address);
     writeln(Lst,NME);
     writeln(Lst,ADR);
     writeln(Lst,CTY,', ',ST,' ',ZIP);
         for X := 1 to 10 do
     writeln(Lst,' ');
end;
```

Fig. 7-47. This include file prints addresses for No. 10 envelopes.

```
{Include file to print No. 10 envelopes}
{NUM10.ADR }

procedure Number10;

var  NAM, CMP, POB, CIT, SID, COD : string[50];
     Y                            : char;

begin
     clrscr;  gotoxy(1,10);
          repeat
     TextColor(11);
     write('Enter name of addressee         ');
     readln(NAM);
     write('Enter company                   ');
     readln(CMP);
     write('Enter street address or P.O.B.  ');
```

```
     readln(POB);
     write('Enter city                       ');
     readln(CIT);
     write('Enter State ID or name           ');
     readln(SID);
     write('Enter zip code                   ');
     readln(COD);
     TextColor(10);
     writeln('-------------------------------------------------');
     write('Entries correct?  (Y/N)          ');
     readln(Y);
          until UpCase(Y) = 'Y';
     writeln(Lst,'                                  ',NAM);
     writeln(Lst,'                                  ',CMP);
     writeln(Lst,'                                  ',POB);
     writeln(Lst,'                                  ',CIT,', ',SID,' ',COD);
end;
```

Fig. 7-48. This include file prints addresses and "FIRST CLASS MAIL" on large manila envelopes.

```
{Include file to print large envelopes first class}
{LRG1.ADR  }

procedure LargeFirst;

var  NAM, CMP, POB, CIT, SID, COD : string[50];
     Y                            : char;

begin
     clrscr;  gotoxy(1,10);
          repeat
     TextColor(11);
     write('Enter name of addressee          ');
     readln(NAM);
     write('Enter company                    ');
     readln(CMP);
     write('Enter street address or P.O.B.   ');
     readln(POB);
     write('Enter city                       ');
     readln(CIT);
     write('Enter State ID or name           ');
     readln(SID);
     write('Enter zip code                   ');
     readln(COD);
     TextColor(10);
     writeln('-------------------------------------------------');
     write('Entries correct?  (Y/N)          ');
     readln(Y);
          until UpCase(Y) = 'Y';
     writeln(Lst,'                                   FIRST CLASS MAIL');
     writeln(Lst,'                                   ================');
     writeln(Lst,' ');
     writeln(Lst,' ');
     writeln(Lst,'                                  ',NAM);
     writeln(Lst,'                                  ',CMP);
     writeln(Lst,'                                  ',POB);
     writeln(Lst,'                                  ',CIT,', ',SID,' ',COD);
end;
```

Fig. 7-49. This include file prints the address on a UPS label.

```
{Include file to print UPS label}
{UNPAR.ADR }

procedure UPS;

var  NAM, CMP, POB, CIT, SID, COD : string[50];
     Y                            : char;

begin
     clrscr;  gotoxy(1,10);
          repeat
     TextColor(11);
     write('Enter name of addressee              ');
     readln(NAM);
     write('Enter company                        ');
     readln(CMP);
     write('Enter street address                 ');
     readln(POB);
     write('Enter city                           ');
     readln(CIT);
     write('Enter State ID or name               ');
     readln(SID);
     write('Enter zip code                       ');
     readln(COD);
     TextColor(10);
     writeln('-----------------------------------------------------');
     write('Entries correct?  (Y/N)              ');
     readln(Y);
          until UpCase(Y) = 'Y';
     writeln(Lst,'                               ',NAM);
     writeln(Lst,'                               ',CMP);
     writeln(Lst,'                               ',POB);
     writeln(Lst,'                               ',CIT,', ',SID,' ',COD);
end;
```

A PERSONAL FINANCE PROGRAM

The PersonalFinances (LEDGER.P) program (Fig. 7-50) creates a number of files that separately store data for taxable income, non-taxable income, and payouts for a total of 20 categories. The program uses eleven files, each of which deals with just one specific aspect of the overall program.

CATEG.FIN (Fig. 7-51) is used to assign the 20 payout categories to a string variable (XX), depending on the value of X at any given moment.

NEW.FIN (Fig. 7-52) is the include file that creates empty files if the program has never before been used, or erases previous entries in order to start a new year or fiscal time period with a set of empty files.

DEP.FIN (Fig 7-53) stores data relative to taxable and non-taxable income. It adds each new entry to previously stored amounts, thus always containing the total to date.

EARN.FIN (Fig. 7-54) is used to enter amounts for taxable and non-taxable income.

EX.FIN (Fig. 7-55) is used to key in the amounts of withdrawals relative to any of the 20 available categories.

PAYMNT.FIN (Fig. 7-56) displays the 20 payout categories over and over again, to permit repeated data entry. Pressing 0 after the last entry will return the program to the main menu.

PF.FIN (Fig. 7-57) displays the income totals and the expense totals to date. It then deducts expenses from the income total, and displays the profit or loss figure up to that date.

HC.FIN (Fig. 7-58) is the include file that a provides an option to produce a hard copy of all 20 payout categories and the amounts that have been paid for each category to date, also printing the final expense total.

WD.FIN (Fig. 7-59) displays the expense totals for each of the 20 categories, plus the final total. It also asks whether or not a hard copy should be printed.

CH.FIN (Fig. 7-60) produces a hard copy of the income totals to date.

INC.FIN (Fig. 7-61) displays the income totals to date, asking whether or not a hard copy is to be printed.

Fig. 7-50. This program keeps a record of your personal finances.

```
{Personal finance record}
{LEDGER.P   }

program PersonalFinances;

var EXPNS                                       : file of real;
    NOTAX, TAX                                  : file of real;
    TPAID,TOTALT, TOTALN, GTOTAL, SUM           : real;
    PAY, PAID, PAIDT                            : array[1..20] of real;
    TDEPOSIT, NDEPOSIT                          : array[1..100] of real;
    Z, X, NUM, WHICH, WH                        : integer;
    XX                                          : string[52];
    R                                           : char;
    BAL, TOT1, TOT2                             : real;

{$I CATEG.FIN    }
{$I NEW.FIN      }
{$I DEP.FIN      }
{$I EARN.FIN     }
{$I EX.FIN       }
{$I PAYMNT.FIN   }
{$I PF.FIN       }
{$I HC.FIN       }
{$I WD.FIN       }
{$I CH.FIN       }
{$I INC.FIN      }

procedure Menu;
begin
     clrscr;  gotoxy(1,5);
     TextColor(10);
     writeln('                              MENU');
     writeln('                              ****');
     writeln;
     TextColor(12);
     write('     1');
     TextColor(13);
     writeln('   Enter new deposits');
     TextColor(11);
     writeln('     -----------------------------------------------');
     TextColor(12);
     write('     2');
     TextColor(13);
     writeln('   Enter payouts');
     TextColor(11);
```

```
    writeln('     ------------------------------------------------');
    TextColor(12);
    write('    3');
    TextColor(13);
    writeln('   Review income totals to date');
    TextColor(12);
    write('    4');
    TextColor(13);
    writeln('   Review outgo totals to date');
    TextColor(12);
    write('    5');
    TextColor(13);
    writeln('   Review balance to date');
    TextColor(11);
    writeln('     ------------------------------------------------');
    TextColor(12);
    write('    6');
    TextColor(13);
    writeln('   Start a new year (Erase previous entries)');
    TextColor(11);
    writeln('     ------------------------------------------------');
    TextColor(12);
    write('    0');
    TextColor(13);
    writeln('   Exit program');
    TextColor(11);
    writeln('     ------------------------------------------------');
    TextColor(14);
    write('    Which?          ');
    readln(WHICH);
        case WHICH of
    1 : Deposits;
    2 : Withdrawals;
    3 : Earnings;
    4 : Expense;
    5 : Balance;
    6 : Start;
    0 : end;
end;

begin
    repeat
    Menu;
    until WHICH = 0;
end.
```

Fig. 7-51. The include file CATEG.FIN establishes expense categories.

```
{Include file assigning categories to variables}
{CATEG.FIN  }

procedure Category;
begin
if X =  1 then XX := 'RENT, MORTGAGE PAYMENT                               ';
if X =  2 then XX := 'GAS, WATER, ELECTRICITY, CLEANING PERSONS ETC.       ';
if X =  3 then XX := 'TELEPHONE, TELEGRAPH ETC.                            ';
if X =  4 then XX := 'FOOD                                                 ';
if X =  5 then XX := 'CIGARETTES, ALCOHOL ETC.                             ';
```

```
if X =  6 then XX := 'RESTAURANTS, ENTERTAINMENT                                ';
if X =  7 then XX := 'DOCTORS, HOSPITALS ETC.                                   ';
if X =  8 then XX := 'MEDICINES                                                 ';
if X =  9 then XX := 'BLUE CROSS/BLUE SHIELD OR SIMILAR                         ';
if X = 10 then XX := 'AMERICAN EXPRESS                                          ';
if X = 11 then XX := 'VISA, MASTER CARD                                         ';
if X = 12 then XX := 'AUTOMOBILE EXPENSES, GAS, INSURANCE                       ';
if X = 13 then XX := 'COMPUTER RELATED EXPENSES, INSURANCE                      ';
if X = 14 then XX := 'OFFICE SUPPLIES, STATIONARY ETC.                          ';
if X = 15 then XX := 'PHOTOGRAPHY, ARTWORK, LAYOUT ETC.                         ';
if X = 16 then XX := 'POSTAGE, SHIPPING                                         ';
if X = 17 then XX := 'CLOTHES, FURNISHINGS, CLEANING                            ';
if X = 18 then XX := 'DUES, SUBSCRIPTIONS, BOOKS, RESEARCH ETC.                 ';
if X = 19 then XX := 'MISC. NON-DEDUCTIBLE EXPENSES                             ';
if X = 20 then XX := 'MISC. TAX-DEDUCTIBLE EXPENSES                             ';
end;
```

Fig. 7-52. The include file NEW.FIN creates new data files.

```
{Include file that creates the data files}
{NEW.FIN  }

procedure Start;
begin
          clrscr; gotoxy(1,10);
     TextColor(12);
     writeln('                                    WARNING!');
     writeln('                                    ********');
     TextColor(14);
     writeln;
     writeln('                        All previous entries will be erased!');
     writeln('                        ------------------------------------');
     writeln;
     write('                        Go ahead?    (Y/N)     ');
     readln(R);
            if UpCase(R) = 'Y' then begin
                 SUM := 0;
     assign(Tax,'TAXABL.DTA');
     rewrite(Tax);
     write(Tax,SUM);
     close(Tax);
     assign(NoTax,'NTAX.DTA');
     rewrite(NoTax);
     write(NoTax,SUM);
     close(NoTax);
     assign(Expns,'COST.DTA');
     rewrite(Expns);
                for Z := 1 to 20 do
     write(Expns,SUM);
     close(Expns);
            end
            else
end;
```

Fig. 7-53. This include file stores deposits and calculates new totals.

```
{Include file registering deposits}
{DEP.FIN  }
```

```
procedure Enter1;
begin
     read(Tax,SUM);
     SUM := SUM + TOTALT;
     rewrite(Tax);
     write(Tax,SUM);
     close(Tax);
end;

procedure Enter2;
begin
     read(NoTax,SUM);
     SUM := SUM + TOTALN;
     rewrite(NoTax);
     write(NoTax,SUM);
     close(NoTax);
end;
```

Fig. 7-54. This include file asks that income data be entered.

```
{Include file asking for earnings input}
{EARN.FIN  }

procedure Taxable;
begin
     clrscr; gotoxy(1,10);
     TextColor(11);
     write('Enter taxable amount          $');
     readln(TDEPOSIT[NUM]);
     TOTALT := TOTALT + TDEPOSIT[NUM];
     Enter1;
     close(NoTax);
     clrscr;  gotoxy(1,10);
end;

procedure NonTaxable;
begin
     clrscr; gotoxy(1,10);
     TextColor(11);
     write('Enter non-taxable amount (incl. refunds)    $');
     readln(NDEPOSIT[NUM]);
     TOTALN := TOTALN + NDEPOSIT[NUM];
     Enter2;
     close(Tax);
     clrscr;  gotoxy(1,10);
end;

procedure Deposits;
begin
        clrscr;  gotoxy(1,10);
     TOTALT := 0;
     TOTALN := 0;
     NUM    := 0;
        repeat
     assign(Tax,'TAXABL.DTA');
     reset(Tax);
     assign(NoTax,'NTAX.DTA');
     reset(NoTax);
     NUM := NUM + 1;
```

```
      TextColor(12);
      write('   1');
      TextColor(13);
      writeln('      Taxable income');
      TextColor(12);
      write('   2');
      TextColor(13);
      writeln('      Non-taxable income & refunds');
      writeln;
      TextColor(14);
      write('        Which?  (0 to quit)      ');
      readln(WH);
           case WH of
         1 : Taxable;
         2 : NonTaxable;
         0 : end;
           until WH = 0;
end;
```

Fig. 7-55. This include file displays withdrawal totals by category.

```
{Include file dealing with expenses}
{EX.FIN }

procedure Enter3;
begin
      assign(Expns,'COST.DTA');
      reset(Expns);
           clrscr; gotoxy(1,2);
           for x := 1 to 20 do begin
      read(Expns,PAIDT[X]);
      PAIDT[X] := PAIDT[X] + PAID[X];
           end;
      rewrite(Expns);
           for X := 1 to 20 do
      write(Expns,PAIDT[X]);
end;

procedure Outlay;
begin
      writeln;
      TextColor(11);
      write('Amount paid out?              $');
      readln(PAY[WHICH]);
      PAID[WHICH] := PAID[WHICH] + PAY[WHICH];
      clrscr;  gotoxy(1,2);
end;
```

Fig. 7-56. This include file asks that withdrawal data be entered.

```
{Include file asking for withdrawal input}
{PAYMNT.FIN  }

procedure Payouts;

label NEXT;

begin
      for X := 1 to 20 do begin
```

```
        PAID[X]  := 0;
        PAY[X]   := 0;
        PAIDT[X] := 0;
        end;
            repeat
        TextColor(10);
        writeln(' 1   RENT, MORTGAGE PAYMENT');
        writeln(' 2   GAS, WATER, ELECTRICITY, CLEANING PERSONS ETC.'
        writeln(' 3   TELEPHONE, TELEGRAPH ETC.');
        writeln(' 4   FOOD');
        writeln(' 5   CIGARETTES, ALCOHOL ETC.');
        writeln(' 6   RESTAURANTS, ENTERTAINMENT');
        writeln(' 7   DOCTORS, HOSPITALS ETC.');
        writeln(' 8   MEDICINES');
        writeln(' 9   BLUE CROSS/BLUE SHIELD OR SIMILAR');
        writeln('10   AMERICAN EXPRESS');
        writeln('11   VISA, MASTER CARD');
        writeln('12   AUTOMOBILE EXPENSES, GAS, INSURANCE');
        writeln('13   COMPUTER RELATED EXPENSES, INSURANCE');
        writeln('14   OFFICE SUPPLIES, STATIONARY ETC.');
        writeln('15   PHOTOGRAPHY, ARTWORK, LAYOUT ETC.');
        writeln('16   POSTAGE, SHIPPING');
        writeln('17   CLOTHES, FURNISHINGS, CLEANING');
        writeln('18   DUES, SUBSCRIPTIONS, BOOKS, RESEARCH ETC.');
        writeln('19   MISC. NON-DEDUCTIBLE EXPENSES');
        writeln('20   MISC. TAX-DEDUCTIBLE EXPENSES');
        writeln;
        write('     Which?    (0 to return to the menu)    ');
        readln(WH);
             if WH = 0 then goto NEXT;
        Outlay;
             until WH = 0;
NEXT:
        Enter3;
end;
```

Fig. 7-57. The include file PF.FIN calculates and displays profit or loss data to date.

```
{Include file determining profit or loss}
{PF.FIN  }

procedure Balance;
begin
     TPAID := 0;
     X     := 0;
     assign(Expns,'COST.DTA');
     reset(Expns);
         repeat
         X := X + 1;
     read(Expns,PAIDT[X]);
     TPAID := TPAID + PAIDT[X];
         until X = 20;
     close(Expns);
     assign(Tax,'TAXABL.DTA');
     reset(Tax);
     read(Tax,SUM);
     close(Tax);
     GTOTAL := SUM;
     TOT1   := SUM;
```

```
     assign(NoTax,'NTAX.DTA');
     reset(NoTax);
     read(NoTax,SUM);
     close(NoTax);
     TOT2   := SUM;
     GTOTAL := GTOTAL + SUM;
     clrscr;  gotoxy(1,10);
     TextColor(11);
     writeln('Total taxable income to date:                $',TOT1:6:2);
     writeln('Total non-taxable income to date:            $',TOT2:6:2);
     TextColor(12);
     writeln('-------------------------------------------------------------');
     TextColor(11);
     writeln('Total expenses to date:                      $',TPAID:6:2);
     TextColor(12);
     writeln('-------------------------------------------------------------');
     BAL := GTOTAL - TPAID;
     TextColor(11);
     writeln('Profit or loss to date:                      $',BAL:6:2);
     gotoxy(60,24);
     TextColor(14);
     writeln('Press any key');
     repeat until KeyPressed;
end;
```

Fig. 7-58. The include file HC.FIN produces a hard copy of the withdrawal data by category.

```
{Include file producing hard copies}
{HC.FIN   }

procedure Print;
begin
     TPAID := 0;
     X     := 0;
     assign(Expns,'COST.DTA');
     reset(Expns);
          repeat
     X := X + 1;
     Category;
     read(Expns,PAIDT[X]);
     writeln(Lst,XX,'        $',PAIDT[X]:6:2);
     TPAID := TPAID + PAIDT[X];
          until X = 20;
     close(Expns);
     writeln(Lst,'Total outlay to date:                        $',TPAID:6:2);
end;
```

Fig. 7-59. The include file WD.FIN displays withdrawal totals by category and asks whether a printout is desired.

```
{Include file dealing with withdrawals}
{WD.FIN   }

procedure Expense;
begin
     TPAID := 0;
     X     := 0;
     assign(Expns,'COST.DTA');
     reset(Expns);
```

```
        repeat
        X := X + 1;
    read(Expns,PAIDT[X]);
    Category;
    TextColor(11);
    writeln(XX,'   $',PAIDT[X]:6:2);
    TPAID := TPAID + PAIDT[X];
        until X = 20;
    close(Expns);
    writeln;
    TextColor(12);
    writeln('Total outlay to date:                          $',TPAID:6:2);
    TextColor(14);
    write('Printout?  (Y/N)     ');
    readln(R);
    if UpCase(R) = 'Y' then begin
    Print;
    end
    else
end;

procedure Withdrawals;
begin
    clrscr;  gotoxy(1,10);
    Payouts;
end;
```

Fig. 7-60. This include file produces a hard copy of income data.

```
{Include file producing hard copies}
{CH.FIN  }

procedure Printout;
begin
    assign(Tax,'TAXABL.DTA');
    reset(Tax);
    read(Tax,SUM);
    close(Tax);
    writeln(Lst,'Total taxable income to date:      $',SUM:6:2);
    GTOTAL := SUM;
    assign(NoTax,'NTAX.DTA');
    reset(NoTax);
    read(NoTax,SUM);
    close(NoTax);
    writeln(Lst,'Total non-taxable income to date:  $',SUM:6:2);
    writeln(Lst,' ');
    GTOTAL := GTOTAL + SUM;
    writeln(Lst,'Total income to date               $',GTOTAL:6:2);
end;
```

Fig. 7-61. The include file displays income data on the screen and asks whether a printout is desired.

```
{Include file dealing with earnings}
{INC.FIN }

procedure Earnings;
begin
        clrscr;  gotoxy(1,10);
```

```
        TextColor(11);
        assign(Tax,'TAXABL.DTA');
        reset(Tax);
        read(Tax,SUM);
        close(Tax);
        writeln('Total taxable income to date:       $',SUM:6:2);
        writeln;
        GTOTAL := SUM;
        assign(NoTax,'NTAX.DTA');
        reset(NoTax);
        read(NoTax,SUM);
        TOT2 := SUM;
        close(NoTax);
        writeln('Total non-taxable income to date:   $',TOT2:6:2);
        GTOTAL := GTOTAL + SUM;
        writeln('Total income to date                $',GTOTAL:6:2);
        writeln;
        TextColor(14);
        write('Printout?  (Y/N)       ');
        readln(R);
        if UpCase(R) = 'Y' then
        Printout
        else
end;
```

A TO Z AND ONE TO FIVE

The last program in this collection is designed to draw and display capital letters and numbers larger than those that can be produced with the 4×6 pixel routine, which become virtually illegible if an attempt is made to use them much larger than the machine-dependent text. The letters and numbers that are produced by this program are a little over one inch high, displayed in the upper left-hand corner of the screen. The size of the letters and their position on the screen can be varied.

The program consists of a main program called LettersAndNumbers (AZ.P, Fig. 7-62) which contains the menu and calls a total of 36 include files, three of which are Graphix Toolbox modules. Of the other 33, two are used to select any of the remaining 31 files to print the 26 letters of the alphabet or any of the 5 digits. These include files are ALPH.IN (Fig. 7-63), which selects the files that print letters, and NUM.IN (Fig. 7-64), which selects the files that print digits. The files LA.IN through LZ.IN (Figs. 7-65 through 7-90) are the ones that draw the letters. N1.IN through N5.IN (Figs. 7-91 through 7-95) draw the digits.

Fig. 7-62. The program AZ.P controls the drawing of alphanumeric characters to be displayed on the screen.

```
{This program produces letters and numbers of any size larger than standard}
{AZ.P  }

program LettersAndNumbers;

var  WHICH, NUMBER  : integer;
     LETTER         : char;

{$I typedef.sys }
{$I graphix.sys }
{$I kernel.sys  }

{$I LA.IN    }
```

```
{$I LB.IN     }
{$I LC.IN     }
{$I LD.IN     }
{$I LE.IN     }
{$I LF.IN     }
{$I LG.IN     }
{$I LH.IN     }
{$I LI.IN     }
{$I LJ.IN     }
{$I LK.IN     }
{$I LL.IN     }
{$I LM.IN     }
{$I LN.IN     }
{$I LO.IN     }
{$I LP.IN     }
{$I LQ.IN     }
{$I LR.IN     }
{$I LS.IN     }
{$I LT.IN     }
{$I LU.IN     }
{$I LV.IN     }
{$I LW.IN     }
{$I LX.IN     }
{$I LY.IN     }
{$I LZ.IN     }
{$I ALPH.IN   }
{$I N1.IN     }
{$I N2.IN     }
{$I N3.IN     }
{$I N4.IN     }
{$I N5.IN     }
{$I N6.IN     }
{$I N7.IN     }
{$I N8.IN     }
{$I N9.IN     }
{$I NO.IN     }
{$I NUM.IN    }

procedure Alpha;
begin
     DrawTheLetter;
end;

procedure Numeric;
begin
     DrawTheNumber;
end;

procedure Menu;
begin
     clrscr;  gotoxy(1,8);
     TextColor(10);
     writeln('                              MENU');
     writeln('                              ****');
     writeln;
     TextColor(12);
     write('                 1');
     TextColor(13);
     writeln('     Print a letter');
```

```
     TextColor(12);
     write('                        2');
     TextColor(13);
     writeln('     Print a number');
     TextColor(11);
     writeln('                        -----------------------------');
     TextColor(12);
     write('                        0');
     TextColor(13);
     writeln('     Exit program');
     TextColor(11);
     writeln('                        -----------------------------');
     TextColor(14);
     write('                        Which?          ');
     readln(WHICH);
         case WHICH of
     1 : begin
         TextColor(11);
         clrscr;   gotoxy(30,12);
         write('Which letter?  ');
         readln(LETTER);
         Alpha;
         end;
     2 : begin
         TextColor(11);
         clrscr;   gotoxy(30,12);
         write('Which number?  ');
         readln(NUMBER);
         Numeric;
         end;
     0 : end;
end;

begin
     repeat
     Menu;
     until WHICH = 0;
end.
```

Fig. 7-63. The include file ALPHA.IN sends the computer to one of 26 procedures, depending on the digit that is to be drawn.

```
{File to select the right procedure}
{ALPH.IN  }

procedure DrawTheLetter;
begin
        case LETTER of
     'A','a'  :  DrawA;
     'B','b'  :  DrawB;
     'C','c'  :  DrawC;
     'D','d'  :  DrawD;
     'E','e'  :  DrawE;
     'F','f'  :  DrawF;
     'G','g'  :  DrawG;
     'H','h'  :  DrawH;
     'I','i'  :  DrawI;
     'J','j'  :  DrawJ;
     'K','k'  :  DrawK;
     'L','l'  :  DrawL;
```

```
        'M','m' :  DrawM;
        'N','n' :  DrawN;
        'O','o' :  DrawO;
        'P','p' :  DrawP;
        'Q','q' :  DrawQ;
        'R','r' :  DrawR;
        'S','s' :  DrawS;
        'T','t' :  DrawT;
        'U','u' :  DrawU;
        'V','v' :  DrawV;
        'W','w' :  DrawW;
        'X','x' :  DrawX;
        'Y','y' :  DrawY;
        'Z','z' :  DrawZ;
           end;
end;
```

Fig. 7-64. The include file NUM.IN sends the computer to one of ten procedures, depending on the digit that is to be drawn.

```
{This file selects the files that draw the numbers}
{NUM.IN  }

procedure DrawTheNumber;
begin
        case NUMBER of
       1 : Draw1;
       2 : Draw2;
       3 : Draw3;
       4 : Draw4;
       5 : Draw5;
       6 : Draw6;
       7 : Draw7;
       8 : Draw8;
       9 : Draw9;
       0 : Draw0;
        end;
end;
```

Fig. 7-65 The include file LA.IN draws the letter A.

```
{This file draws the letter A}
{LA.IN  }

procedure DrawA;

var X1, Y1, X2, Y2,
    X3, Y3, X4, Y4,
    X5, Y5, X6, Y6,
    X7, Y7, X8, Y8,
    X9, Y9, X0, Y0 : real;

begin
  InitGraphic;
  DefineWorld(1,0,1000,1000,0);
  SelectWorld(1);
  SelectWindow(1);
  SetForegroundColor(12);
```

```
  SetBackground(0);
  DrawBorder;
             X1 := 20;
             Y1 := 180;
             X2 := 20;
             Y2 := 100;
             X3 := 20;
             Y3 := 100;
             X4 := 40;
             Y4 := 20;
             X5 := 40;
             Y5 := 20;
             X6 := 60;
             Y6 := 100;
             X7 := 60;
             Y7 := 100;
             X8 := 60;
             Y8 := 180;
             X9 := 20;
             Y9 := 130;
             X0 := 60;
             Y0 := 130;

    DrawLine(X1,Y1,X2,Y2);
    DrawLine(X3,Y3,X4,Y4);
    DrawLine(X5,Y5,X6,Y6);
    DrawLine(X7,Y7,X8,Y8);
    DrawLine(X9,Y9,X0,Y0);

  repeat until KeyPressed;
  LeaveGraphic;
end;
```

Fig. 7-66. LB.IN draws the letter B.

```
{This file draws the letter B}
{LB.IN  }

procedure DrawB;

var X1, Y1, X2, Y2,
    X3, Y3, X4, Y4,
    X5, Y5, X6, Y6,
    X7, Y7, X8, Y8,
    X9, Y9, X0, Y0,
    X11, Y11, X12, Y12,
    X13, Y13, X14, Y14,
    X15, Y15, X16, Y16  : real;

begin
  InitGraphic;
  DefineWorld(1,0,1000,1000,0);
  SelectWorld(1);
  SelectWindow(1);
  SetForegroundColor(12);
  SetBackground(0);
  DrawBorder;
             X1 := 20;
```

```
            Y1  := 180;
            X2  := 20;
            Y2  := 20;
            X3  := 20;
            Y3  := 20;
            X4  := 40;
            Y4  := 20;
            X5  := 40;
            Y5  := 20;
            X6  := 60;
            Y6  := 60;
            X7  := 60;
            Y7  := 60;
            X8  := 40;
            Y8  := 100;
            X9  := 40;
            Y9  := 100;
            X0  := 60;
            Y0  := 140;
           X11  := 60;
           Y11  := 140;
           X12  := 40;
           Y12  := 180;
           X13  := 20;
           Y13  := 180;
           X14  := 40;
           Y14  := 180;
           X15  := 20;
           Y15  := 100;
           X16  := 40;
           Y16  := 100;

      DrawLine(X1,Y1,X2,Y2);
      DrawLine(X3,Y3,X4,Y4);
      DrawLine(X5,Y5,X6,Y6);
      DrawLine(X7,Y7,X8,Y8);
      DrawLine(X9,Y9,X0,Y0);
      DrawLine(X11,Y11,X12,Y12);
      DrawLine(X13,Y13,X14,Y14);
      DrawLine(X15,Y15,X16,Y16);

  repeat until KeyPressed;
  LeaveGraphic;
end;
```

Fig. 7-67. LC.IN draws the letter C.

```
{This file draws the letter C}
{LC.IN  }

procedure DrawC;

var X1, Y1, X2, Y2,
    X3, Y3, X4, Y4,
    X5, Y5, X6, Y6,
    X7, Y7, X8, Y8,
    X9, Y9, X0, Y0 : real;

begin
```

```
  InitGraphic;
  DefineWorld(1,0,1000,1000,0);
  SelectWorld(1);
  SelectWindow(1);
  SetForegroundColor(12);
  SetBackground(0);
  DrawBorder;
           X1 := 20;
           Y1 := 60;
           X2 := 20;
           Y2 := 140;
           X3 := 20;
           Y3 := 60;
           X4 := 40;
           Y4 := 20;
           X5 := 40;
           Y5 := 20;
           X6 := 60;
           Y6 := 20;
           X7 := 20;
           Y7 := 140;
           X8 := 40;
           Y8 := 180;
           X9 := 40;
           Y9 := 180;
           X0 := 60;
           Y0 := 180;

      DrawLine(X1,Y1,X2,Y2);
      DrawLine(X3,Y3,X4,Y4);
      DrawLine(X5,Y5,X6,Y6);
      DrawLine(X7,Y7,X8,Y8);
      DrawLine(X9,Y9,X0,Y0);

  repeat until KeyPressed;
  LeaveGraphic;
end;
```

Fig. 7-68. LD.IN draws the letter D.

```
{This file draws the letter D}
{LD.IN  }

procedure DrawD;

var X1, Y1, X2, Y2,
    X3, Y3, X4, Y4,
    X5, Y5, X6, Y6,
    X7, Y7, X8, Y8,
    X9, Y9, X0, Y0,
    X11, Y11, X12, Y12  : real;

begin
  InitGraphic;
  DefineWorld(1,0,1000,1000,0);
  SelectWorld(1);
  SelectWindow(1);
```

```
  SetForegroundColor(12);
  SetBackground(0);
  DrawBorder;
             X1  := 20;
             Y1  := 180;
             X2  := 20;
             Y2  := 20;
             X3  := 60;
             Y3  := 60;
             X4  := 60;
             Y4  := 140;
             X5  := 20;
             Y5  := 20;
             X6  := 40;
             Y6  := 20;
             X7  := 40;
             Y7  := 20;
             X8  := 60;
             Y8  := 60;
             X9  := 60;
             Y9  := 140;
             X0  := 40;
             Y0  := 180;
            X11  := 20;
            Y11  := 180;
            X12  := 40;
            Y12  := 180;

      DrawLine(X1,Y1,X2,Y2);
      DrawLine(X3,Y3,X4,Y4);
      DrawLine(X5,Y5,X6,Y6);
      DrawLine(X7,Y7,X8,Y8);
      DrawLine(X9,Y9,X0,Y0);
      DrawLine(X11,Y11,X12,Y12);

  repeat until KeyPressed;
  LeaveGraphic;
end;
```

Fig. 7-69. LE.IN draws the letter E.

```
{This file draws the letter E}
{LE.IN  }

procedure DrawE;

var X1, Y1, X2, Y2,
    X3, Y3, X4, Y4,
    X5, Y5, X6, Y6,
    X7, Y7, X8, Y8,
    X9, Y9, X0, Y0 : real;

begin
  InitGraphic;
  DefineWorld(1,0,1000,1000,0);
  SelectWorld(1);
  SelectWindow(1);
  SetForegroundColor(12);
```

```
  SetBackground(0);
  DrawBorder;
           X1 := 20;
           Y1 := 180;
           X2 := 20;
           Y2 := 20;
           X3 := 20;
           Y3 := 20;
           X4 := 60;
           Y4 := 20;
           X5 := 20;
           Y5 := 100;
           X6 := 60;
           Y6 := 100;
           X7 := 20;
           Y7 := 180;
           X8 := 60;
           Y8 := 180;

      DrawLine(X1,Y1,X2,Y2);
      DrawLine(X3,Y3,X4,Y4);
      DrawLine(X5,Y5,X6,Y6);
      DrawLine(X7,Y7,X8,Y8);

  repeat until KeyPressed;
  LeaveGraphic;
end;
```

Fig. 7-70. LF.IN draws the letter F.

```
{This file draws the letter F}
{LF.IN  }

procedure DrawF;

var X1, Y1, X2, Y2,
    X3, Y3, X4, Y4,
    X5, Y5, X6, Y6,
    X7, Y7, X8, Y8,
    X9, Y9, X0, Y0 : real;

begin
  InitGraphic;
  DefineWorld(1,0,1000,1000,0);
  SelectWorld(1);
  SelectWindow(1);
  SetForegroundColor(12);
  SetBackground(0);
  DrawBorder;
           X1 := 20;
           Y1 := 180;
           X2 := 20;
           Y2 := 20;
           X3 := 20;
           Y3 := 20;
           X4 := 60;
           Y4 := 20;
           X5 := 20;
```

```
                Y5 := 100;
                X6 := 60;
                Y6 := 100;

      DrawLine(X1,Y1,X2,Y2);
      DrawLine(X3,Y3,X4,Y4);
      DrawLine(X5,Y5,X6,Y6);

  repeat until KeyPressed;
  LeaveGraphic;
end;
```

Fig. 7-71. LG.IN draws the letter G.

```
{This file draws the letter G}
{LG.IN  }

procedure DrawG;

var X1, Y1, X2, Y2,
    X3, Y3, X4, Y4,
    X5, Y5, X6, Y6,
    X7, Y7, X8, Y8,
    X9, Y9, X0, Y0,
    X11, Y11, X12, Y12,
    X13, Y13, X14, Y14,
    X15, Y15, X16, Y16,
    X17, Y17, X18, Y18    : real;

begin
  InitGraphic;
  DefineWorld(1,0,1000,1000,0);
  SelectWorld(1);
  SelectWindow(1);
  SetForegroundColor(12);
  SetBackground(0);
  DrawBorder;
                X1 := 20;
                Y1 := 30;
                X2 := 20;
                Y2 := 170;
                X3 := 20;
                Y3 := 30;
                X4 := 30;
                Y4 := 20;
                X5 := 20;
                Y5 := 170;
                X6 := 30;
                Y6 := 180;
                X7 := 30;
                Y7 := 20;
                X8 := 50;
                Y8 := 20;
                X9 := 30;
                Y9 := 180;
                X0 := 50;
                Y0 := 180;
               X11 := 50;
               Y11 := 20;
```

```
            X12 := 60;
            Y12 := 30;
            X13 := 50;
            Y13 := 180;
            X14 := 60;
            Y14 := 170;
            X15 := 60;
            Y15 := 170;
            X16 := 60;
            Y16 := 100;
            X17 := 60;
            Y17 := 100;
            X18 := 30;
            Y18 := 100;

      DrawLine(X1,Y1,X2,Y2);
      DrawLine(X3,Y3,X4,Y4);
      DrawLine(X5,Y5,X6,Y6);
      DrawLine(X7,Y7,X8,Y8);
      DrawLine(X9,Y9,X0,Y0);
      DrawLine(X11,Y11,X12,Y12);
      DrawLine(X13,Y13,X14,Y14);
      DrawLine(X15,Y15,X16,Y16);
      DrawLine(X17,Y17,X18,Y18);

  repeat until KeyPressed;
  LeaveGraphic;
end;
```

Fig. 7-72. LH.IN draws the letter H.

```
{This file draws the letter H}
{LH.IN  }

procedure DrawH;

var X1, Y1, X2, Y2,
    X3, Y3, X4, Y4,
    X5, Y5, X6, Y6,
    X7, Y7, X8, Y8,
    X9, Y9, X0, Y0 : real;

begin
  InitGraphic;
  DefineWorld(1,0,1000,1000,0);
  SelectWorld(1);
  SelectWindow(1);
  SetForegroundColor(12);
  SetBackground(0);
  DrawBorder;
            X1 := 20;
            Y1 := 180;
            X2 := 20;
            Y2 := 20;
            X3 := 20;
            Y3 := 100;
            X4 := 60;
            Y4 := 100;
            X5 := 60;
```

```
            Y5 := 20;
            X6 := 60;
            Y6 := 180;

        DrawLine(X1,Y1,X2,Y2);
        DrawLine(X3,Y3,X4,Y4);
        DrawLine(X5,Y5,X6,Y6);

  repeat until KeyPressed;
  LeaveGraphic;
end;
```

Fig. 7-73. LI.IN draws the letter I.

```
{This file draws the letter I}
{LI.IN  }

procedure DrawI;

var X1, Y1, X2, Y2,
    X3, Y3, X4, Y4,
    X5, Y5, X6, Y6,
    X7, Y7, X8, Y8,
    X9, Y9, X0, Y0 : real;

begin
  InitGraphic;
  DefineWorld(1,0,1000,1000,0);
  SelectWorld(1);
  SelectWindow(1);
  SetForegroundColor(12);
  SetBackground(0);
  DrawBorder;
            X1 := 40;
            Y1 := 180;
            X2 := 40;
            Y2 := 20;
            X3 := 30;
            Y3 := 20;
            X4 := 50;
            Y4 := 20;
            X5 := 30;
            Y5 := 180;
            X6 := 50;
            Y6 := 180;

        DrawLine(X1,Y1,X2,Y2);
        DrawLine(X3,Y3,X4,Y4);
        DrawLine(X5,Y5,X6,Y6);

  repeat until KeyPressed;
  LeaveGraphic;
end;
```

Fig. 7-74. LJ.IN draws the letter J.

```
{This file draws the letter J}
{LJ.IN  }
```

```
procedure DrawJ;

var X1, Y1, X2, Y2,
    X3, Y3, X4, Y4,
    X5, Y5, X6, Y6,
    X7, Y7, X8, Y8,
    X9, Y9, X0, Y0 : real;

begin
  InitGraphic;
  DefineWorld(1,0,1000,1000,0);
  SelectWorld(1);
  SelectWindow(1);
  SetForegroundColor(12);
  SetBackground(0);
  DrawBorder;
           X1 := 50;
           Y1 := 20;
           X2 := 50;
           Y2 := 170;
           X3 := 50;
           Y3 := 170;
           X4 := 40;
           Y4 := 180;
           X5 := 40;
           Y5 := 180;
           X6 := 30;
           Y6 := 180;
           X7 := 30;
           Y7 := 180;
           X8 := 20;
           Y8 := 170;

      DrawLine(X1,Y1,X2,Y2);
      DrawLine(X3,Y3,X4,Y4);
      DrawLine(X5,Y5,X6,Y6);
      DrawLine(X7,Y7,X8,Y8);

  repeat until KeyPressed;
  LeaveGraphic;
end;
```

Fig. 7-75. LK.IN draws the letter K.

```
{This file draws the letter K}
{LK.IN  }

procedure DrawK;

var X1, Y1, X2, Y2,
    X3, Y3, X4, Y4,
    X5, Y5, X6, Y6,
    X7, Y7, X8, Y8,
    X9, Y9, X0, Y0 : real;

begin
  InitGraphic;
  DefineWorld(1,0,1000,1000,0);
  SelectWorld(1);
```

```
  SelectWindow(1);
  SetForegroundColor(12);
  SetBackground(0);
  DrawBorder;
             X1 := 20;
             Y1 := 180;
             X2 := 20;
             Y2 := 20;
             X3 := 20;
             Y3 := 100;
             X4 := 60;
             Y4 := 20;
             X5 := 20;
             Y5 := 100;
             X6 := 60;
             Y6 := 180;

      DrawLine(X1,Y1,X2,Y2);
      DrawLine(X3,Y3,X4,Y4);
      DrawLine(X5,Y5,X6,Y6);

  repeat until KeyPressed;
  LeaveGraphic;
end;
```

Fig. 7-76. LL.IN draws the letter L.

```
{This file draws the letter L}
{LL.IN  }

procedure DrawL;

var X1, Y1, X2, Y2,
    X3, Y3, X4, Y4,
    X5, Y5, X6, Y6,
    X7, Y7, X8, Y8,
    X9, Y9, X0, Y0 : real;

begin
  InitGraphic;
  DefineWorld(1,0,1000,1000,0);
  SelectWorld(1);
  SelectWindow(1);
  SetForegroundColor(12);
  SetBackground(0);
  DrawBorder;
             X1 := 20;
             Y1 := 180;
             X2 := 20;
             Y2 := 20;
             X3 := 20;
             Y3 := 180;
             X4 := 60;
             Y4 := 180;

      DrawLine(X1,Y1,X2,Y2);
      DrawLine(X3,Y3,X4,Y4);

  repeat until KeyPressed;
```

```
  LeaveGraphic;
end;
```

Fig. 7-77. LM.IN draws the letter M.

```
{This file draws the letter M}
{LM.IN  }

procedure DrawM;

var X1, Y1, X2, Y2,
    X3, Y3, X4, Y4,
    X5, Y5, X6, Y6,
    X7, Y7, X8, Y8,
    X9, Y9, X0, Y0 : real;

begin
  InitGraphic;
  DefineWorld(1,0,1000,1000,0);
  SelectWorld(1);
  SelectWindow(1);
  SetForegroundColor(12);
  SetBackground(0);
  DrawBorder;
              X1 := 20;
              Y1 := 180;
              X2 := 20;
              Y2 := 20;
              X3 := 60;
              Y3 := 180;
              X4 := 60;
              Y4 := 20;
              X5 := 20;
              Y5 := 20;
              X6 := 40;
              Y6 := 100;
              X7 := 60;
              Y7 := 20;
              X8 := 40;
              Y8 := 100;

    DrawLine(X1,Y1,X2,Y2);
    DrawLine(X3,Y3,X4,Y4);
    DrawLine(X5,Y5,X6,Y6);
    DrawLine(X7,Y7,X8,Y8);

  repeat until KeyPressed;
  LeaveGraphic;
end;
```

Fig. 7-78. LN.IN draws the letter N.

```
{This file draws the letter N}
{LN.IN  }

procedure DrawN;

var X1, Y1, X2, Y2,
```

```
    X3, Y3, X4, Y4,
    X5, Y5, X6, Y6,
    X7, Y7, X8, Y8,
    X9, Y9, X0, Y0 : real;

begin
  InitGraphic;
  DefineWorld(1,0,1000,1000,0);
  SelectWorld(1);
  SelectWindow(1);
  SetForegroundColor(12);
  SetBackground(0);
  DrawBorder;
           X1 := 20;
           Y1 := 180;
           X2 := 20;
           Y2 := 20;
           X3 := 20;
           Y3 := 20;
           X4 := 60;
           Y4 := 180;
           X5 := 60;
           Y5 := 20;
           X6 := 60;
           Y6 := 180;

      DrawLine(X1,Y1,X2,Y2);
      DrawLine(X3,Y3,X4,Y4);
      DrawLine(X5,Y5,X6,Y6);

  repeat until KeyPressed;
  LeaveGraphic;
end;
```

Fig. 7-79. LO.IN draws the letter O.

```
{This file draws the letter O}
{LO.IN  }

procedure DrawO;

var X1, Y1, X2, Y2,
    X3, Y3, X4, Y4,
    X5, Y5, X6, Y6,
    X7, Y7, X8, Y8,
    X9, Y9, X0, Y0,
    X11, Y11, X12, Y12,
    X13, Y13, X14, Y14,
    X15, Y15, X16, Y16  : real;

begin
  InitGraphic;
  DefineWorld(1,0,1000,1000,0);
  SelectWorld(1);
  SelectWindow(1);
  SetForegroundColor(12);
  SetBackground(0);
  DrawBorder;
           X1 := 20;
```

```
            Y1 := 170;
            X2 := 20;
            Y2 := 30;
            X3 := 60;
            Y3 := 170;
            X4 := 60;
            Y4 := 30;
            X5 := 30;
            Y5 := 20;
            X6 := 50;
            Y6 := 20;
            X7 := 30;
            Y7 := 180;
            X8 := 50;
            Y8 := 180;
            X9 := 20;
            Y9 := 30;
            X0 := 30;
            Y0 := 20;
           X11 := 20;
           Y11 := 170;
           X12 := 30;
           Y12 := 180;
           X13 := 50;
           Y13 := 20;
           X14 := 60;
           Y14 := 30;
           X15 := 60;
           Y15 := 170;
           X16 := 50;
           Y16 := 180;

    DrawLine(X1,Y1,X2,Y2);
    DrawLine(X3,Y3,X4,Y4);
    DrawLine(X5,Y5,X6,Y6);
    DrawLine(X7,Y7,X8,Y8);
    DrawLine(X9,Y9,X0,Y0);
    DrawLine(X11,Y11,X12,Y12);
    DrawLine(X13,Y13,X14,Y14);
    DrawLine(X15,Y15,X16,Y16);

  repeat until KeyPressed;
  LeaveGraphic;
end;
```

Fig. 7-80. LP.IN draws the letter P.

```
{This file draws the letter P}
{LP.IN  }

procedure DrawP;

var X1, Y1, X2, Y2,
    X3, Y3, X4, Y4,
    X5, Y5, X6, Y6,
    X7, Y7, X8, Y8,
    X9, Y9, X0, Y0,
    X11, Y11, X12, Y12 : real;
```

```
begin
  InitGraphic;
  DefineWorld(1,0,1000,1000,0);
  SelectWorld(1);
  SelectWindow(1);
  SetForegroundColor(12);
  SetBackground(0);
  DrawBorder;
               X1 := 20;
               Y1 := 180;
               X2 := 20;
               Y2 := 20;
               X3 := 20;
               Y3 := 20;
               X4 := 50;
               Y4 := 20;
               X5 := 60;
               Y5 := 30;
               X6 := 60;
               Y6 := 90;
               X7 := 60;
               Y7 := 90;
               X8 := 50;
               Y8 := 100;
               X9 := 20;
               Y9 := 100;
               X0 := 50;
               Y0 := 100;
               X11 := 50;
               Y11 := 20;
               X12 := 60;
               Y12 := 30;

    DrawLine(X1,Y1,X2,Y2);
    DrawLine(X3,Y3,X4,Y4);
    DrawLine(X5,Y5,X6,Y6);
    DrawLine(X7,Y7,X8,Y8);
    DrawLine(X9,Y9,X0,Y0);
    DrawLine(X11,Y11,X12,Y12);

  repeat until KeyPressed;
  LeaveGraphic;
end;
```

Fig. 7-81. LQ.IN draws the letter Q.

```
{This file draws the letter Q}
{LQ.IN  }

procedure DrawQ;

var X1, Y1, X2, Y2,
    X3, Y3, X4, Y4,
    X5, Y5, X6, Y6,
    X7, Y7, X8, Y8,
    X9, Y9, X0, Y0,
    X11, Y11, X12, Y12,
    X13, Y13, X14, Y14,
    X15, Y15, X16, Y16,
```

```
    X17, Y17, X18, Y18  : real;

begin
  InitGraphic;
  DefineWorld(1,0,1000,1000,0);
  SelectWorld(1);
  SelectWindow(1);
  SetForegroundColor(12);
  SetBackground(0);
  DrawBorder;
                X1 := 20;
                Y1 := 170;
                X2 := 20;
                Y2 := 30;
                X3 := 60;
                Y3 := 170;
                X4 := 60;
                Y4 := 30;
                X5 := 30;
                Y5 := 20;
                X6 := 50;
                Y6 := 20;
                X7 := 30;
                Y7 := 180;
                X8 := 50;
                Y8 := 180;
                X9 := 20;
                Y9 := 30;
                X0 := 30;
                Y0 := 20;
               X11 := 20;
               Y11 := 170;
               X12 := 30;
               Y12 := 180;
               X13 := 50;
               Y13 := 20;
               X14 := 60;
               Y14 := 30;
               X15 := 60;
               Y15 := 170;
               X16 := 50;
               Y16 := 180;
               X17 := 50;
               Y17 := 170;
               X18 := 60;
               Y18 := 180;
      DrawLine(X1,Y1,X2,Y2);
      DrawLine(X3,Y3,X4,Y4);
      DrawLine(X5,Y5,X6,Y6);
      DrawLine(X7,Y7,X8,Y8);
      DrawLine(X9,Y9,X0,Y0);
      DrawLine(X11,Y11,X12,Y12);
      DrawLine(X13,Y13,X14,Y14);
      DrawLine(X15,Y15,X16,Y16);
      DrawLine(X17,Y17,X18,Y18);
   repeat until KeyPressed;
   LeaveGraphic;
 end;
```

Fig. 7-82. LR.IN draws the letter R.

```
{This file draws the letter R}
{LR.IN  }

procedure DrawR;

var X1, Y1, X2, Y2,
    X3, Y3, X4, Y4,
    X5, Y5, X6, Y6,
    X7, Y7, X8, Y8,
    X9, Y9, X0, Y0,
    X11, Y11, X12, Y12,
    X13, Y13, X14, Y14 : real;

begin
  InitGraphic;
  DefineWorld(1,0,1000,1000,0);
  SelectWorld(1);
  SelectWindow(1);
  SetForegroundColor(12);
  SetBackground(0);
  DrawBorder;
             X1  := 20;
             Y1  := 180;
             X2  := 20;
             Y2  := 20;
             X3  := 20;
             Y3  := 20;
             X4  := 50;
             Y4  := 20;
             X5  := 60;
             Y5  := 30;
             X6  := 60;
             Y6  := 90;
             X7  := 60;
             Y7  := 90;
             X8  := 50;
             Y8  := 100;
             X9  := 20;
             Y9  := 100;
             X0  := 50;
             Y0  := 100;
            X11  := 20;
            Y11  := 100;
            X12  := 60;
            Y12  := 180;
            X13  := 50;
            Y13  := 20;
            X14  := 60;
            Y14  := 30;

      DrawLine(X1,Y1,X2,Y2);
      DrawLine(X3,Y3,X4,Y4);
      DrawLine(X5,Y5,X6,Y6);
      DrawLine(X7,Y7,X8,Y8);
      DrawLine(X9,Y9,X0,Y0);
      DrawLine(X11,Y11,X12,Y12);
```

```
  repeat until KeyPressed;
  LeaveGraphic;
end;
```

Fig. 7-83. The include file LS.IN draws the letter S.

```
{This file draws the letter S}
{LS.IN  }

procedure DrawS;

var X1, Y1, X2, Y2,
    X3, Y3, X4, Y4,
    X5, Y5, X6, Y6,
    X7, Y7, X8, Y8,
    X9, Y9, X0, Y0,
    X11, Y11, X12, Y12,
    X13, Y13, X14, Y14,
    X15, Y15, X16, Y16,
    X17, Y17, X18, Y18,
    X19, Y19, X20, Y20,
    X21, Y21, X22, Y22   : real;

begin
  InitGraphic;
  DefineWorld(1,0,1000,1000,0);
  SelectWorld(1);
  SelectWindow(1);
  SetForegroundColor(12);
  SetBackground(0);
  DrawBorder;
              X1  := 20;
              Y1  := 30;
              X2  := 20;
              Y2  := 90;
              X3  := 30;
              Y3  := 20;
              X4  := 50;
              Y4  := 20;
              X5  := 60;
              Y5  := 30;
              X6  := 50;
              Y6  := 20;
              X7  := 20;
              Y7  := 30;
              X8  := 30;
              Y8  := 20;
              X9  := 20;
              Y9  := 90;
              X0  := 30;
              Y0  := 100;
             X11  := 30;
             Y11  := 100;
             X12  := 50;
             Y12  := 100;
             X13  := 50;
             Y13  := 100;
             X14  := 60;
```

```
            Y14 := 110;
            X15 := 60;
            Y15 := 110;
            X16 := 60;
            Y16 := 170;
            X17 := 60;
            Y17 := 170;
            X18 := 50;
            Y18 := 180;
            X19 := 50;
            Y19 := 180;
            X20 := 30;
            Y20 := 180;
            X21 := 30;
            Y21 := 180;
            X22 := 20;
            Y22 := 170;

    DrawLine(X1,Y1,X2,Y2);
    DrawLine(X3,Y3,X4,Y4);
    DrawLine(X5,Y5,X6,Y6);
    DrawLine(X7,Y7,X8,Y8);
    DrawLine(X9,Y9,X0,Y0);
    DrawLine(X11,Y11,X12,Y12);
    DrawLine(X13,Y13,X14,Y14);
    DrawLine(X15,Y15,X16,Y16);
    DrawLine(X17,Y17,X18,Y18);
    DrawLine(X19,Y19,X20,Y20);
    DrawLine(X21,Y21,X22,Y22);

  repeat until KeyPressed;
  LeaveGraphic;
end;
```

Fig. 7-84. The include file LT.In draws the letter T.

```
{This file draws the letter T}
{LT.IN  }

procedure DrawT;

var X1, Y1, X2, Y2,
    X3, Y3, X4, Y4,
    X5, Y5, X6, Y6,
    X7, Y7, X8, Y8,
    X9, Y9, X0, Y0 : real;

begin
  InitGraphic;
  DefineWorld(1,0,1000,1000,0);
  SelectWorld(1);
  SelectWindow(1);
  SetForegroundColor(12);
  SetBackground(0);
  DrawBorder;
           X1 := 20;
           Y1 := 20;
           X2 := 60;
```

```
              Y2 := 20;
              X3 := 40;
              Y3 := 20;
              X4 := 40;
              Y4 := 180;

       DrawLine(X1,Y1,X2,Y2);
       DrawLine(X3,Y3,X4,Y4);

   repeat until KeyPressed;
   LeaveGraphic;
end;
```

Fig. 7-85. LU.IN draws the letter U.

```
{This file draws the letter U}
{LU.IN  }

procedure DrawU;

var X1, Y1, X2, Y2,
    X3, Y3, X4, Y4,
    X5, Y5, X6, Y6,
    X7, Y7, X8, Y8,
    X9, Y9, X0, Y0 : real;

begin
  InitGraphic;
  DefineWorld(1,0,1000,1000,0);
  SelectWorld(1);
  SelectWindow(1);
  SetForegroundColor(12);
  SetBackground(0);
  DrawBorder;
              X1 := 20;
              Y1 := 20;
              X2 := 20;
              Y2 := 170;
              X3 := 20;
              Y3 := 170;
              X4 := 30;
              Y4 := 180;
              X5 := 30;
              Y5 := 180;
              X6 := 50;
              Y6 := 180;
              X7 := 50;
              Y7 := 180;
              X8 := 60;
              Y8 := 170;
              X9 := 60;
              Y9 := 170;
              X0 := 60;
              Y0 := 20;

      DrawLine(X1,Y1,X2,Y2);
      DrawLine(X3,Y3,X4,Y4);
      DrawLine(X5,Y5,X6,Y6);
```

```
      DrawLine(X7,Y7,X8,Y8);
      DrawLine(X9,Y9,X0,Y0);

  repeat until KeyPressed;
  LeaveGraphic;
end;
```

Fig. 7-86. LV.IN draws the letter V.

```
{This file draws the letter V}
{LV.IN  }

procedure DrawV;

var X1, Y1, X2, Y2,
    X3, Y3, X4, Y4,
    X5, Y5, X6, Y6,
    X7, Y7, X8, Y8,
    X9, Y9, X0, Y0 : real;

begin
  InitGraphic;
  DefineWorld(1,0,1000,1000,0);
  SelectWorld(1);
  SelectWindow(1);
  SetForegroundColor(12);
  SetBackground(0);
  DrawBorder;
           X1 := 20;
           Y1 := 20;
           X2 := 40;
           Y2 := 180;
           X3 := 40;
           Y3 := 180;
           X4 := 60;
           Y4 := 20;

      DrawLine(X1,Y1,X2,Y2);
      DrawLine(X3,Y3,X4,Y4);

  repeat until KeyPressed;
  LeaveGraphic;
end;
```

Fig. 7-87. LW.IN draws the letter W.

```
{This file draws the letter W}
{LW.IN  }

procedure DrawW;

var X1, Y1, X2, Y2,
    X3, Y3, X4, Y4,
    X5, Y5, X6, Y6,
    X7, Y7, X8, Y8,
    X9, Y9, X0, Y0 : real;

begin
```

```
   InitGraphic;
   DefineWorld(1,0,1000,1000,0);
   SelectWorld(1);
   SelectWindow(1);
   SetForegroundColor(12);
   SetBackground(0);
   DrawBorder;
              X1 := 20;
              Y1 := 20;
              X2 := 20;
              Y2 := 180;
              X3 := 20;
              Y3 := 180;
              X4 := 40;
              Y4 := 100;
              X5 := 40;
              Y5 := 100;
              X6 := 60;
              Y6 := 180;
              X7 := 60;
              Y7 := 180;
              X8 := 60;
              Y8 := 20;

      DrawLine(X1,Y1,X2,Y2);
      DrawLine(X3,Y3,X4,Y4);
      DrawLine(X5,Y5,X6,Y6);
      DrawLine(X7,Y7,X8,Y8);

   repeat until KeyPressed;
   LeaveGraphic;
end;
```

Fig. 7-88. LX.IN draws the letter X.

```
{This file draws the letter X}
{LX.IN   }

procedure DrawX;

var X1, Y1, X2, Y2,
    X3, Y3, X4, Y4,
    X5, Y5, X6, Y6,
    X7, Y7, X8, Y8,
    X9, Y9, X0, Y0 : real;

begin
  InitGraphic;
  DefineWorld(1,0,1000,1000,0);
  SelectWorld(1);
  SelectWindow(1);
  SetForegroundColor(12);
  SetBackground(0);
  DrawBorder;
             X1 := 20;
             Y1 := 20;
             X2 := 60;
             Y2 := 180;
             X3 := 60;
```

```
            Y3 := 20;
            X4 := 20;
            Y4 := 180;

       DrawLine(X1,Y1,X2,Y2);
       DrawLine(X3,Y3,X4,Y4);

  repeat until KeyPressed;
  LeaveGraphic;
end;
```

Fig. 7-89. LY.IN draws the letter Y.

```
{This file draws the letter Y}
{LY.IN  }

procedure DrawY;

var X1, Y1, X2, Y2,
    X3, Y3, X4, Y4,
    X5, Y5, X6, Y6,
    X7, Y7, X8, Y8,
    X9, Y9, X0, Y0 : real;

begin
  InitGraphic;
  DefineWorld(1,0,1000,1000,0);
  SelectWorld(1);
  SelectWindow(1);
  SetForegroundColor(12);
  SetBackground(0);
  DrawBorder;
            X1 := 20;
            Y1 := 20;
            X2 := 40;
            Y2 := 100;
            X3 := 40;
            Y3 := 100;
            X4 := 60;
            Y4 := 20;
            X5 := 40;
            Y5 := 100;
            X6 := 40;
            Y6 := 180;

       DrawLine(X1,Y1,X2,Y2);
       DrawLine(X3,Y3,X4,Y4);
       DrawLine(X5,Y5,X6,Y6);

  repeat until KeyPressed;
  LeaveGraphic;
end;
```

Fig. 7-90. LZ.IN draws the letter Z.

```
{This file draws the letter Z}
{LZ.IN  }
```

```
procedure DrawZ;

var X1, Y1, X2, Y2,
    X3, Y3, X4, Y4,
    X5, Y5, X6, Y6,
    X7, Y7, X8, Y8,
    X9, Y9, X0, Y0 : real;

begin
  InitGraphic;
  DefineWorld(1,0,1000,1000,0);
  SelectWorld(1);
  SelectWindow(1);
  SetForegroundColor(12);
  SetBackground(0);
  DrawBorder;
           X1 := 20;
           Y1 := 20;
           X2 := 60;
           Y2 := 20;
           X3 := 60;
           Y3 := 20;
           X4 := 20;
           Y4 := 180;
           X5 := 20;
           Y5 := 180;
           X6 := 60;
           Y6 := 180;

      DrawLine(X1,Y1,X2,Y2);
      DrawLine(X3,Y3,X4,Y4);
      DrawLine(X5,Y5,X6,Y6);

  repeat until KeyPressed;
  LeaveGraphic;
end;
```

Fig. 7-91. N1.IN draws the number one.

```
{This file draws the number 1}
{N1.IN  }

procedure Draw1;

var X1, Y1, X2, Y2,
    X3, Y3, X4, Y4,
    X5, Y5, X6, Y6,
    X7, Y7, X8, Y8,
    X9, Y9, X0, Y0 : real;

begin
  InitGraphic;
  DefineWorld(1,0,1000,1000,0);
  SelectWorld(1);
  SelectWindow(1);
  SetForegroundColor(12);
  SetBackground(0);
  DrawBorder;
           X1 := 40;
```

```
                Y1 := 20;
                X2 := 40;
                Y2 := 180;
                X3 := 40;
                Y3 := 20;
                X4 := 30;
                Y4 := 30;
                X5 := 30;
                Y5 := 180;
                X6 := 50;
                Y6 := 180;

         DrawLine(X1,Y1,X2,Y2);
         DrawLine(X3,Y3,X4,Y4);
         DrawLine(X5,Y5,X6,Y6);

  repeat until KeyPressed;
  LeaveGraphic;
end;
```

Fig. 7-92. N2.IN draws the number two.

```
{This file draws the number 2}
{N2.IN   }

procedure Draw2;

var X1, Y1, X2, Y2,
    X3, Y3, X4, Y4,
    X5, Y5, X6, Y6,
    X7, Y7, X8, Y8,
    X9, Y9, X0, Y0,
    X11, Y11, X12, Y12  : real;

begin
  InitGraphic;
  DefineWorld(1,0,1000,1000,0);
  SelectWorld(1);
  SelectWindow(1);
  SetForegroundColor(12);
  SetBackground(0);
  DrawBorder;
                X1 := 20;
                Y1 := 30;
                X2 := 30;
                Y2 := 20;
                X3 := 30;
                Y3 := 20;
                X4 := 50;
                Y4 := 20;
                X5 := 50;
                Y5 := 20;
                X6 := 60;
                Y6 := 30;
                X7 := 60;
                Y7 := 30;
                X8 := 60;
                Y8 := 90;
                X9 := 60;
```

```
            Y9 := 90;
            X0 := 20;
            Y0 := 180;
            X11 := 20;
            Y11 := 180;
            X12 := 60;
            Y12 := 180;

      DrawLine(X1,Y1,X2,Y2);
      DrawLine(X3,Y3,X4,Y4);
      DrawLine(X5,Y5,X6,Y6);
      DrawLine(X7,Y7,X8,Y8);
      DrawLine(X9,Y9,X0,Y0);
      DrawLine(X11,Y11,X12,Y12);

  repeat until KeyPressed;
  LeaveGraphic;
end;
```

Fig. 7-93. N3.IN draws the number three.

```
{This file draws the number 3}
{N3.IN  }

procedure Draw3;

var X1, Y1, X2, Y2,
    X3, Y3, X4, Y4,
    X5, Y5, X6, Y6,
    X7, Y7, X8, Y8,
    X9, Y9, X0, Y0,
    X11, Y11, X12, Y12,
    X13, Y13, X14, Y14,
    X15, Y15, X16, Y16,
    X17, Y17, X18, Y18,
    X19, Y19, X20, Y20  : real;

begin
  InitGraphic;
  DefineWorld(1,0,1000,1000,0);
  SelectWorld(1);
  SelectWindow(1);
  SetForegroundColor(12);
  SetBackground(0);
  DrawBorder;
            X1 := 20;
            Y1 := 30;
            X2 := 30;
            Y2 := 20;
            X3 := 30;
            Y3 := 20;
            X4 := 50;
            Y4 := 20;
            X5 := 50;
            Y5 := 20;
            X6 := 60;
            Y6 := 30;
            X7 := 60;
            Y7 := 30;
```

```
                X8 := 60;
                Y8 := 90;
                X9 := 60;
                Y9 := 90;
                X0 := 50;
                Y0 := 100;
                X11 := 50;
                Y11 := 100;
                X12 := 60;
                Y12 := 110;
                X13 := 60;
                Y13 := 110;
                X14 := 60;
                Y14 := 170;
                X15 := 60;
                Y15 := 170;
                X16 := 50;
                Y16 := 180;
                X17 := 50;
                Y17 := 180;
                X18 := 30;
                Y18 := 180;
                X19 := 30;
                Y19 := 180;
                X20 := 20;
                Y20 := 170;

      DrawLine(X1,Y1,X2,Y2);
      DrawLine(X3,Y3,X4,Y4);
      DrawLine(X5,Y5,X6,Y6);
      DrawLine(X7,Y7,X8,Y8);
      DrawLine(X9,Y9,X0,Y0);
      DrawLine(X11,Y11,X12,Y12);
      DrawLine(X13,Y13,X14,Y14);
      DrawLine(X15,Y15,X16,Y16);
      DrawLine(X17,Y17,X18,Y18);
      DrawLine(X19,Y19,X20,Y20);

  repeat until KeyPressed;
  LeaveGraphic;
end;
```

Fig. 7-94. N4.IN draws the number four.

```
{This file draws the number 4}
{N4.IN  }

procedure Draw4;

var X1, Y1, X2, Y2,
    X3, Y3, X4, Y4,
    X5, Y5, X6, Y6,
    X7, Y7, X8, Y8,
    X9, Y9, X0, Y0  : real;

begin
  InitGraphic;
  DefineWorld(1,0,1000,1000,0);
  SelectWorld(1);
```

```
  SelectWindow(1);
  SetForegroundColor(12);
  SetBackground(0);
  DrawBorder;
              X1 := 60;
              Y1 := 20;
              X2 := 20;
              Y2 := 100;
              X3 := 20;
              Y3 := 100;
              X4 := 60;
              Y4 := 100;
              X5 := 60;
              Y5 := 20;
              X6 := 60;
              Y6 := 180;

     DrawLine(X1,Y1,X2,Y2);
     DrawLine(X3,Y3,X4,Y4);
     DrawLine(X5,Y5,X6,Y6);

  repeat until KeyPressed;
  LeaveGraphic;
end;
```

Fig. 7-95. N5.IN draws the number five.

```
{This file draws the number 5}
{N5.IN  }

procedure Draw5;

var X1, Y1, X2, Y2,
    X3, Y3, X4, Y4,
    X5, Y5, X6, Y6,
    X7, Y7, X8, Y8,
    X9, Y9, X0, Y0,
    X11, Y11, X12, Y12,
    X13, Y13, X14, Y14,
    X15, Y15, X16, Y16  : real;

begin
  InitGraphic;
  DefineWorld(1,0,1000,1000,0);
  SelectWorld(1);
  SelectWindow(1);
  SetForegroundColor(12);
  SetBackground(0);
  DrawBorder;
              X1 := 20;
              Y1 := 20;
              X2 := 60;
              Y2 := 20;
              X3 := 20;
              Y3 := 20;
              X4 := 20;
              Y4 := 100;
              X5 := 20;
              Y5 := 100;
```

```
          X6 := 50;
          Y6 := 100;
          X7 := 50;
          Y7 := 100;
          X8 := 60;
          Y8 := 110;
          X9 := 60;
          Y9 := 110;
          X0 := 60;
          Y0 := 170;
          X11 := 60;
          Y11 := 170;
          X12 := 50;
          Y12 := 180;
          X13 := 50;
          Y13 := 180;
          X14 := 30;
          Y14 := 180;
          X15 := 30;
          Y15 := 180;
          X16 := 20;
          Y16 := 170;

      DrawLine(X1,Y1,X2,Y2);
      DrawLine(X3,Y3,X4,Y4);
      DrawLine(X5,Y5,X6,Y6);
      DrawLine(X7,Y7,X8,Y8);
      DrawLine(X9,Y9,X0,Y0);
      DrawLine(X11,Y11,X12,Y12);
      DrawLine(X13,Y13,X14,Y14);
      DrawLine(X15,Y15,X16,Y16);

  repeat until KeyPressed;
  LeaveGraphic;
end;
```

To change the horizontal position of the letters or digits on the screen, change all values assigned to the X variables identically. To change the position vertically, change the values of the Y variable in the same manner. In other words, if you want to have the character displayed screen center, for instance, add approximately 400 to the X variables and also 400 to the Y variables. Such additions or subtractions, as long as they are consistent, will in no way affect the shape or size of the character.

If you do want to change the size, you can make the characters larger or smaller by adding a multiplication factor to each variable in each L and N include file. In the main program, add a prompt that might read:

```
write('Size?     '); readln(SIZE);
```

and declare SIZE as a global variable of the type real. Then, the changes in the include files would look something like:

```
X1 := 20;                    X1 := X1 * SIZE;
Y1 := 20;                    Y1 := Y1 * SIZE;
```

This would have to be done with each and every variable. Then, if you assign 1 to SIZE, the size of the characters remains unchanged. If you assign any number greater than one such as 1.3 or 2, the size of the characters will be increased accordingly. If you assign a value smaller than one, such as 0.8 or 0.5, the size of the characters will be decreased accordingly.

Appendix A

Copying Distribution Disks

Before using any of the disks that are part of the original distribution packages, you must always make at least one copy of each, after which the originals should be stored in a safe place. It should really not be necessary to mention this, but a number of people ignore this advice, only to find at some future date that they're in trouble, and have to purchase a replacement disk. This involves losses in terms of time as well as money.

Different operation systems, or different versions of the same operating system, might use slightly different routines to copy disks. Regardless of the method, however, you always need to format the work disks onto which you want to copy the originals. With most systems, the routine involves placing the original distribution disk into drive A: and a blank (or to be erased) disk in drive B:. Then, with the A> up, type FORMAT B: and press ENTER (or RETURN).

Once the disk has been formatted, it's ready to be used. I'm currently using PC DOS 3.0, which includes a command named DISKCOPY that can be used to copy entire disks. To do this, with the A> prompt up, type DISKCOPY A: B: and ENTER. If the DISKCOPY command is not available, the routine most likely calls for COPY A:*.* B: and ENTER (or RETURN).

Either system will cause all files contained on the original distribution disk in drive A: to be copied onto your work disk in drive B:. Store the original in a safe place so that you always have one disk in mint condition if something untoward should happen to your work disk.

When you plan to modify or in any way change the material on your work disk, first make a copy of it, also. Then, perform the modifications on the new copy, leaving the original work disk as a true copy of the original distribution disk. Disks are so inexpensive that it would be unwise to try to economize in this area.

Appendix B

Compiling Programs

If you've been writing Turbo Pascal programs, you're certainly familiar with the compiling procedure, and this appendix is probably of no interest to you. On the other hand, especially after a vacation or some other prolonged period of time, you might find that you'd like a quick refresher. So, here are the steps for the compiling procedure that I find most efficient:

1) Place the Turbo Pascal disk into drive A:
2) Place the copy with the to-be-compiled program into drive B:
3) Change the logged drive to B:
4) Type A:TURBO and ENTER
5) With the compiler main menu up, type OCQC
6) Type the work file FILENAME.EXT and ENTER

The program is now being compiled. If the compiler detects any errors and you find that you have to make some changes, such as adding a semicolon, be sure to save the changes by typing ^K^D in order to return to the compiler prompt, >. Then type S to save the edit. After that, type C to start the compiler all over again.

Remember that all the include files with extensions other than .PAS are required for program execution, so they must be on the disk along with the program to be compiled. Otherwise, you'll get error messages because the compiler won't be able to find the appropriate include file when it encounters something that looks like {$I FILENAME.EXT}. Although it is a separate module, it is used by the compiler to be incorporated into the program.

Index

Edited by Marianne Krcma

Other Bestsellers From TAB

☐ **LEARNING C WITH TINY-C**
Have the power, flexibility, and convenience of C . . . for a fraction of the cost of a computer! All you need is this hands-on guide and the tiny-c interpreter (supplied on disk with book). In fact, by the end of Chapter One, you should be able to write, debug, and run tiny-c programs and build software systems based on these programs . . . it's as easy as that! 176 pp., 12 illus., 7″ × 10″. Paperback. Includes dixk for IBM PC® with 128 K.
Paper/Disk $34.90 **Book No. 5160**

☐ **THE WORDPERFECT® BOOK (Covering Versions 4.01 and 4.1)—Scanlon**
Whether you are writing letters, reports, articles, term papers, books, memoranda, legal documents, or financial summaries, this guide will show you how to use WordPerfect's many features to make them more professional. You'll learn to use its built-in Speller and thesaurus, how to draw lines on the screen for creating charts, how to perform mathematical operations, and more! 208 pp., 56 illus. 7″ × 10″.
Paper $16.95 **Hard $24.95**
Book No. 2757

☐ **LOTUS® 1-2-3® SIMPLIFIED—2nd Edition, including Version 2.0—Bolocan**
A book that guides you painlessly from the most basic computer and spreadsheet operations right through the most advanced and powerful operations of 2.0—all in easy-to-follow, logical sequence. Lotus 1-2-3 Version 2.0 is considered one of the most versatile and powerful business software packages available. With this hands-on guide, it can also be one of the easiest to use! 272 pp., 207 illus. 7″ × 10″.
Paper $14.95 **Hard $21.95**
Book No. 2748

☐ **THE POWER OF TURBO PROLOG: THE NATURAL LANGUAGE OF ARTIFICIAL INTELLIGENCE—Roberts**
The newest development in artificial intelligence and expert systems programming is Turbo Prolog—a powerful, super-fast Prolog compiler from Borland International that gives IBM PC, AT, and compatible users programming options previously available only with the latest, most powerful mainframe computers. Now, for the thousands who have invested in Turbo Prolog, or plan to, here's a comprehensive guide that includes wealth of user tips and shortcuts for developing exceptionally powerful and useful artificial intelligence applications using Turbo Prolog. 256 pp., 50 illus.
Paper $14.95 **Hard $22.95**
Book No. 2782

☐ **dBASE III® PLUS—A Comprehensive User's Manual—Bharucha**
Discover how the newest version of Ashton Tate's best-selling relational database management software package—dBASE III PLUS—can make your business programming faster, easier, and more accurate than you've ever imagined possible! If you're upgrading from dBASE II or dBASE III to take advantage of III PLUS's extra management power . . . or you're planning to make III PLUS your first dBASE purchase . . . this is a handbook that you can't afford to miss if you want to tap the full power of dBASE as a programming language. Going well beyond the information included in the standard user's manual, it gives you the hands-on guidance you need to fully understand how dBASE III PLUS works and how to apply it to your own specific data handling needs. 420 pp., 200 illus., 7″ × 10″.
Paper $19.95 **Hard $28.95**
Book No. 2754

*Prices subject to change without notice.

Look for these and other TAB books at your local bookstore.

TAB BOOKS Inc.
P.O. Box 40
Blue Ridge Summit, PA 17214

Send for FREE TAB catalog describing over 1200 current titles in print.

OR ORDER TOLL-FREE TODAY: **800-233-1128**